STREETWISE®

MANAGING A NONPROFIT

STREETWISE®

MANAGING A NONPROFIT

How to Write Winning
Grant Proposals, Work
with a Board, and Build
a Fundraising Program

by John Riddle

Adams Media Corporation
Avon, Massachusetts

A Streetwise® Publication.
Streetwise® is a registered trademark of Adams Media Corporation.

Published by Adams Media Corporation
57 Littlefield Street, Avon, MA 02322. U.S.A.
www.adamsmedia.com

ISBN: 1-58062-698-X

Printed in the United States of America.

J I H G F E D C B A

Library of Congress Cataloging-in-Publication Data
Riddle, John.
Streetwise managing a nonprofit / by John Riddle.
p.   cm.
Includes index.
ISBN 1-58062-698-X
1. Nonprofit organizations—Management. I. Title: Managing a nonprofit. II. Title.
HD62.6 .R54   2002
658'.048—dc21   2002005579

This publication is designed to provide accurate and authoritative information with regard to the subject matter covered. It is sold with the understanding that the publisher is not engaged in rendering legal, accounting, or other professional advice. If legal advice or other expert assistance is required, the services of a competent professional person should be sought.

—From a *Declaration of Principles* jointly adopted by a Committee of the
American Bar Association and a Committee of Publishers and Associations

Cover illustration by Eric Mueller.

This book is available at quantity discounts for bulk purchases.
For information, call 1-800-872-5627.

Visit our exciting small business Web site: www.businesstown.com

CONTENTS

SECTION I: UNDERSTANDING NONPROFIT AGENCIES

SECTION II: GUIDING A NONPROFIT TO SUCCESS

SECTION III: FUNDRAISING 101

CONTENTS

SECTION IV: MARKETING, PUBLIC RELATIONS, AND THE INTERNET

SECTION V: APPENDICES

Understanding Nonprofit Agencies

Nonprofits can be tricky organizations to understand, because they range widely in size, type, geographical reach, mission, employees, and board of directors. This section helps you sort through those details so that you can understand what makes nonprofits—especially yours—tick.

What Is a Nonprofit Agency?

Topics covered in this chapter:

- Types of nonprofit agencies
- IRS Rules and Regulations
- Characteristics of a nonprofit agency

The nonprofit sector of the United States includes thousands of nonprofit agencies such as libraries, hospitals, soup kitchens, animal shelters, and community centers. It is sometimes described as the third sector, the independent sector, the volunteer sector, and the not-for-profit sector.

Whatever name it goes by, a nonprofit agency is simply an organization that is in business to do some type of community service. The organization may feed the hungry, provide shelter to the homeless, or care for elderly people who have no one else to look out for them. A nonprofit agency's mission is simply to *take care of people*. Nothing more, nothing less.

The Many Faces of a Nonprofit

Nonprofit agencies come in a number of flavors, as follows:

Charities—Nonprofit agencies that are exempt under section 501(c)(3) are often called charities, but such organizations do more than provide handouts to needy people: They are also organizations that are religious, educational, scientific, athletic, and protect children and animals. In 1999 more than 650,000 public charities were registered with the Internal Revenue Service (IRS).

Foundations—Many organizations, families, businesses, and even entire communities establish foundations as a way to benefit charitable causes that work toward a better society. Foundations are somewhat more complex than charities due to their internal workings. Government regulations implemented in 1970 imposed stringent reporting requirements on all three types: private foundations, operating foundations, and community foundations. (You can read more about foundations in Chapter 11.) The United States has 40,000 foundations.

Social welfare organizations—Social welfare organizations operate under a different section of the tax code—501(c)(4). Unlike contributions to charities or foundations,

Nonprofits by the Numbers

Just how much of the U.S. economy does the nonprofit sector make up? There are over a million tax-exempt organizations in the country! That's makes this type of organization bigger than the banking and technology/electronics sectors and even the federal government. One in every fifteen Americans is employed by a nonprofit organization.

contributions to social welfare agencies are not tax deductible, and these organizations are allowed to participate in lobbying and some political campaign activities. Some examples include the National Rifle Association (NRA) and the National Organization for Women (NOW).

Professional and trade associations–These organizations are exempt under the tax code section 501(c)(6). Donors who contribute to these organizations are not entitled to a tax deduction but can deduct their contribution as a business expense. This category includes chambers of commerce, business associations, and other organizations that promote the business or professional interests of the community.

Nonprofit agencies have been around for a long time. The idea that charities and other organizations that operate for the public good should be exempt from paying taxes can be traced back through medieval England to ancient times.

Today, while many people argue that nonprofit agencies should not have tax-exempt status, most community leaders, business people, and politicians offer a number of reasons why nonprofits should remain beyond the reach of the IRS.

First, if nonprofit agencies did not exist, they say, the burden would fall on the government to handle the many services that nonprofits provide.

Second, a nonprofit agency offers many benefits to a community, from private schools, hospitals, and day care centers to shelters for homeless people and for stray animals. Every community in the United States benefits from the work nonprofit agencies provide.

Third, it would be exceedingly difficult to determine a dollar value for the services an agency provides on which to base any taxes. Nonprofit agencies provide such a wide array of services the government would be hard-pressed to come up with a fair and equitable way of taxing them.

And fourth, church and state are separate entities. Because religious organizations pay no taxes, the separation of church and state is preserved.

> The idea that charities and other organizations that operate for the public good should be exempt from paying taxes can be traced back through medieval England to ancient times.

IRS Rules and Regulations

Although the IRS recognizes thirty-two different types of tax-exempt organizations according to the 1986 Tax Code (see Chapter 6), the most common type of organization is the 501(c)(3), which is either a private foundation (see Chapter 11) or a public charity. "Charity" is used in its generally accepted legal sense and includes relief of the poor, the distressed, or the underprivileged; advancement of religion; advancement of education or science; erection or maintenance of public buildings, monuments, or works; the lessening of government burdens; lessening of neighborhood tensions; elimination of prejudice and discrimination; defense of human and civil rights secured by law; and the combating of community deterioration and juvenile delinquency. Whew!

The nonprofit is supposed to limit its scope to one or more of the purposes listed in the preceding paragraph. In addition, the assets of an organization must be permanently dedicated to an exempt purpose. In other words, if a nonprofit dissolves, its assets must be distributed for an exempt purpose or be handed over to the federal government or to a state or local government for a public purpose.

The IRS rules and regulations for tax-exempt organizations are radically different from those for for-profit companies. It probably goes without saying, for example, that a tax-exempt organization is not organized or operated for the benefit of private interests, such as for the creator or the creator's family, shareholders of the organization, other designated individuals, or persons controlled directly or indirectly by private interests. And such private interests can't pocket any part of the organization's net earnings. (A private shareholder or individual is a person having a personal and private interest in the activities of the organization.)

Nonprofit organization can't attempt to influence legislation as a substantial part of its activities and may not participate at all in campaign activity for or against political candidates. How does an organization determine whether it has engaged too heavily in such activities to influence legislation? The answer partly depends on the facts and circumstances of each case. But most tax-exempt

Where Does the Money Go?

While nonprofit agencies share many of the same characteristics of for-profit organizations, the chief difference lies in where money that is earned ends up.

In a for-profit organization, money that remains after expenses have been paid can be divided up among shareholders, board members, and employees. For a nonprofit agency, money left over after expenses at the end of the year must be put back into the agency. Those funds are used for expenses, salaries, program, building, or transportation costs.

Many nonprofit agencies operate efficiently and effectively and often turn a profit, which is used to improve the agency and to fulfill its mission.

organizations use Form 5768 (*Election/Revocation of Election by an Eligible Section 501(c)(3) Organization to Make Expenditures to Influence Legislation*) as a guide.

Characteristics of a Nonprofit Agency

According to IRS regulations, a nonprofit agency has the following characteristics:

- Provides a service for the public benefit by filling a need in the community
- Is a private organization, incorporated and separate from any government agency
- Is governed by a volunteer and uncompensated board of directors
- Does not distribute profits but reinvests in programs at the agency or for capital improvements

Educate But Don't Agitate

For purposes of a section 501(c)(3) organization, lobbying and political activities are two different creatures and are subject to different sets of rules. Some small amount of lobbying is usually acceptable. Political activities, however, are an absolute no-no. A tax-exempt organization may not participate in or intervene in (including the publishing or distributing of statements) any political campaign on behalf of or in opposition to any candidate for public office.

But there are gray areas. For example, organizations can sponsor debates or forums to educate voters. But if the forum or debate shows a preference for or against a certain candidate, it becomes a prohibited activity. The motivation of an organization isn't relevant in determining whether the political campaign prohibition has been violated. Activities that encourage people to vote for or against a particular candidate, even on the basis of nonpartisan criteria, violate the prohibition of political campaigning.

For more information on this topic, visit our Web site at www.businesstown.com

Chapter 2

Crafting a Mission Statement

Topics covered in this chapter:

- **What your mission statement should say**
- **How to develop a vision statement**
- **Your guiding principles**

L egally speaking, a mission statement is required before a non-profit organization is incorporated. But the importance of mission statements extends beyond the legal imperative. Your nonprofit agency's mission statement is the first thing that people learn about your organization. If your statement does not define your agency and what services it provides, it might be time to take a second look at it.

> Your mission statement explains why your nonprofit agency was created in the first place.

What Is a Mission Statement?

Your mission statement explains why your nonprofit agency was created in the first place. It states the reason you provide the services you do. It is short enough to be memorized easily, but long enough to get your point across so that no one has any doubts about what you do in the nonprofit world.

Many mission statements also include a list of goals (results you plan to achieve) and/or objectives (the means by which you plan to meet your goals) that relate to the mission. If you decide to go this route—and many nonprofits do—still write a short, easily remembered mission statement that precedes your list of goals and objectives. See the "Sample Mission Statements" section at the end of this chapter for an idea of how long, how short, how simple, and how complex mission statements can be.

Mission statements in the business world are sometimes called "vision statements" and are often confused with guiding principles or value statements. These terms require some clarification.

A vision statement is exactly what it sounds like: When you close your eyes and think about the potential for your nonprofit, what vision do you see? Whom are you helping? In what community do they live and work? How and how much are you helping? What problems are you eradicating or easing? In what way are you making people's lives better?

Many people believe that the term "mission statement" should be thrown out the window and replaced by the term "vision statement." They believe that the best mission statements articulate the vision you see for your organization in the future. Others believe that a vision is only a starting point, and when you have a clear vision, you can write a mission statement that tells the world why you exist today. Whatever term you choose to use, don't lose sight of the fact that a mission statement exists simply to tell people why your nonprofit organization exists.

Guiding principles, also called value statements, are usually a list of good behaviors that the organization would like to see its staff members, volunteers, and boards of directors use in their everyday interactions as representatives of your organization. Guiding principles often discuss how donors, colleagues, and community members should be treated, stressing the need for respect, valuing diversity, and so on. While guiding principles are important conduct guides that can accompany a mission statement, they usually do not explain why the organization exists in the first place.

Knowing What to Do with a Mission Statement

The truth is, when you mention the term "mission statement" to most people, they either crack up or their eyes glaze over. Mission statements can be funny or worse; they can be insulting, especially when the organization—nonprofit or for-profit—isn't coming close to fulfilling its mission but still has the mission statement neatly framed in the lobby.

Ideally, a mission statement should be a ready-made answer for anyone who asks what your organization does. That's why it has to be written in everyday language and should be simple enough to memorize. Whenever anyone—from your next-door neighbor to the person interviewing you at your biggest fund-raising event—asks you the purpose of your organization, you don't have to hem and haw. You know.

In addition, a mission statement should guide your everyday activities and the activities of every staff member, volunteer, and board of directors members. Every action you take should be directly related to fulfilling the mission of your organization. If you're continually working on tasks that have nothing to do with your mission

> A mission statement should be a ready-made answer for anyone who asks what your organization does.

statement, either your statement is no longer relevant or you're spending your time ineffectively.

Put your mission statement on every piece of literature you send out and put it on the home page of your Web site (see Chapter 17). The mission statement conveys to potential donors and volunteers what you do: They can quickly decide whether your organization's mission meshes with their own values and whether they want to be involved.

Developing a Mission Statement

To develop your first mission statement, bring together a small group of people to develop the statement, and then test your drafts with your larger organization to get feedback. When organizing the group be sure to include a diverse cross-section (in terms of job responsibilities) of your larger organization as well as your organization's best writer; you'll need his or her writing skills to draft a compelling statement.

Before your first meeting, send an e-mail or memo explaining the purpose of the group and ask each team member to answer the following questions and to bring their written responses to the meeting:

- Why do we exist?
- What constituency do we serve?
- What services do we provide?
- What needs of our constituency do we satisfy?
- Who else provides similar services?
- How are we unique?

Start the first meeting with an honest discussion of why a mission statement is necessary as well as why some people on the team think it's not necessary. Oftentimes team members may think a mission statement is a waste of time and need to understand how simple—and how effective in your everyday decisions—a mission statement can be.

Next, begin sharing the team member's individual responses to the questions about the organization. This is not an opportunity to judge or berate people's answers, but to thoughtfully read and build

To develop your first mission statement, bring together a small group of people to develop the statement, and then test your drafts with your larger organization to get feedback.

off of some of the answers to those key questions. The key to this discussion is to arrange it as a free-flowing brainstorming session, where no idea is a bad one and no negative comments are allowed. See Chapter 8 for the lowdown on brainstorming, but here are some guidelines in a nutshell:

- Allow any idea to be discussed, even if it doesn't appear to have any merit.
- Eliminate all negative statements such as, "That'll never work." "We've tried that before." or "We can't possibly pull off something like that."
- Establish a clear agenda and don't stray from it. You're trying to come up with a mission statement, not the Bill of Rights.
- Throw out rules—just go with the flow.
- Keep the first session short, and schedule as many sessions as you need to nail down your draft statement.
- Assign someone to take notes of every single idea mentioned. Whenever you get stuck, review the notes up to that point.

As you brainstorm and take notes, you're attempting to come to consensus on the mission statement, piece by piece. If the team can agree on just a few words, consider that part done and move on to another part. Use "xxx" or "blah, blah, blah" to fill in the words that you haven't yet agreed on.

Whatever you do, don't string five sentences—one from each team member, for instance—into a meaningless mission statement. Although this technique may keep all the key players happy, its result is unworkable hodgepodge. You can't organize your day around five versions of what people think the organization is all about. Consensus isn't about divvying up the mission statement so that everyone gets a piece; it's about agreeing about and cooperating on the short, meaningful statement of why your nonprofit exists.

Ultimately, you want to come up with a short, one- to three-sentence statement of twenty to fifty words and present it to the larger organization. At that meeting, again encourage a frank discussion about how people feel about mission statements and how you view

> Ultimately, you want to come up with a short, one- to three-sentence statement of twenty to fifty words and present it to the larger organization.

them. Ask for feedback on word choices or sentiments in the statement that staff members, volunteers, and board members are uncomfortable with. Don't, however, dicker over punctuation and grammar—your trusty writer will take care of that.

Keep revising it until everyone is satisfied with the mission statement. Don't let anyone get so exasperated that he or she gives up. Stay patient and keep at it until the statement is a perfect answer to the question, "What do we do?"

Reviewing and Refreshing an Existing Mission Statement

Take a fresh look at your mission statement every year or two or whenever you experience great change: moving to a new location, growing or shrinking your staff, expanding (or departing from) your established constituency, offering more (or fewer) services, or setting new goals. Your existing mission statement may still fit perfectly or may need a complete overhaul.

If you're making a second (or third or fourth) revision of your existing mission statement because your organization has changed, follow each of the steps listed in the preceding section without spending time to discuss the importance of a mission statement. If, however, you're modifying your mission statement because your existing one never did adequately convey why your organization exists, spend extra time discussing the importance of a mission statement with people in your organization. If they've seen a useless statement in the lobby for a few years, it may be the laughingstock of your organization. Hear what members of your organization have to say about mission statements, and then express how you would like to see a new statement used in the future.

> Take a fresh look at your mission statement every year or two or whenever you experience great change: moving to a new location, growing or shrinking your staff, expanding (or departing from) your established constituency, offering more (or fewer) services, or setting new goals.

Sample Mission Statements

The following mission statements are examples from the real world. They are not judged here as being good or bad, effective or ineffective, because mission statements that seem useless to one person may have the power to rally an entire organization of supporters. They all do, however, serve as good examples for you to review and share with your team members.

The Human Society of the United States

The mission of the Animal Research Issues section is to reduce and eventually eliminate harm to animals used in research, testing, and education, through the promotion of alternative methods and other means. We seek to foster an awareness of, and respect for, the individual interests of these animals within the scientific community and the general public. The section will strive for the highest standards of scholarship and professionalism in pursuit of its mission.

World Wildlife Fund

Known worldwide by its panda logo, World Wildlife Fund (WWF) is dedicated to protecting the world's wildlife and wild lands. The largest privately supported international conservation organization in the world, WWF has more than 1 million members in the United States alone. Since its inception in 1961, WWF has invested in over 13,100 projects in 157 countries.

WWF directs its conservation efforts toward three global goals: protecting endangered spaces, saving endangered species, and addressing global threats. From working to save the giant panda, tiger, and rhino to helping establish and manage parks and reserves worldwide, WWF has been a conservation leader for more than 38 years.

The Nature Conservancy

To preserve the plants, animals, and natural communities that represent the diversity of life on Earth by protecting the lands and waters they need to survive.

The International Red Cross

The International Committee of the Red Cross (ICRC) is an impartial, neutral and independent organization whose exclusively

> The mission of the Animal Research Issues section is to reduce and eventually eliminate harm to animals used in research, testing, and education, through the promotion of alternative methods and other means.

humanitarian mission is to protect the lives and dignity of victims of war and internal violence and to provide them with assistance. It directs and coordinates the international relief activities conducted by the Movement in situations of conflict. It also endeavors to prevent suffering by promoting and strengthening humanitarian law and universal humanitarian principles.

The American Red Cross

The American Red Cross is a humanitarian organization, led by volunteers, that provides relief to victims of disaster and helps people prevent, prepare for, and respond to emergencies. It does this through services that are consistent with the congressional charter and the fundamental principles of the International Red Cross and the Red Crescent Movement.

Locks of Love

Locks of Love is a not-for-profit organization that provides the highest quality hair prosthetics to financially disadvantaged children with medical hair loss. Most of the Locks of Love recipients have lost their hair due to a medical condition known as *alopecia areata,* which has no known cause or cure. These prostheses help to restore their self-esteem and self-confidence, which enables them to face the world and their peers.

The Compassionate Friends

The mission of The Compassionate Friends is to assist families toward the positive resolution of grief following the death of a child of any age and to provide information to help others be supportive. The Compassionate Friends is a national nonprofit, self-help support organization that offers friendship and understanding to bereaved parents, grandparents, and siblings. There is no religious affiliation and there are no membership dues or fees. The secret of TCF's success is simple: As seasoned grievers reach out to the newly bereaved, energy that has been directed inward begins to flow outward and both are helped to heal.

The American Red Cross is a humanitarian organization, led by volunteers, that provides relief to victims of disaster and helps people prevent, prepare for, and respond to emergencies.

Dallas Ronald McDonald House

Existing to serve and sustain families when catastrophe strikes the most cherished part of their lives, their children.

People for the Ethical Treatment of Animals

People for the Ethical Treatment of Animals (PETA), with more than six hundred thousand members, is the largest animal rights organization in the world. Founded in 1980, PETA is dedicated to establishing and protecting the rights of all animals. PETA operates under the simple principle that animals are not ours to eat, wear, experiment on, or use for entertainment.

PETA focuses its attention on the four areas in which the largest numbers of animals suffer the most intensely for the longest periods of time: on factory farms, in laboratories, in the fur trade, and in the entertainment industry. We also work on a variety of other issues, including the cruel killing of beavers, birds and other "pests," and the abuse of backyard dogs.

PETA works through public education, cruelty investigations, research, animal rescue, legislation, special events, celebrity involvement, and direct action.

> We also work on a variety of other issues, including the cruel killing of beavers, birds and other "pests," and the abuse of backyard dogs.

Amnesty International (mission and vision)

Amnesty International's vision is of a world in which every person enjoys all of the human rights enshrined in the Universal Declaration of Human Rights and other international human rights standards. In pursuit of this vision, Amnesty International's mission is to undertake research and action focused on preventing and ending grave abuses of the rights to physical and mental integrity, freedom of conscience and expression, and freedom from discrimination, within the context of its work to promote all human rights.

National Rifle Association (NRA)

To establish and enhance the NRA's leadership role in support of law enforcement officers' training through schools, competition, services, and programs. This is accomplished through:

- The personal instruction of firearms instructor development schools by staff and industry recognized adjunct instructors.
- The exposure of every student to the broadest base of techniques, tactics, and technical and teaching knowledge in order to produce the highest attainable level of skills required to effectively perform his/her role as a firearm instructor.
- The continual updating, refining, and revising of our methods, concepts, tactical/technical applications, and teaching methods.
- The facilitation of tuition-free schools by outside entities engaged in similar law enforcement goals and objectives.
- The National Police Shooting Championships.
- The Jeannie E. Bray memorial college scholarship fund.
- The securing of discounted body armor for those officers whose departments do not provide it.
- The production of the quarterly LEAD newsletter.
- The active and aggressive marketing of our programs to all segments of the law enforcement community.

Our ultimate goal is the saving of lives and prevention of injuries through the safe, effective, and timely use of the law enforcement firearm. This is done by providing the law enforcement firearm instructor with the knowledge, skills, and abilities necessary to teach their students how to "WIN A LETHAL ENCOUNTER!"

National Public Radio (NPR)

> NPR is committed to the presentation of fair, accurate, and comprehensive information and selected cultural expressions for the benefit of, and at the service of our democracy.

NPR is committed to the presentation of fair, accurate, and comprehensive information and selected cultural expressions for the benefit of, and at the service of our democracy. NPR is pledged to abide scrupulously by the highest artistic, editorial, and journalistic standards and practices of broadcast programming. NPR is committed to providing diverse and balanced viewpoints through the entirety of its programming. NPR recognizes that its credibility in the minds of the general population is its most precious asset and must be protected. Even a rigorously managed programming organization may inadvertently depart from its own standards and practices, and abuse its freedom and power to inform and entertain. NPR is dedicated to identifying such transgressions if they occur, correcting them, and acting to prevent repetition.

Public Radio International

The mission of Public Radio International is to engage listeners with distinctive radio programs that provide information, insights, and cultural experiences essential to understanding a diverse interdependent world.

New Orleans Area Habitat for Humanity

New Orleans Area Habitat for Humanity is dedicated to building houses in partnership with God's people, whereby families are empowered to transform their own lives; and to eliminating poverty housing in the New Orleans area while serving as a catalyst to make decent shelter a matter of conscience and action. New Orleans Area Habitat for Humanity is an affiliate of Habitat for Humanity International, an ecumenical Christian not-for-profit organization. To achieve our bold mission, we form partnerships with a variety of donors and volunteers who want to make a tangible difference in this city. Individuals from all walks of life unite with congregations, businesses, organizations, and foundations to build or renovate houses. Habitat then sells those houses to partner families at cost, with no profit and no-interest 15 to 30 year mortgages. Habitat works because the affordable house payments offer the families capital, rather than charity.

> To achieve our bold mission, we form partnerships with a variety of donors and volunteers who want to make a tangible difference in this city.

National Endowment for the Arts

The mission of the National Endowment for the Arts (NEA) is to broaden public access to the arts and to expand opportunities for educational experiences in the arts for Americans of all ages.

The NEA, in partnership with State and local arts agencies, arts organizations, foundations, the corporate community, and other government agencies, supports programs to benefit at-risk youth, their families, and their communities through involvement in the arts.

Grants to organizations to support arts-based youth programs are typically awarded through the Education and Access and the Partnership, Planning, and Stabilization Divisions of the NEA.

Delaware Theatre Company

The Delaware Theatre Company is a cultural, educational, and community-service organization whose purpose is to create theatre of the highest professional quality in Delaware and thereby enrich the cultural life of the area.

Mothers Against Drunk Driving

The mission of Mothers Against Drunk Driving is to stop drunk driving, support the victims of this violent crime, and prevent underage drinking.

Rotary International

The mission of Rotary International is to support its member clubs in fulfilling the Object of Rotary by:

- Fostering unity among member clubs;
- Strengthening and expanding Rotary around the world;
- Communicating worldwide the work of Rotary; and
- Providing a system of international administration.

UNICEF

UNICEF is mandated by the United Nations General Assembly to advocate for the protection of children's rights, to help meet their basic needs, and to expand their opportunities to reach their full potential.

UNICEF is guided by the Convention on the Rights of the Child and strives to establish children's rights as enduring ethical principles and international standards of behavior towards children.

UNICEF insists that the survival, protection, and development of children are universal development imperatives that are integral to human progress.

> The mission of Mothers Against Drunk Driving is to stop drunk driving, support the victims of this violent crime, and prevent underage drinking.

UNICEF mobilizes political will and material resources to help countries, particularly developing countries, ensure a "first call for children" and to build their capacity to form appropriate policies and deliver services for children and their families.

UNICEF is committed to ensuring special protection for the most disadvantaged children—victims of war, disasters, extreme poverty, all forms of violence and exploitation, and those with disabilities.

UNICEF responds in emergencies to protect the rights of children. In coordination with United Nations partners and humanitarian agencies, UNICEF makes its unique facilities for rapid response available to its partners to relieve the suffering of children and those who provide their care.

UNICEF is nonpartisan and its cooperation is free of discrimination. In everything it does, the most disadvantaged children and the countries in greatest need have priority. UNICEF aims, through its country programs, to promote the equal rights of women and girls and to support their full participation in the political, social, and economic development of their communities.

UNICEF works with all its partners towards the attainment of the sustainable human development goals adopted by the world community and the realization of the vision of peace and social progress enshrined in the Charter of the United Nations.

> UNICEF is nonpartisan and its cooperation is free of discrimination.

American Cancer Society

The American Cancer Society is the nationwide community-based voluntary health organization dedicated to eliminating cancer as a major health problem by preventing cancer, saving lives from cancer, and diminishing suffering from cancer through research, education, advocacy, and service.

The Max Foundation

The Max Foundation is a nonprofit organization dedicated to improve the lives and survival rates of patients with leukemia and other blood-related diseases, especially children with a Hispanic or Latin American origin. We pledge to give each patient who suffers from leukemia a chance to access every possible resource in the quest for a cure. We dream of a day when all patients can be cured from this devastating illness, no matter the region of the world where they happened to be born.

The Susan G. Komen Breast Cancer Foundation

To eradicate breast cancer as a life-threatening disease by advancing research, education, screening, and treatment.

Reading Is Fundamental (RIF)

RIF develops and delivers children's and family literacy programs that help prepare young children for reading and motivate school-age children to read regularly. Through a national network of teachers, parents, and community volunteers, RIF programs provide books and other essential literacy resources to children, at no cost to them or their families. RIF focuses its highest priority on the nation's neediest children, from birth to age 11.

The Salvation Army

The Salvation Army, an international movement, is an evangelical part of the universal Christian church. Its message is based on the Bible. Its ministry is motivated by the love of God. Its mission is to preach the gospel of Jesus Christ and to meet human needs in His name without discrimination.

Goodwill Industries

Goodwill Industries will actively strive to achieve the full participation in society of people with disabilities and other individuals with special needs by expanding their opportunities and occupational capabilities through a network of autonomous, nonprofit, community-based organizations providing services throughout the world in response to local needs.

The World Alliance of Neuromuscular Disorder Associations

To encourage and facilitate cooperation between national associations, in order to help people with Neuromuscular Disorders and work towards a cure and eradication of the disorders.

> Through a national network of teachers, parents, and community volunteers, RIF programs provide books and other essential literacy resources to children, at no cost to them or their families.

To represent the interests of people who have Neuromuscular Disorders and their families in every nation without consideration of race, religion, or political belief, so that people with the disorders are accorded care and dignity.

To facilitate swift dissemination of information on treatment and research findings which may be of use to Neuromuscular Disorder Associations around the world.

To be accepted by the World Health Organization as the appropriate authority to be consulted, and to make suggestions, on issues affecting people who have Neuromuscular Disorders and their families, researchers, and service providers.

To make effective representation, when necessary, to individual Governments to ensure they are aware of the needs of their citizens with Neuromuscular Disorders and their families.

To encourage the formation of Neuromuscular Disorder Associations in countries without existing bodies, by providing information and advice.

To develop strategies for better care and services for people with Neuromuscular Disorders and advise and support for their families.

TOPSoccer

To foster the physical, mental, and emotional growth and development of America's youth through the sport of soccer at all levels of age and competition.

Special Olympics

To provide year-round sports training and athletic competition in a variety of Olympic-type sports for individuals with mental retardation by giving them continuing opportunities to develop physical fitness, demonstrate courage, experience joy and participate in a sharing of gifts, skills, and friendship with their families, other Special Olympics athletes, and the community.

To encourage the formation of Neuromuscular Disorder Associations in countries without existing bodies, by providing information and advice.

For more information on this topic, visit our Web site at www.businesstown.com

Guiding a Nonprofit to Success

This section provides you with the tools you need to manage your nonprofit to success. Here, you find out how to build a team of paid employees and organize a network of volunteers. You also find out how to work with a board of directors—even when they disagree with you—and how to manage your day-to-day tasks efficiently.

Chapter 3

Building a Nonprofit Team

Topics covered in this chapter:

- **Special characteristics of nonprofit employees**
- **Ways to empower nonprofit employees**
- **Where to find volunteers**

anaging people comes easily for some people, but for many managers of nonprofit organizations, it can be a real challenge because the employees are often a breed apart. This chapter helps you understand what motivates nonprofit employees and volunteers so that you can inspire them to achieve great success for your nonprofit.

Employees of Nonprofits Are a Breed Apart

Did you know that most employees at nonprofit agencies are earning far less than they could if they worked for a for-profit company? Ever wonder why people would settle for less money and fewer benefits? The answer is quite very simple: employees of nonprofits are a different breed.

They don't think like typical employees of for-profit companies. Most of those employees have their own agenda. They know what they want to get out of their work experience. They know they can climb their way up to the top of the corporate ladder and jump from company to company without feeling bad about whom they are leaving behind.

Typical nonprofit employees, however, are not like that. They work for your nonprofit organization because they have a passion for its mission. They believe in the cause, whether it's saving the whales, feeding the hungry, or counseling people with problems.

Whatever the reason, nonprofit employees are a valuable commodity, and they should be thanked every day. They should be told, "Great job!" as often as possible. They should know that they are valued and appreciated just for working at your nonprofit agency.

Sadly, if you took a poll of some nonprofit agency workers, you would probably find that many of them don't feel appreciated, and are on the verge of burning out. They are overworked, underpaid, and unappreciated, yet they keep on going. They keep on helping others in need. They always put themselves last and others first. If you had that kind of loyalty in a for-profit company, you would be at the top of the *Fortune* 500 list in a hurry.

So, with that in mind, when is the last time you, as a nonprofit manager, made your employees feel good? When is the last time you

> Typical nonprofit employees work for your nonprofit organization because they have a passion for its mission.

made your employees feel appreciated and special just for coming into work that day? Has it been awhile since you even talked to some of your employees? If you haven't told your employees how much you appreciate them, stop reading and do it right now. You'll feel better, and they will, too.

Is it no wonder that many nonprofit managers have a difficult time attracting new employees? Especially when they are forced to do so on a shoestring budget?

Stacey Cook, Executive Director for Project Fit America (PFA), believes that it is possible to attract good employees to work for a nonprofit agency, though only as a result of trial and error. "You can interview, organize pay packages and benefits, but at the end of the day, the best staff are people who find a home in your cause," she says. "We have found no magic bullet here. We place an ad in the paper and pray."

Cook says the most successful hires are those who are committed to the cause and have the potential to make the cause their career. It may sound dramatic, but it is true. There is no way to compete with the big bucks often available. On the other hand, not everyone wants to work sixty to ninety hours a week in the corporate world and take home the stress of managing a high volume of customers and the frustration with the office politics of a corporate ladder that can often lead to a dead end.

"Working for a nonprofit may not mean no money," she says. "You can establish performance-based incentives and create a work environment that honors the human being and not the dollar bill. More people walk away from high paying jobs because they do not feel valued, and find the work empty. Not everyone has to have BMW parked in their garage and a vacation in Europe. There are a good deal of folks who want to contribute to their household finances, build savings, and not have a stress level at warp speed 10."

A quality nonprofit organization should put "golden handcuffs" on staff the way for-profit business does. When you find super employees, you are wise to find ways to let them know they are exceptional and to retain them. Those people are succeeding because they have embraced and embodied your mission goals. Look at what you can do to create a quality workplace.

Ten Ways to Empower Nonprofit Employees

Here are ten ways to help your nonprofit employees embrace their job and your agency's mission:

1. Treat them with respect and support them.
2. Be a good role model. Employees will look to you for leadership and guidance.
3. Build relationships with employees. Create a sense of trust and a system of support and fairness.
4. Have a plan. No one can operate without one.
5. Set reachable goals. When you reach them, set new ones.
6. Pay them fairly, and use bonuses whenever possible.
7. Realize that everyone at your nonprofit agency is "family." And families should stick together in good times and in bad.
8. Offer training, even when you think you cannot afford it. Employees will appreciate your efforts and reward you by working harder.
9. Communicate with your staff often. Hold staff meetings, send memos or e-mails.
10. Take time to laugh. No one needs to get so wrapped up in their jobs that they cannot take time to laugh.

What has worked for Cook is to give benefits unique to the workplace. For instance, the dress code in her organization has changed to "clean and covered." The staff does not work nights or weekends. Flex hours are available. Duties are shared; everyone pitches in to lick stamps or help produce a media piece. Employees are partners in a cause.

Cook also uses a variety of methods to attract academic staff to work in the field for their project. "This aspect of our nonprofit has overflow applications and a constant stream of employment inquiries," she explains. "We have never had to advertise for these positions and have the cream of the crop submitting resumes for consideration. Since our work is academically based in the schools, we literally subcontract working professionals who have the right credentials for our field of work. They take a couple days each month and go in field for us to work with schools directly. We pay them a fee for the day and all related expenses.

"They enjoy getting hands-on again with schools and become valuable mentor-teachers to the students at the new school that has just recently received a PFA donation and are just beginning their work on our project. It is a perfect marriage of field experience, enthusiasm, and partnership. In addition, this provides us with cost containment for our budgets and allows us to attract top-level players who really want to work for a nonprofit, but cannot afford to give up their current salaries and positions to make this transition."

What Employees Want

Sadly, many nonprofit managers don't have a clue about what their employees really want from their jobs. This section helps you pin down what many nonprofit—as well as for-profit—employees are looking for. Employees want:

> *Recognition*—they want management to know they exist and that they are doing their best to get their job done.

> *Responsibility*—the chance to show management they can handle the pressure.

The Importance of Assistants

Every time Stacey Cook, Executive Director for Project Fit America, a program dedicated to promoting cardiovascular health in kids grades K to 12, has advertised for an administrative assistant at a starting salary of $26,000, she has received no fewer than fifty people calling to apply.

A recent hire did such a great job and "wrapped her arms around our work" that she was given a $5,000 raise for two years running. "We made her raise our funding priority, because without high quality in-house administrative support, it is very difficult to maintain the level of service necessary to retain strong donor and grant recipient relations," says Cook. "This was an investment for us, and it will come back to us tenfold."

Opportunity–to advance up the employment ladder. While advancement is not always possible in a nonprofit agency, managers can create positions that will help employees "advance."

A safe work environment–No one wants to work in an environment that has more than an acceptable risk of danger.

A fair wage–Even though you are managing a nonprofit agency, your employees do not want to feel they are underpaid compared to what the agency can afford to pay them.

Goals they can meet–Are you helping your employees set goals that are reachable? Are you setting a good example to your employees and volunteers by being a goal oriented nonprofit leader? If you haven't set goals in a while, start out with small ones and slowly increase as time goes on. When employees see that you are meeting your goals, it will be an incentive for them to meet their own goals.

How to Inspire Staff, Board, and Clients

Managers of a nonprofit have a number of steps they can take to inspire staff. Consider the following.

Step one: Have a goal. Without a goal you're dead in the water and you won't know what to do next. You as a manager need to make it common knowledge that everyone is working toward a common goal, a goal that helps fulfill the mission statement.

Step two: Create a plan. Now that you have a goal, you need a plan to help you achieve that goal. Great managers develop plans that are unique to both their and the agencies' needs and situations. You know the culture of your nonprofit agency better than anyone else, so you are in the best position to create a plan to achieve your goals.

Step three: Have the right attitude. Attitudes are contagious, so make sure your attitude is a positive one. With the right attitude, you and your employees can meet any challenge.

Step four: Put other people first. As a nonprofit leader, you have the option of putting everyone else first. And when you do that, you are showing everyone that you care and value your employees and your agency. When that happens, people are inspired to do their very best.

Step five: Never give up. When the going gets tough and people feel they can go no further, they will look to their leader for guidance and inspiration. What better way to inspire your staff, employees, and clients than by never giving up? Keep moving forward. Find a way to make it work. Look for creative solutions to those problems that seem to face you every day.

Why Employees Excel or Fail

As a nonprofit manager it is within your power to create a work environment that is conducive to excellence. With some limits, you hold the key to getting your employees to excel. Using an incentive and reward program is just one way to motivate employees to perform at their best level possible. For example, you can create an employee of the month award. When employees have the possibility of winning an award, it creates a pattern of excellence. Remember, people want to be recognized for the job they have done, and offering an agency-wide award is an excellent opportunity.

Another way to recognize employees' contributions is to have a suggestion box and reward people for their suggestions. Just because you are a nonprofit agency does not mean you cannot reward people for excellent ideas on how to improve their world of work. You can offer time off or ask local businesses to donate free dinners or merchandise as rewards.

Admittedly, you can be the best manager the nonprofit world has ever seen but still have an employee who is failing to meet expectations. But there is hope, once you acknowledge why employees fail at their job.

For one thing, they may be having health problems. If that is the case, help them find a solution, even if it means contacting their health insurance company on their behalf.

Alternatively, underperforming employees may not be getting the support they need from you. Are you giving your employees the tools and support they need to get their job done?

They may not be happy with their job. When is the last time you asked an employee if they were happy at work?

Or they may be having financial problems. This can be a sticky area to talk about, but sometimes an employee's financial problems will spill over into the workplace, even at a nonprofit agency.

Building a Better Carrot

Does you nonprofit agency have an employee incentive program? If you think your agency cannot afford one, think again; it does not have to cost a bundle to be effective.

For example, many nonprofit agencies have employee incentive programs in which employees receive free dinners at local restaurants that have been generously donated by merchants.

If you want to know what employees would consider to be an excellent incentive program, draft a questionnaire and distribute it all around. Keep it simple. Ask a few simple questions and suggest ideas from your own perspective of what would make a great employee incentive program.

You will end up with a good list from which to choose and from that will flow an incentive and reward program tailored to your individual nonprofit agency.

Finding Volunteers

Want to know the best-kept secret in nonprofits? Volunteers. That's right. Without volunteers, your fund-raising plans and perhaps even your direct services will be difficult to implement.

Some people have argued that volunteerism is dead, simply because people in our society are busier with everyday tasks, due to the increased numbers of single-parent households, more households with both parents working, and people moving away from where they were born in search of a better quality of life. But that's not true. People still find time to volunteer.

Nonprofit agencies across the country report that new volunteers are coming forward all the time, asking how they can become involved and make a difference. Millions of volunteers are investing their time, energies, and unique abilities to help solve the critical problems facing nonprofit agencies. These new volunteers come forward because they know they are providing a valuable service that might go undone if they do not step up.

More than half of the people living in the United States volunteer at some point in their lives for at least a few hours per week. And when asked, nearly all agreed to help. Yet how often do you ask for volunteers? Without those valuable volunteers to help make your services and goals come true, you might find yourself looking at a budget shortfall.

> Nonprofit agencies across the country report that new volunteers are coming forward all the time, asking how they can become involved and make a difference.

Understanding Why People Volunteer

According to a survey by Blue Moon Communications, the ten most popular reasons why individuals volunteer their time are:

1. They desire to serve others.
2. They have a sense of pride in helping.
3. They want to make a difference.
4. They want to help someone in need.
5. They were asked to volunteer.
6. They want to share their special gift or talent.
7. They want to feel good about themselves.
8. They are looking for a cause to believe in.

9. They volunteer because no one else has.
10. They volunteer because it is exciting for them.

Where to Look for Volunteers

Looking for volunteers but don't know where to turn? Here are several resources:

- *United Way*–Many United Way organizations have Loaned Executive programs. Some corporations will loan you an executive for up to one year to help your nonprofit agency.
- *Small business associations*–Try your local chamber of commerce, the Public Relations Society of America, and other business associations to see what type of volunteer programs and committees they have.
- *Service organizations*–Whether it is Rotary, Lions Club, Kiwanis, or some other local service organization, they are all good sources for volunteers. Consider providing a speaker at their next luncheon to introduce your nonprofit agency and mission.
- *Labor unions*–Organized labor in every community has always been ready to lend a hand when asked. Many projects would not be possible without the support of several local labor unions that provided dozens of skilled volunteers when asked.
- *Fraternities and sororities*–Whether it is their sense of wanting to help the community or just to satisfy community service requirements, every college and university has a steady supply of energetic, hard-working volunteers.
- *High schools*–Many high schools have service organizations or National Honor Society chapters that are looking for ways to donate their time.
- *Civic associations*–Many local civic associations are always glad to help out and supply a few volunteers for a worthy nonprofit project.
- *Churches and religious organizations*–While they are nonprofit agencies themselves, they also know the value of volunteers and rarely hesitate to answer the call for help.

> Many United Way organizations have Loaned Executive programs. Some corporations will loan you an executive for up to one year to help your nonprofit agency.

• *Association of Retired Persons*—Check with your local chamber of commerce or look in the Yellow Pages of your telephone book for information about SCORE (Service Corp of Retired Executives) and RSVP (Retired Senior Volunteer Professionals). Both are excellent sources of qualified volunteers.

Ways to Get People to Volunteer

The first rule for recruiting volunteers is to make every prospective volunteer feel special. When people feel wanted or needed they are more likely to respond to your appeal for help and lend a hand, even if they are already busy. Be enthusiastic when asking people to volunteer. Your attitude should be contagious.

Remember to send a thank-you card or note, and not just when their job is completed. People need to hear how much they are appreciated at other times as well.

Once they sign up, put their job description in writing and make sure they understand what is expected before they come on board as a volunteer. Be candid about deadlines that must be respected. If a volunteer tells you up front that he or she does not think a task can be completed before a deadline, don't make matters worse for everyone by having that person fill a volunteer position "because no one else was available."

If training is necessary, allow ample time for someone to not only complete the training but also feel comfortable in using new skills.

If and when you run into turbulence, never give up on a volunteer. Volunteers can suffer from burnout just like any staff member. Rotate volunteer positions when time and conditions permit.

Finally, recognize that volunteers are human and that family emergencies are bound to happen. Always have a back-up person to call.

Case Study: How One Nonprofit Created a Unique Volunteer Program

Even though the American Red Cross has one of the world's most readily recognized symbol (a pair of red rectangles that form a cross),

Why People Don't Volunteer

Ever wonder why people don't volunteer? Blue Moon Communications, a fund-raising consulting firm in Delaware, conducted a survey and came up with the following reasons:

• Because no one asked me to (Stop stalling and start asking.)

• The work might be too physically demanding (Are you asking too much from your volunteers?)

• I don't have enough time (Allow for flexible schedules and times.)

• They don't have child care (Can your nonprofit agency provide this service for your volunteers?)

• I don't have transportation (Provide a shuttle service.)

• I might have to incur other financial costs, such as meals and parking fees (Offer free meals and snacks and make sure free parking is available.)

• I'm afraid I won't know how to operate equipment (Offer training and make your volunteers feel good about any office equipment they might have to use, such as fax machines, computers, or the telephone system.)

the Delaware Chapter of the American Red Cross wanted to create a unique volunteer program to recruit newer and younger volunteers. The organization's many brainstorming sessions resulted in the creation of the 485 Club: A Shade of Hope. The number 485 is the shade of red that printers use to produce the Red Cross logo.

The club began recruiting professionals from area banks, insurance companies, and other corporations that employed thousands of people in their twenties and thirties. The group of volunteers who ran the club met once a month and developed their own goals: to assist the local chapter in their fund-raising efforts, to help increase public awareness and knowledge about the Red Cross, to assist in recruiting new leadership for the local board of directors, to promote volunteerism throughout the community for the benefit of the Red Cross, and to help build diversity into the Delaware Chapter of the American Red Cross.

Within a few months, the club had attracted young professionals who were more than eager to lend a hand. One volunteer said she met many new people and was glad to be doing something positive for her community. Another volunteer reported that young professionals have a civic responsibility and that the club provided them with an opportunity to meet that responsibility.

See what happens when you brainstorm to create new ways to attract volunteers?

> One volunteer said she met many new people and was glad to be doing something positive for her community.

For more information on this topic, visit our Web site at www.businesstown.com

Chapter 4

Working with a Board of Directors

Topics covered in this chapter:

- **How to build a board of directors**
- **Running a smooth board meeting**
- **How to handle disagreements with your members**

I n this chapter, you find out what a board of directors really is and how to work with its members. From understanding the positions on the board to knowing how to fill them to understanding how to work through disagreements with board members, this chapter helps you develop a newfound appreciation for the board of directors as a partner in nonprofit excellence.

Building a Better Board

What is the perfect board? As any nonprofit manager on the planet will tell you, the perfect board is one that shows up for all of the regularly scheduled meetings and takes its mandate to govern seriously, is committed to fundraising, and embraces the agency's mission statement.

It's crucial that every nonprofit agency recruit the best volunteers from the community to serve on the board of directors. But finding and convincing outstanding community leaders to serve on your board of directors can be difficult. Being methodical in your search certainly helps. Keep an up-to-date list of potential volunteers. Start clipping newspaper and magazine articles about board members from other local nonprofit agencies who are in the news. When their term is up, they may be looking for another agency to serve. Write down why you think prospects would be assets to your nonprofit agency. List any special skills or community contacts they have as well. Refer those potential candidates to your board's nominating committee.

Create a board application that is easy to fill out and clearly defines the opportunities that are available. Have the applications, as well as brochures and other literature about your agency, handy at all times. You never know when someone may stop in and inquire about serving as a volunteer on your board.

If a potential volunteer is uncertain, invite him or her to an upcoming board meeting. (Just make sure that no controversial topics are on the agenda that may cause a heated board meeting.)

And before confirming an appointment, make sure that potential volunteers do not have any conflict of interest with your nonprofit agency.

Essential Questions

The following are the types of questions that should be asked of prospective board members:

- Personal contact information (name, address, phone, e-mail)
- Relevant experience (either as a board member or employment)
- Reason for being interested in serving with the nonprofit agency
- Areas of expertise
- Other volunteer commitments

Who's Who on the Board

The best way to make your board of directors move forward is to have the proper board officers and committees in place. That way people know what is expected of them and what needs to be done.

Most boards are made up of at least four officers:

President–runs board meetings and works closely with the executive director to ensure the agency operates smoothly and without any problems.

Vice President–moves into the top position at board meetings if the president is not in attendance and serves as a committee chairperson on an as needed basis.

Five Ways to Find Mr. and Ms. Right

You want to stack your board with the best and brightest but are unsure where they're hiding. Here are five suggestions on how to ferret them out.

1. Place a "Help Wanted" advertisement in a corporate newsletter. Most company newsletters allow local nonprofit agencies to place free ads or send in information about their needs. What better place to recruit board members than right at the corporate level?
2. Ask each board member to bring the name of one potential board member to the next meeting. No exceptions. If they fail to bring a name, they must pay a fine of $100 as a contribution to the agency.
3. Keep an eye on the volunteers who are already serving in other capacities at your agency. Sometimes you will find some great members who never thought about serving on the board before they were asked.
4. Have your local chamber of commerce newspaper or newsletter run an interview with your board president. It's the perfect opportunity to talk about the wonderful things your agency is doing and to talk about potential volunteer opportunities.
5. Network with local professional organizations such as the Junior League, SCORE, and Lions Club. Ask your contacts if they know of any potential volunteers who would make good board members.

Secretary—records the minutes at every board meeting and makes sure everyone receives a copy after they are typed and proofread.

Treasurer—handles the budgeting, accounting, and nonprofit finances. Some will argue that this is the most important board position. The treasurer is also chairperson of the board finance committee.

Boards have a number of common standing committees. The development committee is responsible for setting the fund-raising goals for the agency. It is made up of at least two board members who are enthusiastic about fundraising along with the executive director and director of development.

The finance committee assists the treasurer with all financial matters for the agency. It is also responsible for creating the agency's budget and for making adjustments to that budget on as needed basis.

The program committee ensures the programs of the agency are in place and are carried out in accordance with the mission statement.

The nominating committee is responsible for finding new volunteers in the community to serve on the board. This committee should meet frequently and always be on the lookout for new talent.

How Many Board Members Do You Really Need?

This question could be debated endlessly and never be settled. Will your nonprofit agency operate more smoothly if you have a smaller board or a larger board? Even board consultants disagree on the subject. Many nonprofits find they can get along with between eight and ten board members, while others swear they need forty or more board members to get anything done.

To answer the question with a question: How many members do you think you need? Those agencies that typically have smaller boards will sing the praises of their size. But nonprofit agencies that have a large board of directors and are having a great time will no doubt vote for a larger board size. It's up to your board of directors to decide. Sometimes the size of the board is dependent upon the size of the nonprofit agency. If it is a small nonprofit agency, odds

Survey Other Agencies

If you are wondering how many board members other nonprofit agencies in your local community have, check with your United Way office. Managers there often have that information on hand. If they don't, survey other agencies yourself. Pick up the telephone and call a few other nonprofit managers; sharing information among agencies can help everyone move forward.

are they will have fewer board members than would a much larger nonprofit agency.

New nonprofit agencies also tend to have smaller boards because they tend to take the time to recruit the right number of volunteers who will guide and serve the organization.

What Makes a Board Member Tick?

One of the roles you play as manager of a nonprofit organization is to do whatever you can to help your board members do their job as stewards and governors of the nonprofit. It will be easier for you to do that once you learn why people volunteer to become board members.

People volunteer to serve on a board for a variety of reasons. They may believe in the mission of the nonprofit agency and be excited about helping that agency succeed to the fullest extent. They may be impressed with the leadership of the agency or how the agency serves its community. Perhaps they're looking for an opportunity to serve as a volunteer or for ways to improve their community. Family ties to the nonprofit may feed a sense of obligation to serve in some capacity. For some people, a seat on the board gives prestige and the respect of their peers and business associates.

Once they take their place on the board, what do members expect from the organization? They expect:

Accurate, up-to-date information in all areas, especially regarding fundraising, budgeting, and public relations

Accountability: Most board members are drawn from the business community and are held accountable to their superiors, so they expect the same from the nonprofit agency.

Board meetings to accomplish something

To ask questions and get honest answers

To be appreciated for their volunteer efforts

To serve where needed.

The Board Meeting: Dream or Nightmare?

In the perfect nonprofit world, every board meeting is productive and friendly. In reality, there are hundreds, if not thousands, of horror stories about unruly board meetings circulating among nonprofit managers.

To avoid wasting everyone's time and testing their patience, have an agenda prepared ahead of time and stick to it. One of the biggest problems facing board members is trying to fit everyone's personal agenda into every meeting. It's just not going to happen, so make sure the executive director and board chairperson put together an agenda ahead of time and are professional in handling the items to be discussed.

Another wise move is to have board resolutions prepared ahead of time. This step will save time during the meeting and avoid having members stumble over the wording for every board resolution during the meeting.

Send each board member the agenda and any supporting paperwork at least one week ahead of time. That way everyone can prepare questions and come to the meeting better prepared.

Don't meet too often. Some nonprofit agencies have only three or four board meetings a year. Depending on the size of the agency, you will need to meet more or less frequently. Fewer meetings will also help to encourage good attendance, which in turn will help guarantee having a quorum.

Serve refreshments at every board meeting. Volunteers are busy people and it does not take much to serve light refreshments.

Make sure someone takes good minutes, and have those minutes transcribed and sent to board members on a timely basis. The minutes do not have to be pages long, either. Keep them short and to the point so they reflect what took place at the meeting.

When Board Members Disagree with You

It's bound to happen sooner or later and when it does you might feel as if the world is collapsing under your feet. If it is any consolation,

Keep Your Eye on the Clock

Don't fall into the habit of making your board meetings too long. Some nonprofit agencies have board meetings that last for three or four hours, which is a recipe for a snoozefest, and much too long for a productive board meeting. Try to limit your board meetings to two hours or less. Once board members realize that the meetings do have a time constraint, it will be easier for them to attend.

board members and nonprofit managers h¯ve been having disagreements for a long time.

If a board member disagrees with you, it will usually be about a specific point. I have found the best way to smooth things over is to ask the disgruntled board member to come up with an alternative solution. Guess what? In most cases, the disagreement goes away.

But keep the negotiating table open for all options. If board members do not like the idea for a fund-raising event you want to go forward with, ask them what parts of the event they don't feel comfortable with. Odds are they really aren't against the entire event, just one or two particular aspects. Ask for their input, and get them to tell you what would make them feel better about the problem.

What is worse than having board members disagree with you is having board members disagree with each other. It can get downright ugly.

The first thing to remember is to ensure board meetings follow *Robert's Rules of Order*. The book is probably used as a basis for more meetings in the United States than any other. It will help you maintain order and, hopefully, keep your next board meeting from turning into chaos.

If you know ahead of time that a controversial issue will be on the agenda at the next board meeting, do what you can do diffuse the situation before the meeting takes place. Send a memo to board members outlining the agenda, and remind them that one or more items are important but must be discussed calmly and rationally.

One executive director I worked with always had ice cream and all of the toppings to make sundaes. She thought that if people were eating ice cream and having a good time, it would be harder to get into arguments and resort to name calling. She was right; it worked every time.

Use Board Members' Gifts

Are you taking advantage of your board members' gifts? I don't mean the financial gifts; I'm talking about their other ones. Some board members are skilled at public relations; are you asking them to serve on public relations committees?

Other board members might be wizards at financial statements and should be assisting with financial matters.

Make sure you survey all new board members and see what gifts they bring to your nonprofit agency.

Should the Board Make Everyday Decisions?

The answer to this question is no. The board should rarely get involved in day-to-day decisions. There are, however, exceptions to the rule. The executive director and the appropriate board committees get together and create policies for the nonprofit agency. Those polices are then approved and implemented by the executive director and other agency staff. If the executive director fails to implement those policies, the board president may decide to step in and temporarily take control of the operation.

Chapter 5

Improving Your Day-to-day Management Skills

Topics covered in this chapter:

- **Playing multiple roles**
- **Time management tips**
- **Setting your schedule**

I f you are a nonprofit manager, especially at a smaller agency, you often have to wear many hats. In addition to being the executive director, you will sometimes have to act as bookkeeper, accountant, secretary, fund-raising professional, and baby sitter. But if you're like most nonprofit managers, you're up to the challenge of figuring out how to manage these tasks and still grow your own career. This chapter shows you how.

Your Career as a Nonprofit Manager

If you think you would enjoy a career as a nonprofit manager, then here is a gold star for you. Nonprofit agencies need good managers, and if you have those skills, there is a nonprofit nearby that can use your help, expertise, and enthusiasm. Rest assured, many people who work for nonprofit agencies find it fulfilling and rewarding. They feel their time and effort are being invested in a good cause, one that is serving their local community.

While you probably will not get rich working as a manager at a nonprofit agency, the salaries have been increasing in the past few years. Many executive directors started their careers as a social workers, development directors, or even volunteers. They worked their way up the nonprofit ladder until they reached the top of the organization. The rewards, in terms of money and benefits, may not be in line with comparable jobs in the corporate world, but you will be able to make a decent living while helping society.

Wearing Multiple Hats

Here are some tips to help you play the multiple roles that are often required at a nonprofit and maintain your sanity at the same time.

Keep your staff and board informed. There's nothing worse than trying to do everything yourself when it is not necessary. When you share information about the agency's needs and problems, others may suggest creative solutions to those challenges.

Keep a priority list, and review it often. What is a priority in the morning might not be the same priority in the late afternoon, and most times you have little or no control over situations that might arise. For example, the boiler in your building gives out, and suddenly you're scrambling to get emergency repairs and funding to take care of the problem.

Delegate whenever possible. The trick to getting six things done at the same time is to find good people to assist you. Most nonprofit employees are not motivated by money and benefits, so use their loyalty and give them the chance to pitch in when they are needed.

Take fifteen minutes a day and relax. Go for a walk, read a book, or take a power nap. Whatever you decide, devote a quarter of an hour during the workday to yourself.

Keep your to-do lists in shape. It is okay to have a to-do list, but don't let the list get so clogged with tasks that you don't get any of them accomplished. Review your lists carefully and regularly, and feel free to reprioritize the tasks listed, as situations change.

Don't look at problems as problems. Think of them in terms of challenges and opportunities and they will be easier to overcome.

Be proactive instead of reactive. Don't panic and act on impulse; think things through and look for the best possible solution.

Becoming Super Organized

What do your desk and office look like these days? Are they nice and neat, with everything filed and organized the way it should be? Or has it been days or even weeks since you've even seen the top of your desk? If you are looking at a mound of paper, you are not alone. Many nonprofit managers wear so many hats they find their desktops filled with endless piles of important papers.

It all starts when you place one piece of paper into a pile. Before you know it, the mail arrives and is sorted into still more piles on your desk. People drop off other files and important papers that must be dealt with immediately, and before you know it, you have more paper than you can handle.

Here are some tips to help you organize your work life:

- File papers immediately; no excuses, no exceptions.
- Delegate tasks whenever possible.
- Learn new time management techniques and use them.

Take a Management Test

Just how good a manager do you think you really are? Take our quiz and discover your management ability. Answer Yes or No to each of the following statements:

1. I am confident in my ability to manage people.
2. My attitude is always positive.
3. I believe that people are basically good.
4. I consider myself an organized manager.
5. I can delegate when necessary.
6. I can handle change when the need arises.
7. I consider myself a creative problem solver.
8. I have a good handle on time management.
9. Employees consider me a leader.
10. I am a firm believer in the planning process.

If you answered Yes to all ten statements, you are a great manager in the nonprofit world. If you answered No to any of the statements, it is time to take a serious look at them and make any necessary adjustments on your end.

• Set up a tickler file system so that important dates and papers are not lost in the system.
• Stop procrastinating.
• Stop writing notes on little scraps of paper.
• Schedule some free time each and every day.
• Encourage your employees and volunteers to become organized and efficient.
• Make appointments and keep them.
• Don't waste your time at useless meetings.

Time Management Tips for Nonprofit Managers

Benjamin Franklin is believed to have said, "Time is the stuff of which life is made." You can't fault his thinking; time is something that we all share equally, no matter how much money we earn or what Ivy League school we graduated from. We all have twenty-four hours in a day and seven days a week.

It is how we manage our time that separates one person from the next. Successful business owners learned long ago how to master time management techniques, and you can learn them as well. And if you say you are too busy to learn new time management techniques, something is likely wrong, because people who have learned how to manage their time well always find time for something new in their schedule.

Ask yourself, Do I manage time or does time manage me? For many nonprofit managers, it seems as if they are slaves to the monster known as time. They bounce from one crisis to the next, and can never seem to ever get caught up with their list of things that really need to be accomplished.

One of the best tips to keep in mind when trying to manage your affairs is to spend some time each day planning and organizing your schedule. Organize in a way that makes sense to you. Some people do well with a wall calendar while others need a fancy day planner. Find something that works for you and use it.

Learn from the Masters

Every manager wants to be successful, so why not duplicate successful nonprofit management styles that you have learned and been exposed to over the years?

Maybe it is time to reread an excellent book about leadership or management in a nonprofit setting, this time with a pen and notebook in hand. Have you attended a workshop or seminar at which you learned successful leadership styles, tips, and techniques? Review your notes and apply what you learned.

Think also about managers you have worked for over the years. Some have been effective and others have been brutal. Learn to duplicate the successful management styles of those good ones, and your job as a leader will be easier.

Next, guard your time. Do not allow others to steal it from you. It's yours and it is up to you to decide how your time will be spent.

Be proactive and not reactive when it comes to time management. In other words, do not simply react when something goes wrong. Find a way to fix the problem before it becomes a crisis.

Make a decision and stick with it. But be ready to swerve if there is a bump in the road.

Realize that you will never please everyone at all times. If you persist in being a chronic pleaser, you will deplete your precious currency of time. A related reminder is to stop trying to respond to every crisis. Let someone else handle the unexpected problem the next time it arises; let others take responsibility instead of you giving up your valuable time to jump in and save the day.

Have confidence in your ability to manage your own time. If you don't have confidence in yourself, how can you expect others to trust you?

Don't let paperwork pile up. Clean out your briefcase. Get rid of all of those old papers that you have been carrying around needlessly. Learn to live clutter free, and suddenly you will become more organized and have more time on your hands.

Keep an appointment diary. Make sure you know what is taking place when you begin your workday. Don't overbook.

Keep a time diary for thirty days. Record every fifteen minutes of your workday; then evaluate everything that took place and make recommendations to yourself that will improve how well you use your time.

Be considerate of other people's time as well. Remember that people work at different paces; just as you do not want to have someone waste your time, you do not want to be the person who wastes someone else's time either.

Have an action list. Put things on this list that you want to accomplish each day, no matter what problems or interruptions may materialize.

Use the eighty-twenty rule. This rule states that 80 percent of your reward will come from 20 percent of your effort. The trick comes, however, when you try to identify what 20 percent of your effort is really needed.

Communication Traps to Avoid

Being an effective communicator does not mean having a silver tongue and smooth delivery. It does mean developing your skills at listening and speaking with clarity. Keep these ideas in mind.

- Don't tune out when people talk. Some managers in nonprofit agencies use "selective listening" and end up hearing only part of what someone is saying. Don't be so busy that you can't pay attention when people are talking to you.

- Don't send out conflicting messages. You may say something with your voice but if your body language is not sharing that same message, you end up delivering mixed messages.

- Be crystal clear when communicating. Don't say to an employee, "I need this done as soon as possible." Instead, give the employee a firm deadline. Say "I need this report finished by Friday morning."

- Don't just put your communications in writing. People need face-to-face instructions as well.

Be a good listener. When people talk to you, don't interrupt them until they are finished, even if you have to bite your tongue.

Learn how to multitask. Brainstorm ways you can complete two tasks at the same time. For example, if you take the train to your business, use that time to work on important papers or to review trade journals.

Finally, stop watching the clock. Time will go much slower for you if you stop worrying about what time it is all the time.

How Your Schedule Can Make or Break Your Day

It may be a self-evident fact, but harried managers often can forget that an effective schedule can make or break their day. With the right schedule, you will get ten times more tasks accomplished than you would with the wrong schedule.

How can you tell if your schedule is the right one? Ask yourself these questions:

- Am I leaving time in my schedule to return telephone calls and e-mails?
- Am I leaving time in my schedule to eat at least one nutritious meal while I am on the job?
- Am I leaving time in my schedule to meet with other staff members?
- Am I leaving time in my schedule to send thank-you notes to donors and friends?
- Am I leaving time in my schedule to communicate my agency's needs to local corporations and businesses?
- Am I leaving time in my schedule to meet with volunteers as needed?
- Am I leaving time in my schedule for professional development?
- Am I leaving time in my schedule for a little rest and relaxation?

- Am I leaving time in my schedule for fund-raising activities?
- Am I leaving time in my schedule for building relationships with leaders in the community?

Know When to Delegate and When Not To

As a nonprofit manager, do you know when to delegate and when to avoid it at all costs? Many managers of nonprofits have difficulty delegating a task to an employee, board member, or a volunteer; and there is no shortage of reasons why. They are afraid that the task will not be done right or will not be done at all.

They are afraid that they will lose control of the project or task. They are afraid that no one will understand its importance. Or they are afraid that they will be in trouble if the project they delegate is not done properly.

Do you notice the common denominator? It is fear. Most nonprofit managers are simply afraid to delegate, and that fear is causing them more headaches and work for themselves. Effective delegation allows managers a chance to achieve their goals by using the talents of employees, volunteers, and board members.

The best corporate leaders and managers have learned early on in their careers to surround themselves with talented coworkers and associates who help them meet their goals and objectives. The same truths hold for nonprofit agencies. If you have the chance to delegate, take it.

Delegation Traps to Avoid

There is some finesse involved in delegating tasks. For one thing, don't just assign a task and wait for results. Meet with the people who now have the responsibility to carry out your assignment. Make sure they all know what is expected of them and when the project is due.

Avoid delegating a complex project to a new employee who does not know the culture of the organization. It takes new employees almost a year or two to get to know the inner workings of a non-

---

Change from Within

As a nonprofit manager, your job includes implementing change at your agency, which can be almost a daily event. But employees, even at nonprofit agencies, often resist any type of change in their work environment. It doesn't matter how or why a change takes place. It's simply human nature; people will usually tense up when they find out a new procedure has been introduced or an existing policy has been changed.

The secret to introducing change into the nonprofit workplace successfully is to involve the employees at every level. In a brainstorming session, sit everyone down and ask them for their input. When nonprofit employees feel they have a hand in the changes, it will be easier for them to accept those innovations.

profit agency. If you do give a new recruit an important project, make sure he or she understands what needs to be done and how it can be best accomplished.

Remember that delegation involves teamwork. The best team is the one in which members support one another and get the job done.

Mistakes will happen, so stay in touch with those people now responsible for carrying out your instructions.

Finally, don't think you can delegate everything. Some managers like nothing better than offloading all their tasks to underlings, leaving nothing for themselves. That is a recipe for disaster.

Letting Go

Often the hardest job a manager in a nonprofit organization will face is simply how to manage and "let go." In other words, how to empower employees and volunteers to tackle the jobs and then step back and allow them to complete their assignments.

Look! Six Balls in the Air!

Ever go to the circus and watch the juggler toss clubs into the air as if it were nothing? Ever get jealous of the juggler's ability? Don't fret, because with the proper motivation, you too can learn how to juggle six tasks at once. Consider the following advice.

Save professional reading to do at your desk while you are eating lunch. And if you want to read only one or two articles out of the entire journal or magazine, clip them out. Otherwise you may find yourself wasting time browsing articles that you really are not interested in.

If you commute using public transportation, use your time wisely by reading important documents, dictating letters, or working on your laptop.

Eliminate distractions from your work area. Focus on what helps you get the job done, not what keeps you from performing it well.

Anticipate problems and be flexible with your schedule. Keep creative solutions on standby in case the need arises.

Be an action-oriented person. In other words, take action and don't just talk about the task or problem at hand.

Focus on the big picture and concentrate on what you can do to get to that big picture.

Develop a time management plan that works for you, and build plenty of flexible time into that plan.

For many managers, that is easier said than done. Whether it is the fear of failure or the need to be in control at all times, many managers are their own worst enemy. They make it difficult to get the job done, and they don't realize what they are doing.

As a busy manager you no doubt have many responsibilities and should not expect to have to do everything by yourself. You need to guard against the only-I-can-do-the-job syndrome that attacks many managers in nonprofit agencies. Once you realize that you are leading a team, you can start trusting that team to get the job done.

Secrets of Successful Delegation

Want to become a wizard at delegating tasks? Here is some advice.

- Set goals for projects and then look for the best people to help you carry out those goals and objectives.

- Be a firm believer in teamwork. It takes a team to run a good nonprofit agency.

- Don't be a control freak. Learn to know when it is okay to let go.

- Monitor the delegation process through meetings, e-mail updates, memos, and face-to-face meetings.

- Reward the people who have successfully completed their delegated tasks. Once people learn that you are willing to put your money where your mouth is and reward good work, they will be eager to help whenever the opportunity arises.

For more information on this topic, visit our Web site at www.businesstown.com

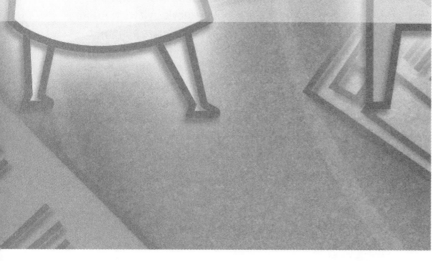

Chapter 6

Paperwork: Corporate Bylaws and Financial Statements

Topics covered in this chapter:

- Setting up your bylaws
- Where to find a auditing firm
- Tax requirements for a nonprofit

I n this chapter, you find out more about the part of management that nearly everyone hates: paperwork. You discover how to prepare and abide by the bylaws of your nonprofit, how to keep your financial records in top shape for the Internal Revenue Service (IRS), and how to find the best auditing firm for your agency's needs. Don't let the paper trail discourage you from becoming the best nonprofit manager you can be.

Nonprofit Bylaws

Bylaws are the rules and regulations that govern your nonprofit agency's operations. No matter what type of nonprofit you run—even if you run a very small organization—you need bylaws. Check with your state agency that regulates nonprofit organizations for any special requirements you must meet, but use this chapter as a starting point.

Bylaws help your board of directors carry out the agency's mission. They will include information such as:

> Bylaws help your board of directors carry out the agency's mission.

- How many board members need to be on the board at one time
- Length of term on board
- Any limits on board membership
- How many board members are required for a quorum
- Descriptions of the duties of key agency employees

The best bylaws deal with the needs of your own nonprofit agency. Don't just copy another nonprofit agency's bylaws word for word. Be creative and add items to your bylaws. Smart nonprofit agencies make sure they use bylaws to their advantage. For example, many agencies have bylaws that address the number of board meetings that board members must attend, or face dismissal. Other bylaws can address the fund-raising requirements for board members.

There are plenty of sample bylaws available to use as models for your own. To research good examples of nonprofit bylaws on the Internet, surf to the Web site at *www.fdncenter.org/learn/faqs/samplebylaws.html.* You will find links to about a dozen sample bylaws. Also look for a bylaw sample in Appendix B of this book.

Check with your local library, too, to see whether it carries reference volumes with sample bylaws for you to review. Examine at least six samples of real nonprofit bylaws before you put your pen to the paper and draft your own.

Financial Reporting

Every manager of a nonprofit agency needs a good financial helper. Sometimes that helper will be a bookkeeper, an accountant, an accounting clerk, the treasurer from the board, or simply a volunteer who is good with figures.

Whether you like it or not, the paperwork must be kept in order. Your financial reports to the appropriate government agencies must be filed on time; these documents are then available for public inspection. The reason for timely reporting is simple. If the general public perceives that something is wrong with your nonprofit agency or that you are hiding something, your reputation will quickly diminish. You will no longer be thought of as a nonprofit agency that is doing great things. Instead, people will wonder what you are up to.

Where to Find a Great Auditing Firm

Every nonprofit eventually needs a certified public accounting firm to provide an annual audit. Don't make the mistake committed by too many managers who open the Yellow Pages and without some thought pick the accountant around the block.

A better way is to ask for a referral from other nonprofit agencies in your community or from the local United Way. United Way officials will know which CPA firms and independent CPAs work with member agencies.

When interviewing potential auditing firms, ask for samples of other nonprofit audits they have prepared. If they don't have any or they haven't done one in five or more years, cross them off your list.

Ask to meet the people who will be handling your audit. How experienced are they? Who are the support people in their office handling your nonprofit audit?

Liability Insurance and More

Make sure your bylaws spell out the requirements for directors' and officers' liability insurance. More than a dozen such insurance plans are available. Check with other local nonprofit agencies to see what directors' and officers' liability insurance company they are using. Obtain sample policies and compare rates before deciding on the best one.

Before you write any bylaws that address banking and financial transactions, check with your local bank branch offices to see whether any special laws or regulations govern or address nonprofit agencies and monetary rules.

Also ask specific questions about costs. You don't want to be surprised when a bill comes in for more than you thought.

Filing Requirements for Nonprofit Agencies

Generally, tax-exempt organizations must file an annual information return. Tax-exempt organizations that have annual gross receipts of less than $25,000 are not required to file the annual information return. Churches and certain religious organizations, certain state and local instrumentalities, and other organizations are exempt from having to file an annual return.

The IRS defines thirty-two distinct types of tax-exempt organizations, which are listed in Table 6-1, along with the annual IRS form the organization is required to file. Find your type of organization to determine which type of annual return your organization must file.

Note that the IRS could have assigned names to the types of organizations, as it does to hurricanes and planets, but chose, instead, to use an ever-confusing numeric system. The numbers that identify the types of organizations refer to specific sections of the 1986 Tax Code, which you *never* want to read, if you can help it.

Table 6-1: IRS Classification of Tax-Exempt Organizations

Type	Description	Annual Return Required
501(c)(1)	Corporations organized under acts of Congress (including federal credit unions)	None
501(c)(2)	Title holding corporation for an exempt organization	990 or 990EZ
501(c)(3)	Religious, educational, charitable, scientific, literary, public safety, sports, cruelty-prevention organizations	990, 990EZ, or 990-PF
501(c)(4)	Civic leagues, social welfare organizations, and local associations of employees	990 or 990EZ
501(c)(5)	Labor, agricultural, and horticultural organizations	990 or 990EZ

Table 6-1: IRS Classification of Tax-Exempt Organizations, *continued*

Type	Description	Annual Return Required
501(c)(6)	Business leagues, chambers of commerce, real estate boards, and so on	990 or 990EZ
501(c)(7)	Social and recreation clubs	990 or 990EZ
501(c)(8)	Fraternal beneficiary societies and associations	990 or 990EZ
501(c)(9)	Volunteer employees' beneficiaries associations	990 or 990EZ
501(c)(10)	Domestic fraternal societies and associations	990 or 990EZ
501(c)(11)	Teachers' retirement fund associations	990 or 990EZ
501(c)(12)	Benevolent life insurance associations, mutual ditch or irrigation companies, mutual or cooperative telephone companies, and so on	990 or 990EZ
501(c)(13)	Cemetery companies (conducting burials and related activities)	990 or 990EZ
501(c)(14)	State-chartered credit unions, mutual reserve funds	990 or 990EZ
501(c)(15)	Mutual insurance companies or associations	990 or 990EZ
501(c)(16)	Cooperative organizations to finance crop operations	990 or 990EZ
501(c)(17)	Supplemental unemployment benefit trusts	990 or 990EZ
501(c)(18)	Employee-funded pension trust (created before June 25, 1959)	990 or 990EZ
501(c)(19)	Post of organization of past or present members of the armed forces	990 or 990EZ
501(c)(20)	Group legal services plan organizations	N/A
501(c)(21)	Black lung benefit trusts	990-BL
501(c)(22)	Withdrawal liability payment fund	990 or 990EZ
501(c)(23)	Veterans organizations (created before 1880)	990 or 990EZ
501(c)(25)	Title holding corporation or trusts with multiple parents	990 or 990EZ
501(c)(26)	State-sponsored organization providing health coverage for high-risk individuals	990 or 990EZ
501(c)(27)	State-sponsored workers' compensation reinsurance organization	990 or 990EZ
501(d)	Religious and apostolic associations	1065
501(e)	Cooperative hospital service organizations	990 or 990EZ
501(f)	Cooperative service organizations or operating educational organizations	990 or 990EZ
501(k)	Child-care organization	990 or 990EZ
501(n)	Charitable risk pools	990 or 990EZ
521(a)	Farmers' cooperative associations	990-C

Which Forms to File

As you can see in Table 6-1, most tax-exempt nonprofits have to file Form 990 (*Return of Organization Exempt From Income Tax*) or Form 990EZ, the *short form.*

Form 990-EZ is designed for use by small tax-exempt organizations and nonexempt charitable trusts. An organization may file Form 990EZ instead of Form 990 only if its gross receipts during the year were less than $100,000 and if its total assets at the end of the year were less than $250,000. If your organization fails to meet either of these conditions, you can't file Form 990-EZ and must file Form 990. All private foundations exempt under section 501(c)(3) must file Form 990-PF.

All of these forms are due by the fifteenth day of the fifth month after the end of your organization's accounting period. If you fail to file a required return, you organization is subject to a penalty of $20 a day. The same penalty applies if your organization fails to give correct and complete information or required information on its return. The maximum penalty for any one return is $10,000 or 5 percent of the organization's gross receipts for the year, whichever is less. If the organization has gross receipts in excess of $1 million, the penalties are increased to $100 per day with a maximum penalty of $50,000.

Taxes You May Have to Pay

Even though an organization is recognized as tax exempt, it still may be liable for tax on its unrelated business income. A tax-exempt nonprofit that has $1,000 or more gross income from an unrelated business must file Form 990-T (*Exempt Organization Business Income Tax Return)*. This form is in addition to the annual information return. The Form 990-T of a tax-exempt nonprofit must be filed by the fifteenth day of the fifth month after the tax year ends. (An employees' trust must file Form 990-T by the fifteenth day of the fourth month after its tax year ends.) A tax-exempt organization's Form 990-T is not available for public inspection.

Tax-exempt nonprofits must make quarterly payments of estimated tax on unrelated business income. An organization must make

File on Time!

The worst thing you can do is fail to file your official tax forms on time. You will not only have to pay a penalty but also be perceived as being a nonprofit agency that is having financial problems. Remember, people's perceptions are their reality, so if the public perceives something to be wrong at your agency (even though everything is okay), your reputation as a nonprofit manager will be on the line.

estimated tax payments if it expects its tax due for the year to be $500 or more.

Every employer, including a tax-exempt nonprofit, who pays wages to employees is responsible for withholding, depositing, paying, and reporting federal income tax, social security taxes (FICA), and federal unemployment tax (FUTA) for such wage payments, unless that employer is specifically excepted by statute from such requirements or if the taxes are clearly inapplicable.

Tax-exempt nonprofits must make their last three annual information returns and their approved application for recognition of exemption with all supporting documents available for public inspection. The organization is required to provide copies of these documents upon request without charge (other than a reasonable fee for reproduction and copying costs). Penalties are provided for failure to comply with these requirements.

> Tax-exempt nonprofits must make their last three annual information returns and their approved application for recognition of exemption with all supporting documents available for public inspection.

For more information on this topic, visit our Web site at www.businesstown.com

Fundraising 101

In this section you will learn the basics of fundraising and what goes into making a great fund-raising special event. You will be given the rules for successfully obtaining corporate contributions and information about the different types of corporate contributions. Also included is information on organizing a direct-mail campaign, along with tips on how to create the perfect direct-mail piece. By the time you are finished reading this section, you will know what fundraising is and how you can create a successful fund-raising program that will work at your non-profit agency.

Making Fundraising Your Best Friend

Topics covered in this chapter:

- **What is fundraising**
- **Who should manage a nonprofit's finances**
- **How to start a fund-raising program**

Chapter 7

> Raising funds is tough, competitive work and you must be prepared to devote your all to achieve your goals.

Everyday in the United States some type of fund-raising activity takes place. It may be a special event, a direct-mail pitch, or a request to a corporation or a foundation for funding. Unfortunately, a large percentage of those efforts fail. Pick up any daily newspaper in any major city and chances are you will read a headline forecasting more doom and gloom for a local nonprofit agency. While many experts agree that tough economic times make it difficult for charities to raise money, they also point out that the key for surviving and thriving is to plan ahead.

Unfortunately, not everyone understands the planning process that is involved in conceiving and launching a successful fund-raising campaign. Raising funds is tough, competitive work and you must be prepared to devote your all to achieve your goals. Yet, all too often, managers become discouraged when their plans fail to make it past the drawing board.

A Lesson from the Playground

I speak from experience. When my eldest daughter began attending Brookside Elementary School in Newark, Delaware, my wife and I attended the school's open house in late September. After meeting with teachers, the parents were invited to the cafeteria for refreshments. During that time the president of the Parent and Teacher Association announced that the school had raised a few hundred dollars and wanted to use the money to purchase new playground equipment. She asked if anyone would be interested in looking through playground equipment catalogs and help decide what to buy. As I raised my hand to volunteer, little did I realize that my life would be changed forever.

I took home the catalogs, and after seeing what could be bought for the small amount of money the school had raised, I was disappointed. All of the big, exciting equipment cost thousands of dollars, and we only had a few hundred to spend. I was beginning to get disappointed.

At that stage of my life I was working as a researcher and writer for an educational consulting company. My job required me to spend quite a bit of time at the University of Delaware library. The next day when I visited the library I began to research playground equipment; I wanted to find out who made the best, how much the equipment cost, how long it lasted, and how safe it was.

During my research the name Robert Leathers kept surfacing. Headlines from magazines and newspapers read, "Robert Leathers Builds Another Dream Playground!" and "Kids Vote Robert Leathers the Playground King!" I was beginning to get curious. Just who was this Robert Leathers? Why he was so successful in building playgrounds for schools all across the United States?

Eventually I found what I was looking for. It turned out that Robert Leathers was an architect based in Ithaca, New York, and was known for his designs in the luxury housing market. When he had volunteered to build a playground for his child's school, his services were suddenly in demand. Schools and children begged Leathers to come to their town and to help them build their own dream playground.

Within a few years Robert Leathers became so popular with his playground building techniques that *Sesame Street, Sixty Minutes*, and other television programs sought him out. He was the cover story for many national news magazines. By this time I knew what I wanted for Brookside Elementary: I wanted a Robert Leathers playground!

His playground building technique included visiting the school and meeting with the children, and asking them what *they* wanted. It did not matter if the children wanted a fort, castle, maze, pirate ship, or some other creation. If the children wanted it in their playground, Robert Leathers drew up plans and told them how it could be done. He even had a complete package that showed the school and parents what they needed to do in order to make their dream playground become a reality.

I collected as much information as I could and contacted his organization in New York to find out how Brookside Elementary could organize and build what had been referred to in *Time* as "the Disneyland of playgrounds."

A few weeks later I presented my findings at the PTA meeting. Everyone seemed excited when I showed them the photographs and sketches from other dream playground projects. Within minutes the parents and the teachers in attendance wanted one of those giant wooden structures at Brookside Elementary. That is, until I told

> Within a few years Robert Leathers became so popular with his playground building techniques that *Sesame Street, Sixty Minutes*, and other television programs sought him out.

them how much it would cost: "All we have to do is raise $40,000 and recruit 1,500 volunteers who will work twenty hours a day for five days, and our dream will become a reality!"

I might as well have thrown cold water over the entire group. Suddenly, dreams were shattered when everyone agreed that it could not be done, and that the entire idea of a dream playground might work for other schools, but no way could our community pull off such a huge project. It took several more meetings before the principal caught my enthusiasm and said that maybe, just maybe, it might work.

Ten months later we all proudly attended the ribbon cutting ceremony for Brookside Elementary's Dream Playground Project. We had indeed raised enough money and even recruited more than enough volunteers to achieve our goal. It was not only hard work but also fun.

My point in sharing this story is not to brag about what our playground committee was able to accomplish, but to illustrate the point that if you believe in a fund-raising project, nothing should get in your way. Do not let anything discourage you.

It doesn't matter what your nonprofit mission is. You can be busy saving the rain forests, the whales, or endangered wildlife. You can be operating a soup kitchen, a family counseling center, or community center. You can even be a small elementary school wanting something better for your children. If you believe in your project, nothing will stand in your way. You can and will find the right fund-raising approach to meet your goals. With a little research and the proper planning, you can be on the road to fundraising success.

Fundraising can be frightening to people who have never been involved in such projects. The odds against success can be frightful. But it doesn't matter if you are new to the wonderful world of fund raising or a seasoned pro who is looking for some new ideas to try. If you believe in your project and it becomes your passion, there is no way it can fail.

What Is Fundraising?

Most people believe fundraising is simply the act of asking a person or an organization for a donation. That is only partially correct. True

> Fundraising can be frightening to people who have never been involved in such projects.

fundraising goes deeper than that: The people you're asking for donations must believe deeply in the mission of your organization. (See Chapter 2 for more on mission statements.) Create a passion about your cause, and you'll create loyal donors.

Fundraising is an important aspect of any nonprofit organization, and the people involved in the fund-raising field know firsthand how a good fund-raising program is crucial to their very existence. Too many agencies make the mistake of thinking that just because they are in business, people will send them money. Without skilled and creative fund-raising professionals, many nonprofit agencies would cease to exist.

Too often, nonprofits conduct public relations and communications as if it were a hostage situation. Michael Ertel, Public Relations and Employee Communications Manager at Marketplace Bank and board member of the Orlando Chapter of the Public Relations Society of America, has seen this phenomenon at work. He describes it this way, "If this doesn't happen, if we're not bailed out, if we're not given publicity or we're not given money from a certain source for one reason or another, this service will go away. Little Timmy will no longer be able to have this service available to him." Ertel adds, "That is a very dangerous way to do public relations. It's like a soldier walking onto a battlefield with a white flag already in his hands saying, 'I know we're going to lose, but, if you can bail us out, we'll float above water.' And then the [nonprofits] wonder why no one wants to fund them."

Ertel says no one wants to fund an organization or firm that is not a success. "If a company were going out to the stock market and saying, 'Our company is about this close to going out of business, but we want you to give us money so we can stay in business because we're a really good company,' they wouldn't get any buyers," he says.

In a similar way, communicating to your community about the successes of your organization should not be doom and gloom: We are about to go out of business, so out of the goodness of your heart send money. Instead, the nonprofit agency should position itself as a viable community partner, working toward social change and social activities.

Why People Give

According to a survey conducted by Blue Moon Communications, the following are the most typical reasons why people donate money to a cause.

1. Belief in the cause
2. Recognition and honor
3. For a tax deduction
4. Family tradition
5. Religious beliefs
6. Joy
7. Guilt
8. Fear
9. To make a difference

Who Is Responsible for Fundraising?

In the year 2000, individuals gave more than $152 billion to nonprofit charities, according to the American Association of Fundraising Counsel. That's a lot of money but the big question is, Who is responsible for raising the money? Who is in charge of making sure that people have an opportunity to make a donation?

Stacey Cook, executive director for Project Fit America, will tell you that it is everyone's job. "There is not a person in any capacity of the organization that is not important to fund raising," she says. "By that I mean that every aspect of the organization from the mail room to the board room needs to be impeccable in order to attract and retain donors."

Some nonprofit agencies have the luxury of having a full-time or a part-time development director whose job description usually spells out how he or she is responsible for raising a specific dollar amount during a fiscal year. But just because you have the luxury of a staff development officer with a well-defined job description does not mean that fundraising will always be successful. Millie DeAnda, Executive Director of the Greater Dallas Crime Commission, believes fundraising begins and ends with the board of directors. "The board members are responsible for the organization's financial condition, and that includes being actively involved in fund raising," she says.

Board members are a vital component of every fund-raising plan and they should be involved to help make every campaign a rousing success. Board members have the ability to reach out to corporations, foundations, and area businesses when it comes to raising money. They are hard working volunteers who clearly have a passion for your nonprofit agency. So use those volunteers to your advantage and get them involved, at least on the board level, in every fund-raising campaign.

Fundraising as Priority One

Do you eat, drink, and sleep fundraising? If you are, then you are working way too hard. It is true that fundraising should be your number one priority, but you don't have to let it consume your life. With

Make the Community Link

The most important thing a nonprofit can do is position itself as a viable community member, according to Michael Ertel, Public Relations and Employee Communications Manager at Marketplace Bank.

"Most nonprofits that I see don't necessarily position themselves in the community the way that other businesses position themselves as a good resource, a well-intentioned resource, not a resource for business," he says. "And that's unfortunate because a lot of nonprofits do conduct themselves in a manner much like a business but they don't do their public relations in the same fashion."

the proper planning fundraising can be an exciting opportunity, one that you're not likely to forget for a long time. But unless your group is part of a well-known charitable organization, you may run into difficulty trying to raise the funds you need. Once fund raising becomes your number one priority, however, the process will become easier.

In 1990, when I was hired as the development director of the Delaware Adolescent Program, they had no fund-raising program in place. They had survived for nearly twenty-five years without having to worry about fundraising because the doctors who had created the organization also funded it. But the founders had retired a few years earlier, and now the program was desperate for funds. So they advertised for the position of development director, which I answered.

For almost two years prior to that time, I was a partner in a special events company called Great Events. We produced special events for both for-profit corporations and nonprofit agencies, and I had seen my fair share of successful nonprofits. The one common factor among those successful nonprofits was their ability to make fundraising their number one priority. That did not mean that everything else took a back seat, just that the reason they were so successful and could accomplish everything in their mission statement was *because* they concentrated on their fund-raising efforts.

They recruited the best volunteers. They held the best special events. They wrote the best direct-mail solicitation letters. They wrote the best grants. In other words, they did everything they possibly could do to make their fund-raising programs a success.

Getting everyone at your nonprofit agency to agree that fund raising should be the number one priority is not as easy as it sounds. You will meet obstacles along the way. The obstacle I faced was trying to convince the people who hired me as their new development director that the fund-raising program had to be a team effort and not something that I alone would take care of. While I was certainly the person to spearhead the fund-raising program, I still needed the support of the executive director, the board, the staff, and all of the volunteers.

They were not an easy sell. The executive director who hired me thought she was too busy to become involved in the fund-raising program. She also did not want me to bother the board with any

Fundraising Is Friend Raising

As a manager of a nonprofit agency, you need to raise money but you also need to "raise friends."

What is involved in friend raising? Invite people to see what your agency can do or to become a part of your organization as a volunteer. Invite people to share the good news about your agency with their friends, family, coworkers, and business associates.

Every nonprofit agency needs friends and funds. But you'll never raise the funds without those all-important friends. So what have you done lately to make friends?

fund-raising ideas or events. But after a few weeks of meetings and countless memos, everyone in the organization finally saw that if fundraising became a priority, they would soon be able to meet their fund-raising goals.

It took a few months before the board agreed to even put fundraising on their meeting agenda. But once they did, they started to come alive with excitement. They clearly wanted to become involved. Finally I had everyone on the same page, and fundraising became the agency's number one priority.

How to Start a Fund-raising Program

If you don't have a fund-raising program in place right now, then you must be one of only a handful of nonprofit agencies in the United States with a large enough endowment to fund all your programs. But if you are struggling and need to create a good fund-raising program, or if you have a fund-raising program in place but feel it is time for an overhaul, follow these simple steps to create a fund-raising strategy.

Step one: Create a fund-raising committee. This committee should consist of at least two board members who are enthusiastic about fundraising and several people from the management level of your nonprofit—the executive director, associate executive director, development director, and planned giving director. Ideally, your fund-raising committee will consist of five to seven people. This way when you hold a meeting, if one or two members have a last minute appointment and cannot attend, you will at least have enough people to discuss your fund-raising agenda.

Step two: Put your fund-raising goals in writing. It sounds simple enough, but many nonprofit agencies do not bother to put down on paper specific fund-raising goals. They have a ballpark figure in mind but don't really know how much they want to raise. Or worse, they do not know how to go about raising that amount of money. If you need to raise $50,000 over the next year, write it down. Once you have a specific fund-raising goal in mind, your job will be made much easier.

Step three: Develop a plan of action. In other words, what do you think you need to do in order to raise that $50,000? Can you write a grant for that amount? Do you need to plan a special event? Will a direct-mail campaign do the trick? How about looking into federal government grants? .

The best plan of action will involve a realistic look at how much you believe can be raised from various sources. Can you really expect to hold a special event to raise that much money? Or should you only expect a small percentage of the fund-raising goal to come from an event? Will the rest of the funds be raised from grants, direct mail, or government money? This step is important, so take your time and develop a plan of action that will work for your nonprofit agency.

Step four: Revise your plans. The fund-raising committee must constantly stay on top of your agency's fund-raising efforts, and must be ready to revise the fund-raising plans if necessary. Suppose you have budgeted for $10,000 to be raised through your direct-mail solicitation campaign but only $7,000 has come through, with only a few days left until it is over. Where will you get the remaining $3,000 that you need?

Smart nonprofit managers always have a Plan B ready to roll. An example of a Plan B could be a special event fund-raising party, in which you invite people to a big night of music, dancing, a silent auction, and lots of fun. Or Plan B could call for an emergency grant fund-raising campaign. Some foundations around the country have specific emergency fund-raising funds available. When I was the development director at a nonprofit agency in Delaware, I was able to obtain emergency funding from the Longwood Foundation, a local foundation that also gives grants to nonprofits around the country.

Step five: Share those plans. Don't just sit back, form a fund-raising committee, come up with a goal, and a strategy to meet that goal. Instead, share your fund-raising plans with everyone who is connected with your nonprofit agency: board members, staff, volunteers, and donors. Everyone should be aware of your fund-raising plan and be kept informed of your progress.

> Smart nonprofit managers always have a Plan B ready to roll.

Fund-raising Software

Are you using fund-raising software at your nonprofit agency? If you are, congratulations. If you are not, then you'd better get busy and find out how fund-raising software can save you time and help you raise more money.

As a nonprofit manager, you want to make sure you have the best fund-raising software on the planet. With the best fund-raising software you will be able to take your nonprofit agency to a level of excellence that you have not experienced in the past.

Fund-raising software helps you target different donors with unique messages, track the effectiveness of a fund-raising campaign—whether a direct-mail piece or a special event—identify and recognize your largest donors, and continue to build your base of donors.

Fund-raising software is an effective tool for any nonprofit, but the software costs money, as does the purchase and maintenance of the hardware, training for existing and future employees, and expansion and future. It's a big investment, so make sure you need it. If you run a small organization and are using a low-tech system that is working well or if you receive nearly all of your funding from one or two donors, don't invest in fund-raising software. If, however, you feel that your current system of soliciting and tracking donations is causing you to lose potential donation opportunities and, therefore, not fulfilling your mission (see Chapter 2), you'll want to consider investing in fund-raising software that you can afford. In addition, if your organization needs more funds to expand your current operations, you'll want to consider fund-raising software.

Before looking at your options, however, think about what to want fund-raising software to do for you. Determine your specific needs based on your plans, as in the following:

- We need to start a direct-mail campaign for our new initiative.
- Each year, we need to identify donors who have not cotributed during the previous year and contact them by telephone.
- We need to send thank-you letters within two weeks of receiving donations.
- We need to increase the average amount of each donation.

You may want to rate your list from most important to least important, in case a potential software that fits your budget can't do everything you want it to.

> If you run a small organization and are using a low-tech system that is working well or if you receive nearly all of your funding from one or two donors, don't invest in fund-raising software.

Think also about your future needs. You know the future goals for your organization: How will your decision to purchase new software help with those goals?

Don't complete this activity on your own. Ask other key members of your staff to do the same, and then meet to share ideas. Beware, however, of people who have worked with a particular type of software and want you to purchase it so that they don't have to learn a new system. That software may not be right for your organization.

Now determine how much money you can make available to spend on fund-raising software and new or upgraded hardware, training, and so on. Go over your budget from top to bottom to squeeze out every last dollar and then set an upper limit. You may meet up with a sharp salesperson, so keep your upper limit fresh in your mind.

Also determine how pressing your needs are: Can this system wait for six months, after your big fund-raising event is over and you don't have the pressure of planning that event and implementing new software? Or do you need it right away so that you can meet your fund-raising goals for this year?

Contact a computer consultant or salesperson to look at products only after you are clear on your fund-raising goals, available budget, and timing. You'll then be wowed by expensive software with lots of bells and whistles that probably does everything you want it to. Be careful, however, not to overbuy. Every dollar you spend on unnecessary software features is money you can't spend on services for your constituents. Keep in mind what you need your software to do and make sure it can do that effectively. Anything else is a waste.

When comparing software, look at the following hidden costs:

- Hardware—Will your existing hardware work with the new software? If not, will new hardware or hardware upgrades fit your budget?
- Third-party software—Do you need other software to print letters, generate labels, send e-mails, and so on? Find out exactly what other software you'll need before making a decision about fund-raising software.
- Add-ons—Will you need to pay more for your fund-raising software to also manage special event management, keep

> Determine how much money you can make available to spend on fund-raising software and new or upgraded hardware, training, and so on.

track of volunteers, mesh with your existing accounting system, and so on? Or is that included in the price of the fund-raising software?

- Setup—Will the software company load the software onto your organization's computer and test to make sure it's operating properly? If not, how much will that cost you in in-house resources?
- Support—Is technical support free, or do you pay for onsite visits and phone calls? Do you have to sign up for year-long technical support every year? And if you do, will the company be in business in a year? Check the company's track record.
- Training—Is training required, or is the software so simple that you don't need training? Will the company train your existing staff for free? If not, how much will training cost? Will it be onsite or offsite? Can you train one or two staff members and have them train the rest of your staff? How will you train future staff members?
- Upgrades and revisions—How often is the software revised and do you have to upgrade each time?
- Existing data—Can all your existing data move easily to the new software, will someone on your staff need to rekey all that information, or can the software company convert your existing data (usually for a fee)?
- Down time—Will your existing system be out of commission while the new system is installed and tested? Can this be done during nonwork hours?

Buying and using fund-raising software won't be without glitches, no matter how well you plan. Just be sure to anticipate surprises and roll with the punches. Eventually, this, too, shall pass. Take good notes so that your next software decision—whether to buy something new or upgrade your existing software—will be a little easier.

> Buying and using fund-raising software won't be without glitches, no matter how well you plan.

Chapter 8

Special Events

Topics covered in this chapter:

- **Using creative special events to raise funds**
- **How to make an event cost effective**
- **Tips for a successful fund-raiser**
- **How to find sponsors**
- **Keeping event costs down**

Some nonprofit managers are not really sure what a fund-raising special event is all about. Ever wonder why some nonprofit agencies raise lots of money holding special events while others lose money every time they attempt to hold one? The secret is in learning the ABCs of special events. Once you master the basics, you will be ready for any special event idea that comes along.

What Is a Special Event?

Special events can be fun and exciting, and even raise money and awareness of your organization and its mission. Choose the wrong event, however, and your dream can quickly turn into a nightmare.

Many nonprofit agencies decide to hold a special event without giving it much thought. They believe that all they have to do is to come up with an idea, have a few meetings, and then volunteers, money, and good publicity will all materialize. If only it were that easy.

With a little extra careful planning and research, it is possible to build the perfect special event. The most important thing to remember is this: Just because a special event worked for one nonprofit agency does not mean it will work for yours.

The key to success in any special event is creativity. In today's highly competitive environment you need to be highly creative when it comes to offering a special event. You cannot just mail invitations to a black tie dinner and expect contributions to roll in. Your event needs to be special and offer something different, especially if it is the first time the event is being held in your town.

Creating an Event with a Twist

Many successful fund-raising special events are based in part on other events. While it is a good idea to collect information on other special events taking place around the country, be careful that you don't end up suffering from information overload. Here's an example of how I came up with a special event idea with a twist:

While racking my brain for a creative special event idea, I found myself flipping through a copy of the *Guinness Book of World Records*. I knew that many nonprofit agencies from all across the

> The key to success in any special event is creativity.

country were holding special events based on ideas in this book. For some unknown reason the creative side of my brain kept searching for something different to do.

Then it hit me. Why not try for a Guinness World Record by assembling the largest group of people dancing the "twist" at one time? I checked through the book and couldn't find any groups that had ever tried to set a world record in that category. So I contacted the Guinness office and they gave me the official guidelines to set a new Dance Record in the "Twist" category. And because it was going to be a new category, our nonprofit agency needed at least 5,001 people dancing the Twist at one time. Almost ten years earlier another nonprofit agency in our town had attempted to play the world's largest game of musical chairs—with 10,000 people. So I was confident the community was ready for a new, exciting, and creative special event.

I convinced everyone at the nonprofit I was working at that the event would be a success. I chose a local horse racetrack to be the venue for the event, knowing that there would be a good crowd on a Saturday afternoon. It would give everyone an opportunity to come out, participate in a world record event, and have a day of family fun. The racetrack had a picnic grove that included a Moon Bounce and children's games, so everyone agreed that it would be the perfect location.

After several brainstorming meetings, our fund-raising committee developed more than a dozen creative ways to raise money with this special event. I came up with the idea of asking Chubby Checker to perform his famous song in person at the event, but when I contacted him he said he would love to come, but had a previous singing engagement on that day. But he did record several Public Service Announcements that aired on local radio stations. (See Chapter 15 for more on PSAs.) Chubby urged people to come out and "twist and twist again."

We also had hundreds of volunteers wear buttons that read, "Ask me how you can Twist your way into a world record!" The buttons were successful because almost every one who read one ended up asking the person for more information. And since we were only asking for a $5 contribution to participate in the Twist event, the people wearing those cute little buttons raised hundreds of dollars a day.

> After several brainstorming meetings, our fund-raising committee developed more than a dozen creative ways to raise money with this special event.

Another key factor in the success of the event was to ask local businesses and corporations to sponsor teams of "twisters" made up of employees and their friends and families. Many businesses made a $500 contribution and told groups of their employees to take their families and have a good time. Almost two dozen corporations wrote about the event in their company newsletters before it took place. That sparked competition among different departments to see who could get the most people out to twist.

Alas, Mother Nature did not want to cooperate on that Saturday afternoon. It rained so hard that many of the people who had purchased tickets didn't show up to dance to the Twist. Although we did not set the Guinness Book of World Records in that new category, we had plenty of fun and raised lots of money!

Getting and Staying Fresh

If you are running an established special event, one that has raised money year after year, the worst thing you can do is to dust off last year's file, get out the volunteer list, and schedule the date. These are things you could do in your sleep: offer the same menu, send out the same invitation (printed with new colors, of course), hold it at the same location. Keep this up and you're bound to keep getting last year's funds. In other words, new people won't come out to your event and past supporters will become tired of attending "the same old event as last year!"

When I was working as a development director I got the idea to hold a silent auction at one of our special events. But I wanted our silent auction to be different, something that people would talk about when they went home. So instead of the usual dinners at local restaurants and free flowers from the local florist, I created a silent auction that featured nothing but celebrity items.

Obtaining celebrity items was easier than I had ever imagined. Just think how your special event will be the talk of the town by having items in your silent auction that includes a Stephen King autographed bestseller, a signed Randy Travis T-shirt, a golf glove signed by Arnold Palmer, and script from the soap opera *General Hospital,* signed by the entire cast.

Creative Fundraising

New creative special events are usually combinations of existing events. For example, instead of a stuffy black tie gala, hold a family black tie event. Let the kids dress up too, and serve fun finger foods and Shirley Temple drinks. Add excitement by staging the event at an unconventional location: a barn, a skating rink, a department store, a train station, or even an airport hanger.

Being creative at a gala can also save money. Instead of costly flower arrangements, put items on the table and invite the guests to make their own centerpieces. Give prizes for the best ones that are made. Try something different, such as a wet T-shirt contest. Instead of wearing the T-shirt you have to throw it the farthest. Consider adding additional moneymaking ventures, such as a silent auction, to your existing special events.

Getting famous people to part with something is not as difficult as you may think. As long as you plan your celebrity silent auction four to six months ahead of time, you should be able to obtain memorabilia from celebrities in all walks of life. Thanks to America's never-ending interest in celebrities, auctions that feature donated items from famous people are now taking place all across the country.

Are Special Events Cost Effective?

The answer to that question is, "It depends." Specifically, it depends on whom you ask. Special events can be very costly, but they can also be very cost effective. When I ran my special event business we created several Halloween events that made the clients some money but not as much as they had hoped for. But other special events we hosted ended up making so much cash we couldn't count it fast enough.

Special events can raise large sums of money, but the nonprofit agency has to have an established track record of putting on successful events. It requires a lot of work, volunteer effort, donor cultivation, faith, and plenty of luck. For these reasons, larger nonprofit agencies tend to find it easier to host a special event fund-raising function. They have larger budgets, more volunteers, and access to resources that many smaller nonprofit agencies don't often have.

Remember, your goal in finding the perfect special event is an important one. When you explore your ideas in greater depth and things are looking bleak, it is better to cancel a special event on the drawing board than to continue with an idea that can end up being a disaster. Consider each of the following questions very carefully.

Is this event appropriate for your nonprofit agency?

If you are with a religious organization, for example, the general public may not approve of an event that features alcoholic beverages or charitable gambling. If your fund-raising idea committee has decided on a Monte Carlo night, try switching to a '50s theme and hold your event in a local malt shop. And instead of charitable gambling, hold a silent auction featuring celebrity memorabilia with a twist: obtain items from celebrities who were famous in the '50s. By

How to Find Celebrity Addresses

First rule—use as many sources as possible. While there are several books for sale that feature addresses of celebrities, many are only the addresses of their booking agencies. If you find more than one celebrity listed at the same address, chances are pretty slim that your request for a donated item will be honored.

You can contact an author by writing to the publicity department at his or her publishing company. Or you can go to the library and look in *Who's Who of American Authors*. Other celebrity addresses can be found in the different *Who's Who* volumes.

Most celebrities now have their own Web site, and it is possible to contact them via e-mail from their home page. Many nonprofit agencies report receiving responses from at least half of the celebrities they contacted.

When writing to celebrities asking for donations, don't use a form letter. I always had a better response rate when I sent each one a personalized letter.

Get the News Out

When sending out press releases to the media about your special event don't forget to include company newsletters. They are always looking for local community news, especially when it may affect employees and their families. And follow up with a telephone call to make sure it was received. That gives you a good excuse to ask them when they will be publishing information about your special event.

If you are trying to get your local newspaper to write a feature story about your upcoming event, sometimes it is easier to work with a freelance writer who regularly has his or her byline in that newspaper. The next time you read your newspaper notice that the staff reporters have a byline under the headline. A notation in the byline that says "Special to the Post" indicates that a freelance writer or stringer wrote the article. These writers usually can call in the "hot tip" to their editor and get the assignment to write the article.

And don't forget to offer free tickets to local radio stations in exchange for promotional consideration.

Lastly, include your mission statement in all news releases and other announcements about your special event.

making a few simple changes and improvement to your plan, you can make that type of a special event work for your nonprofit agency.

Do you have sufficient volunteers to make this special event work?

If you are a very small nonprofit agency do not make big plans for any special events that require more volunteers than you have. To illustrate, here is an example from small group that had big plans about a decade ago. Julie Gold is the singer/songwriter who wrote that Grammy Award–winning tune *From A Distance*, popularized by Bette Midler. While most people only remember the Bette Midler version, Julie Gold toured the country and sold out concert halls singing her popular song, along with dozens of other tunes she had written and recorded. Someone at a small nonprofit agency decided it would be a good idea if Julie Gold performed at a benefit concert and raised money for the agency's cause. It was a good idea: Julie Gold would donate her time, travel from New York City at her own expense, and perform two shows on a Friday evening. Even the theater where she was to perform donated space.

The nonprofit agency made its big mistake when it decided it did not have to be involved in selling the tickets. The agency's managers failed to understand the golden rule of any special event. Ads don't sell tickets. Radio announcements don't sell tickets. Newspaper stories don't sell tickets. People sell tickets! While those other activities all contribute to the overall success of a fund-raising special event, you need people to sell tickets to make the event a winner. In this case, because no one wanted to sell tickets to the Julie Gold concert, the event was canceled and a potential moneymaking event turned into an embarrassment for those involved. Remember to make sure you have enough people necessary to take your event from start to finish, and to make it a huge success.

Will the event raise enough money to warrant the time and energy it will take to produce it?

If you plan a special event that raises $60,000 but your expenses are $56,000, can you justify that much time and effort for a

$4,000 net profit? For some nonprofit agencies the answer will be yes. Each group and event needs to be considered on an individual basis. If a special event brings hundreds of people together who eventually become members of an organization, then the goal of attracting new people has been met, despite the fact that only $4,000 is raised. On the other hand, if an organization is trying to raise a larger amount of money but somehow failed to get enough sponsors to cover their costs, then netting $4,000 seems like too much time and energy for such a small return.

Can your event withstand any competition?

If you have decided to hold a walk-a-thon in the autumn and you suddenly discover that two other nonprofit agencies are also holding that type of an event at the same time, you might want to reconsider waiting until spring to hold yours. While it is true that some large nonprofit agencies such as the American Heart Association and the Juvenile Diabetes Foundation are able to hold a walk-a-thon on the same weekend or close to the same date as another agency, you might find that you are competing for the same walkers.

In Delaware, for example, the Lutheran Community Services is supported by almost twenty Lutheran churches in the state. When they want to hold a walk-a-thon on a Saturday morning in the fall, and it happens to be the same time the American Heart Association is having their annual walk-a-thon, they don't have to worry about recruiting walkers. The Lutheran churches will supply enough walkers to make their special event a big success. But if your agency doesn't have a pool of volunteers, think twice before scheduling your special event the same weekend as another nonprofit agency.

Check with your local United Way office and chamber of commerce office. Both organizations usually publish a calendar of special events for the coming year. And don't forget to check in your local newspaper for advertisements or articles for other nonprofit special events, and be on the lookout for fliers that are on display in local store windows.

How Much Should You Spend?

When budgeting for a special event, it's not unusual to spend 50 to 60 percent of the amount of money raised for expenses. In your special events fund-raising budget make sure you include every possible expense. Don't get caught short because you forgot to budget for printing, advertising, food, security, or some other expense.

Here is a sample special event budget for an art auction:

Expenses

Food	$2,000
Wine	$300
Decorations	$500
Entertainment	$700
Printing	$600
Postage	$300
Total Expenses	**$4,400**

Income

80 couples @ $100 each	$8,000
Raffle	$1,000
Silent Auction	$2,000
Proceeds from Art Auction	$6,000
Total Income	$17,000
Less Expenses	$4,400
Net Profit	**$12,600**

Special Event Tip Sheet 1

Here is some wisdom gleaned from special event planning pros.

- Set your fund-raising goal. Nothing becomes dynamic until it first becomes specific.
- There's no such thing as luck. Your key to success lies in persistence. Persistence produces results.
- Have a flip chart, magic markers, or a chalkboard at your brainstorming sessions. Write your ideas in color; creative people are visual thinkers.
- Get everything donated. Recruit people who love to ask for donations of goods and services.
- Don't forget name tags for staff, volunteers, security, and board members.
- Make sure to form a cleanup committee.
- Explore every moneymaking opportunity for your special event. Take advantage of the fact that several hundred people could be gathered in one area, and provide them with ample means to spend their money.
- Create an action team to spearhead your special event committee.
- Use every possible connection you have to make your event a success. Ask your doctor or dentist to buy tickets for themselves and their friends, for example.
- Take extra special care of the VIPs who will be attending the event.
- When looking for potential sponsors for your next special event, keep new businesses in mind. They are always searching for a way to do something positive for the community.
- Do only what you can do, and do it well, and recognize when it's time to bring in outside help, such as a special events consultant.
- Keep lines of communication open among staff, volunteers, vendors, the media, and everyone else who will have any involvement with the event.
- When the special event is over, send a thank you to everyone who was involved in making it happen.
- If your event is a rousing success, consider making it the "first annual" one.
- If your special event did not go as well as you had hoped, don't panic. Sit down and evaluate what went right and what didn't work.

Special Event Tip Sheet 2

Here is more wisdom gleaned from special event planning pros.

- When budgeting for the income you expect from your special event, be as realistic as possible. Don't get caught up in wishful thinking.

- Work on your budget as the event gets closer. Revise any changes in income or expense projections as they occur.

- If your special event needs a permit from your city or town, apply for one well in advance. Leave ample time to get the necessary insurance. Before holding any type of contest, game, or other charitable gambling activity, consult with the state's attorney general's office. They will be able to tell you if what you are planning to do is legal and if a permit is required.

- Don't forget to ask your own organization's vendors to sponsor your next special event, and have partial sponsorship slots available.

- Successful special events require a cheerleader who can rally everyone to do their very best. Recruit that cheerleader early on in your planning process.

- Decision-makers for small businesses do not have a lot of time, so if you are asking them for a donation of a product or service, put your request in writing on the agency's letterhead. Keep the request short and sweet, and you will see positive results.

- Offer training to your volunteers. Many might be inexperienced when it comes to working on a special event committee.

- After the event is over conduct a thorough financial review. If your special event has been taking place over a number of years, see if you are increasing the amount of money you are making.

- If you decide to hold some type of raffle at your event include some big-ticket items. People are more likely to purchase a raffle ticket if the quality of the prize makes it worthwhile. Travel agencies can always donate trips to exotic places, and airlines can sometimes donate airfare.

- Promote upcoming special event on bumper stickers.

Brainstorming for Dollars

Brainstorming is one of the most effective ways for groups to work together in finding creative solutions. Individuals, businesses, and nonprofit agencies have developed brainstorming as a major facet of their creative policies. Walt Disney was a strong believer in the process, and look at what he was able to create!

The basic rules to keep in mind are discussed in the following sections.

Allow Any Idea to Be Discussed

Some of the best ideas have started out as what sounded like crazy nonsense. But if your committee is free to discuss any ideas, regardless of how impossible they sound, that original idea may well spawn others, ultimately creating fantastic, workable ideas in the process.

Eliminate Negativity

Tell everyone in your brainstorming session that negative comments such as, "That'll never work." "We've tried that before." or "We can't possibly pull off something like that." are not allowed at this meeting. In fact, you should prohibit any negative comments during a brainstorming session. Let reality come back into play when you're reviewing the ideas that came from the brainstorming session, but that's another meeting with a completely different agenda.

Remember that even if you tell your group that negative talk isn't allowed (and be sure to give examples!), you'll have to stay vigilant. The first time someone gives a negative response, nip it in the bud. Acknowledge the comment, explain how it can keep good ideas from coming up, and then move on with more good ideas.

Establish a Clear Agenda

Explain in the initial minutes of the session what you're trying to accomplish. Here are some examples:

> Some of the best ideas have started out as what sounded like crazy nonsense.

- "We're here to think of special events or promotional activities that can make the public more aware of the services we offer."
- "We need to come up with potential corporate sponsors who would be a good fit for our annual 5K road race."
- "We're going to spend twenty minutes discussing any possible activity that we can include in our annual Fall Festival."

Throw Out Rules

Besides a hard-and-fast rule about keeping the talk positive, don't bother with other rules. Go with the flow, even if that means allowing people to interrupt each other, go back to topics that were discussed ten minutes earlier, talk about projects they've worked on at other organizations, and so on.

Keep the Sessions Short

If your brainstorming meeting is at the beginning of the day, limit your first session to thirty minutes so that everyone in your meeting stays fresh. Keep in mind that thirty minutes at the end of the day can be a really long time to brainstorm. You won't get new, fresh ideas if people are tired or half-asleep.

Assign Someone to Take Notes

During the session, have someone write all of the ideas on a chalkboard, marker board, overhead projector transparency, or some other large surface that everyone can see. The note taker doesn't have to have any special skills, but should write down *every idea*—not just ones that he or she deems "good." Every idea is worth writing down. And even if you have only a partial solution to a problem, suggest it so that it is written down. It could spark someone to come up with the rest of the idea or solution.

> If your brainstorming meeting is at the beginning of the day, limit your first session to thirty minutes so that everyone in your meeting stays fresh.

Special Event Tip Sheet 3

Here's more advice from special event planning pros.

- Always plan for more than enough parking spaces at any special event. If people cannot find a convenient place to park, they might not bother to show up at all.

- Art departments in high schools and colleges are always a good source of free graphic design and printing assistance. Students may also satisfy a community service requirement by helping out on your project.

- Be realistic about the number of people who will attend your first special event. If you are a small nonprofit agency that does not have a large pool of volunteers and supporters, don't expect thousands of strangers to show up in black tie outfits carrying blank checks. Start small and slowly build attendance.

- If your nonprofit agency is thinking about holding a murder mystery dinner as a fundraiser, keep in mind that Halloween is the most popular and successful time of the year for this type of event.

- Remember that the nature of fund raising is to take risks. Be prepared to take some risks to make your special event a success.

- If you are thinking about purchasing special event software to help plan your event, get the names of some other nonprofit agencies that have been using the software for a few years. Ask them if they had to do it all over again, would they still purchase the software, and do they really think it was worth the expense?

- Before you begin your fund-raising efforts, make sure you have the energy, direction, and enthusiasm necessary for success.

- Recognize that planning is a complex process. Some people are good at it, while others are not. Recruit good planners on your special event team.

- Start a resource file composed of newspaper clippings, magazine and journal articles, and other relevant fundraising information about other nonprofit agencies and their special events. Draw on it often for ideas.

Quantity, not Quality, Rules

It is difficult to work with only a short list of creative ideas. These ideas will be further discussed in other meetings and forums, and if you have only one idea, the future discussions won't have much depth. The exception to this guideline is if you hit on what appears to be a fantastic idea early on, and each subsequent idea keeps building on and refining that first one. What you'll probably end up with is a well-honed idea with great potential.

Don't Give Up!

The last half of the brainstorming session is usually better than the first. It takes the first half to get all the usual responses and habitual solutions out of the way. When these are removed, you are left with new and creative ideas and solutions to your fund-raising needs. In the same way, second and third brainstorming sessions— provided they're not scheduled on the same day or even in the same week—are usually more productive than the first. The group gets more comfortable with each other and shares its most outlandish ideas, which is exactly what you're going for.

> The last half of the brainstorming session is usually better than the first.

Special Event Ideas

Having trouble brainstorming ideas for your special event? This section lists three ideas that just may work for you.

A Carnival

Did you know that many of the major carnival companies that travel around the country will pay a nonprofit agency a fee to host a fund-raising carnival for them? Fees can range anywhere from $5,000 to $15,000 depending upon a variety of factors. Plus, you can also receive a percentage of the ticket sales from rides and carnival games. Check in your local telephone book under Carnivals to see if anyone in your region has placed an ad or a listing. The carnival companies usually advertise in many different telephone books and directories. You can also look for carnival companies using an Internet search engine.

After you find a carnival company you would like to work with, the first thing you need to do is to check references. Ask for the names and contact information for at least three other nonprofit agencies with whom they have dealt with in the past two years. And make sure you contact those references. Don't rely just on letters of reference that appear in a sales brochure or catalog. Those can be easily faked, and unfortunately, some carnival companies' practices are less than stellar.

After the carnival company has passed your thorough inspection, your next step is to look for a suitable location. Usually the carnival company will specify how large an area they will need for their rides, equipment, food concessions, games, and other things they usually bring with them. (The worst thing you can do is to book a carnival into a location that is too small. You need to allow plenty of space for parking and for people to walk around.)

Most of the carnival companies will print up professional looking posters for you to distribute in the area. Make sure you get an ample supply, and make sure you have more than enough volunteers ready to drive around and post them everywhere. But the best public relations that can happen for a carnival to be successful is to be located in a high-traffic shopping center—either on a major highway or road or one that has a few anchor stores that attract thousands of people at day. Word of mouth will quickly spread about your carnival, and by the end of the first day everyone in town will know where you are located and what you are doing.

Check to see if the carnival company will rent your nonprofit agency a booth or two. When I did my first fund-raising carnival I rented a duck pond booth and a wheel of chance booth. For a flat fee of $200, our agency was free to charge whatever we wanted, and we could keep the proceeds all to ourselves. But you need to factor in the cost of prizes (those stuffed animals aren't cheap), and make sure you have enough volunteers ready to work in the booth for all of the hours you will be open. (And make sure your volunteers aren't giving away all of your prizes, either. We found out one soft-hearted

> The worst thing you can do is to book a carnival into a location that is too small.

volunteer was giving away stuffed animals to people who lost. He felt sorry for them, but he was costing us big time!)

An Art Auction

Did you know that it's very easy to hold an art auction as a fund-raising special event? And you don't have to be an expert in the field of art, either. Professional art auction companies will come out and run this event for you. Again, check in your local telephone book Yellow Pages to see if anyone is listed in your region. If you don't find anyone listed there, get on the Internet and try your favorite search engine. You'll find at least a half a dozen companies to choose from.

Don't forget to check references for art auction companies, as well. After you have selected a company to work with, your next agenda item will be to select a location to hold the event. If your nonprofit agency has a large multipurpose room that will hold a large crowd, and still have room for the art work, then you might want to consider using your own space. The biggest expense in holding an art auction is typically the room rent and food. So if you have a space that will work, use it. However, remember that an art auction is in the "upscale" special event category, so if your agency is located in a poor section of town or your room hasn't been painted in twenty years, think about where else you can hold it.

Ask a local printer to donate the cost of printing tickets and flyers to publicize the event. Most printers will say yes when they find out their name will be listed as a sponsor of an art auction. When thinking about food and beverages, you have your choice. When I did my first art auction, we used a local country club. We wanted to make it a very upscale, fun event for everyone who attended. But the rent and the cost of the food and alcohol were very expensive, and it cut into our profits more than we had thought it would. (FYI: If you've never operated an event with an "open bar," I'm going to suggest that you don't. It can get quite costly, and it's very difficult to estimate how many drinks people will really have.)

Most of the art auction companies will supply the auctioneer, but your agency will have to supply about a dozen or so volunteers.

> If your nonprofit agency has a large multipurpose room that will hold a large crowd, and still have room for the art work, then you might want to consider using your own space.

These volunteer positions are very important, so make sure you have reliable people who are committed to fill those slots.

You will make money from the sale of the admission tickets, and the art auction will give you a percentage of the money they make from auctioning off their art objects. I have seen small crowds spend lots of money on art, so don't think you can't make any money with this type of a special event.

Merchandise Sales

Sooner later nearly every nonprofit will become involved in some type of merchandise sales as a way to raise money. Whether you decide to sell gift wrap, pizza, candy, Christmas trees, or cookies, this type of fund-raising activity can be quite successful.

First, look at your bottom line. How much does your nonprofit agency need to make selling some type of merchandise? And don't be too shy about it, either. If you need to raise a quick $5,000 to repair a heater, realize that it can be done successfully through merchandise sales.

Remember to keep in mind the following ten rules of merchandise sales:

1. Always obtain samples of the products you will be selling. If the company won't send you a sample of their product, don't even consider selling it.
2. Always ask for three references, preferably from a nonprofit group similar to your own (soup kitchen, PTA, health agency, etc.). Make sure you contact those references and see if they were really pleased working with that particular company. Ask them if the merchandise was first class, and whether it was well received by their customers.
3. Negotiate everything! And we mean everything! Some companies promise you a 50 percent profit margin (which seems to be standard in the industry), while others offer you only a 20 or 30 percent profit margin. And some companies will offer a sliding scale that makes them look very attractive.

A Silent Auction

Get local merchants to donate gift certificates, products, services, etc. And don't forget to include a few celebrity items in your silent auction. You want people to be talking about this event when they leave, so next year it will be bigger and more successful.

But be realistic; how many items will you have to sell before you make any money?

4. Tell them you want free shipping and handling. Most of them will offer free shipping if you ask; if you don't ask, they won't offer. (Remember, they are in business to make money as well.)

5. Ask about their policy on damaged and broken merchandise. Who is responsible? And how long will it take to get replacement merchandise shipped and delivered to you?

6. Discourage children and volunteers from selling merchandise door to door. (In some states it is against the law to sell door to door.)

7. Collect the money before the order is shipped. Although some companies will give you the option of paying for their merchandise thirty days after it has been received, make sure everyone prepays for their order. (You would be surprised how many people "change their mind" after they order something and then refuse to pay for it when it arrives.)

8. Accept credit cards. Credit card billing is not as difficult as it used to be. Check with the merchandise company to see if they have a plan where customers can pay via credit card.

9. Throw a big "Thank You" party for the volunteers, staff, supporters, and anyone else who took the time out of their busy schedules to help make your merchandise sale a success. (Contact a local restaurant to see if there is space to hold a big thank you party; they may even donate some food and beverages if you ask.)

9. Send thank-you notes to everyone who buys something from your organization. They will be surprised, and your nonprofit will be remembered as an agency that cares about its supporters.

> Send thank-you notes to everyone who buys something from your organization.

Getting on the Sponsorship Train

Sponsorships can be a wonderful coup for your special event. Getting a small business or a local corporation to underwrite some or all of the expenses for the event isn't as difficult as it sounds, as long as you emphasize the right opportunities that your event offers.

The first thing experts say is to sell sponsor benefits ("Over 3,000 people will sample your food product and see your logo.") and not features ("Over 3,000 people will be at our event."). Don't present a potential sponsor with an extensive menu of options. Instead, present a package that has been custom designed for that particular business or corporation.

Send effectively worded sponsorship proposals to several companies at the same time, and follow up each proposal with a telephone call. For example, if you're looking for a pizza company to sponsor an event, send a sponsorship proposal to Domino's, Pizza Hut, Papa John's, and local pizza companies. Let them bid to become the sponsor.

Under only the rarest circumstances should you allow the sponsor to set the price. Include a standard fee or partial sponsorship opportunity as well.

And don't let the sponsor write the contract for sponsorship. Have a contract ready to sign that spells out exactly what they will be getting in exchange for their support.

Remember, the key to a really successful special event is to have someone else pay all of the bills. So when you are in the planning stages, set realistic goals, especially if you've never had a sponsor in the past. Don't overlook in-kind contributions of products or services when seeking sponsorship help. For example, if you're having difficulty getting a company to pay your printing expenses for an event, ask two or more small print shops to donate their services in exchange for being listed as a sponsor.

How to Find Companies to Sponsor Special Events

Where do you find companies willing to become sponsors? Start by noticing which companies have already sponsored events in your community. When you attend other events, take note of their sponsors. Often sponsors are thanked in a newspaper advertisement or brochure. Start a clipping file of potential sponsors, then contact those companies to see who is in charge of nonprofit sponsorships.

> Send effectively worded sponsorship proposals to several companies at the same time, and follow up each proposal with a telephone call.

A number of places are sources for leads. The chamber of commerce usually publishes a calendar of events for its community, and many fund-raising events will most likely be included. Check to see who is sponsoring what event.

The United Way office also publishes a calendar of events for member agencies. Check to see who are their sponsors.

The business section of your local newspaper publishes announcements of businesses that are sponsoring local nonprofit events, so start looking for those stories and file them for future use. The same goes for posters and fliers in store windows, on community bulletin boards, and at other places.

Lastly, make sure you send out sponsorship information to local advertising agencies because many businesses rely on their ad agencies to find them a suitable special event to sponsor.

If you want to hold a big special event fund-raising activity, you will most likely need to have a sponsor or two to help pay for all or most of your expenses. Recruit the best people possible for the sponsorship committee. It is an important committee and should be made up of people who aren't afraid to send out sponsorship materials and to make follow-up telephone calls and in-person visits.

Sometimes it takes from three to six months to obtain a major sponsor for a nonprofit event, so don't wait until the last minute and try to find one.

Getting Sponsors on Board

In the ideal world, whenever you plan a special event, sponsors seek you out and beg for a chance to pay all of your expenses. Unfortunately, we do not live in that world, and usually it's the nonprofit agency that goes around to the businesses and corporations begging for them to become a sponsor. Yet while it is true that the competition for sponsorship dollars is increasing, the number of companies wanting to become sponsors of special events has increased.

But just how do you go about getting a sponsor to pay for all or part of your special event expenses? Simplicity. Simplicity is the secret to winning sponsorship dollars. Keep your request simple,

> If you want to hold a big special event fund-raising activity, you will most likely need to have a sponsor or two to help pay for all or most of your expenses.

and remember the key decision factor that will affect every decision: the company will need to ask themselves, "What's in it for me?"

That's right. It may sound selfish, but if a corporation or a business is going to pay out hundreds or even thousands of dollars, they will want to know how it will benefit *them*. Once you learn the fine art of convincing sponsors how they will benefit from becoming a sponsor, you will have no trouble getting all of your expenses paid.

When I was heading up the Brookside Elementary School's Dream Playground project, our committee came up with a way for local businesses to sponsor different parts of the playground. Here is a partial listing of the special features that our playground had and how much it would cost each sponsor to pay for them. (Keep in mind that the entire playground was a wooden structure.):

- Truck: $500
- Castle with a haunted house: $3,500
- Pirate ship: $1,500
- Sandbox: $1,000
- Tire tunnel: $1,500
- Wiggly bridge: $2,000
- Bench: $500
- Outdoor classroom: $5,000
- Race car: $2,000
- Fort: $2,500

After we broke all of our needs down into simple terms, local businesses were willing to consider being either a whole or a partial sponsor; we had no problem obtaining sponsors to pay for all of our special features.

Sample Sponsorship Proposal (Fictional)

The National Walk Association is asking Giant Mart to be the major sponsor of our annual special event walk. We are asking Giant Mart to do the following:

- Provide cash sponsorship of $25,000
- Recruit team leaders throughout each of the Giant Mart stores in our county

After we broke all of our needs down into simple terms, local businesses were willing to consider being either a whole or a partial sponsor.

- Appoint a senior-level manager to serve on the local walk site committee
- Tag local newspaper and radio ads in the tri-county area
- Provide people who walk with official T-shirts or hats
- Have the store managers set goals within each store and challenge departments to compete with each other
- Produce posters and flyers to display in all Giant Mart stores in the tri-county area
- Provide an adequate number of volunteers on the day of the event (number to be determined from the walk committee)
- Have a table inside each Giant Mart store where shoppers can sign up for the special event
- Host a party at each Giant Mart store for employees and their families who participate in the special event

In exchange, the National Walk Association will:

- Allow Giant Mart to use the National Walk Association logo and trademarks in your advertising and internal communications
- Include your corporate logo on all printed materials relating to the special event
- Promote Giant Mart's sponsorship in all media releases, banners, signs, and flyers
- Distribute Giant Mart's circulars and discount coupons on the day of the special event
- Distribute official thank-you certificates to all Giant Mart employees who participate

Remember to keep your sponsorship proposals short and sweet. For the Brookside Dream Playground Project discussed in the preceding section, we simply put together a one-page flyer, with return information on the bottom for a sponsor to fill out and send along with a check. I have seen some nonprofit agencies put together a forty-page document outlining their sponsorship policies and rules. (Most business owners and corporate contribution officers prefer a smaller, simpler request.)

> Remember to keep your sponsorship proposals short and sweet.

Keeping Special Event Costs Down

You can always hope that a sponsor will offer to pay for your fund-raising expenses, though the chances of this happening are slim. There are some ways to keep special event expenses to a minimum while you're waiting for a sugar daddy sponsor.

- Always ask for a nonprofit discount. If you don't ask a hotel, restaurant, or other venue for a nonprofit discount, you won't get it.
- Order materials in bulk if an event will run over several years.
- Be on the lookout for local entertainers who will likely be less expensive than a well-known national act. As long as the music is good, donors won't care who is providing the entertainment for them.
- Look for local merchants who do not mind donating services such as printing, advertising, marketing, or food.
- When getting a price for printing (if you have to pay, that is), ask about a price break if you include the printer's logo at the bottom of the fliers.
- Ask large corporations if their security department can provide security at your event (if you need it).

> Always ask for a nonprofit discount. If you don't ask a hotel, restaurant, or other venue for a nonprofit discount, you won't get it.

Putting All Your Special Event Ideas Together in an Example

Suppose your nonprofit agency is looking to plan a fund-raising special event, but you're not quite sure how to move things forward. The following example shows how a local nonprofit agency might plan its first ever Family Fun Festival.

Scene: a local nonprofit agency

Characters: executive director, fund-raising professional, board member

Executive director: "Well, I know how we can make this Family Fun Festival work, because last week I spoke with a friend of mine in

Baltimore, and their agency ran a similar event. It went smoothly, and they also raised big bucks!"

Board member: "Oh yes, I think I read about that special event in the newspaper. But hey, didn't they have a sponsor who paid for all of their expenses? And what do you think our chances of finding a sponsor to pay for all of our expenses are? I don't want to get too far with these plans until we know what our true cost will be."

Fund-raising professional: "Yes, they did have a sponsor, and it was the fifth year the event had taken place. Since it was held in the atrium of the local hospital, it was easy to get doctors and other professionals to stop by. I'm not so sure we should do exactly what they did, but maybe we could take some of their ideas that worked and brainstorm some of our own."

Everyone agrees, and then the brainstorming session begins.

Executive director: "All right, before we begin, let's review the rules of this brainstorming session. First, there are no 'bad ideas.' Every suggestion will be written on the chalkboard for careful consideration. Second, we want as many ideas as possible. Remember, in brainstorming, quantity, not quality, is the rule of the hour. And finally, this brainstorming session will last only thirty minutes. No longer, no shorter. Any questions?"

Results of Brainstorming Session

For the next half an hour, people shouted out suggestions, ideas, and thoughts as if there were no tomorrow. In fact, it turned out to be a very successful session. Here's a review of the ideas that were written down on the chalkboard.

The session sparked the following ideas for:

Possible locations to hold the special event:

- Town park
- Local shopping center
- Gymnasium at the local community college
- Country club

> Every suggestion will be written on the chalkboard for careful consideration.

Entertainment possibilities:

- Local high-school marching bands
- Local rock and roll bands
- Local country and bluegrass bands
- Karate school demonstrations
- Gymnastics school demonstrations
- Barbershop quarter
- Local cheerleading squads
- Choirs from local churches

Food and beverages possibilities: (The job of the people in the brainstorming session is not to think about cost or other details, but to think only of possibilities.)

- Hire a catering company.
- Ask local fast food companies to donate food services.
- Sell vendor spaces to different food vendors.
- Have nonprofit agency volunteers make and sell food.
- Ask Pepsi or Coke to donate soft drinks.
- Have only snack foods (chips, pretzels, peanuts, and so on).

Potential activities:

- Face painting
- Clowns
- Balloons
- Magicians
- Hayrides
- Pumpkin decorating contest
- Grab bags
- Carnival-type games
- Cake walk
- Raffle
- Silent auction
- Candy sales
- Bingo
- Square dancing
- Twist contest

Ask local fast food companies to donate food services.

- Pictures taken with costumed characters
- Book sale
- Flea market
- Antique sale

Miscellaneous ways to generate additional income:

- Sell spaces to local craft vendors and make sure the event is listed as "Family Fun Festival and Craft Fair."
- Sell spaces to local vendors (such as travel agencies, restaurants, insurance companies, banks, cell phone companies, and so on).
- Charge admission to enter the event (or have a basket available for collecting donations upon entering).
- Ask other local nonprofit agencies to rent space (at a reduced rate) and publicize the services they offer the community.
- Sell T-shirts and hats with the name and logo of the non-profit agency.

Potential publicity and public relations: (You can find out more about public relations in Chapter 16.)

- Send press releases to the local newspapers and magazines.
- Send public service announcements (PSAs) to the local radio stations (see Chapter 15).
- Invite a local radio station to broadcast live from the event.
- Place advertisements in local newspapers (Ask for a special nonprofit rate or ask the newspaper to become a corporate sponsor and donate the ads).
- Have flyers printed and placed in store windows all over town.
- Have posters printed and displayed at the local mall.
- Send announcements to all businesses and ask for their employees to come out and support the event.
- Have local supermarkets insert flyers into the bags of each shopper.
- Contact local radio stations and ask about doing a call-in interview with a local on-air personality who can help promote the event.
- Contact the local schools and have notices sent home with each student.

Send announcements to all businesses and ask for their employees to come out and support the event

Decisions Made from Brainstorming Ideas

Armed with all of those ideas, the three people from that local nonprofit agency formed a fund-raising committee and went forward with their plans. Here's what they decided on:

Event location—While each of the other ideas (town park, local shopping center, and country club) were good ones, it was finally decided that the event would take place in the gym at the local community college. Since it was the first year for this event, the committee didn't want to worry about a rain date (or low attendance because of rain), so they immediately ruled out outdoor locations. And they thought it would be easier to get space donated at the community college.

Event entertainment—Guess what? They ended up having every one on the list. Because the event was going to run from 9:00 A.M. to 9:00 P.M., they wanted to make sure there was plenty of entertainment to keep the crowds happy with nonstop entertainment during the entire event. Plus, with so many children and youth appearing in many of the entertainment venues, it meant that plenty of parents would be attending as well.

Event food and beverages—The committee took a little longer to reach agreement about food, but finally agreed that a local catering company would be hired to sell family type foods: hot dogs, hamburgers, pizza, etc. (The caterer agreed to come in and run the entire operation at no cost to the nonprofit agency, and they donated a portion of the money they made that day.) The caterer also said it was okay to sell vendor space to other people selling foods such as cotton candy, popcorn, candy apples, and so on. A snack food company donated small bags of chips and pretzels; each person who came through the door received a free bag of snacks. (That freebie helped many people feel they should drop a few coins or dollars into the donation basket.)

Event activities—The committee was able to incorporate most of the activities from their brainstorming list. That meant

> While each of the other ideas (town park, local shopping center, and country club) were good ones, it was finally decided that the event would take place in the gym at the local community college.

that plenty of fun was available for family members of all ages. A local farmer brought both a hay wagon for a hayride and enough bales of straw and hay to make a maze; he donated all of the proceeds from these two events to the agency.

Miscellaneous ways to generate additional income—Once again, everything from the brainstorming session made it to the final event. Craft vendors, business vendors, other nonprofit agencies, and even the T-shirts and hats (donated by a local bank) were sold.

Publicity and public relations—Since the committee lacked experience in this area, they contacted the local chapter of the Public Relations Society of America (PRSA), who provided the expertise they needed. With the help of the PRSA volunteer, the nonprofit agency successfully promoted the Family Fun Festival and Craft Fair to the local community. They were able to implement everything from their brainstorming list, with the exception of having the local radio station broadcast live at the event. They found out that many radio stations charge a substantial fee to broadcast live at special events. The committee decided not to look for a sponsor to pay for the radio broadcast that year, but would look for a sponsor at next year's event. One other suggestion the PRSA volunteer made really paid off. The volunteer suggested that the nonprofit agency ask each of the five local banks to pay one thousand dollars each to be listed as sponsors of the event. All five agreed and the nonprofit made $5,000 even before the event began!

> Since the committee lacked experience in this area, they contacted the local chapter of the Public Relations Society of America (PRSA), who provided the expertise they needed.

Income and Expenses for the Event

Over a six-week time period the committee mailed flyers to local businesses and crafters, asking them to participate in the special event. Even though the event was still three months away, the nonprofit agency offered an "early bird discount" to those people who responded before a certain date. Sometimes the discount was only for ten or twenty dollars, but the idea paid off. Most of the vendor spaces were sold by the time the early bird deadline expired.

Here's a breakdown of the budget for this first Family Fun Festival and Craft Fair:

Income: $15,000

- Craft vendors: space enough for 80 @$40 each = $3,200
- Business vendors: space for 40 @$60 each = $2,400
- Nonprofit agencies: space for 20 @ $20 each = $400
- Donations at front door: average $1.00 each = $2,500
- Raffle drawings: 500 tickets sold, split 50/50 = $500
- Sponsors: Five banks @ $1,000 each = $5,000
- Hay rides/maze = $500
- T-shirt/hat sales = $500

Expenses: No expenses (everything was donated)

Net income from this event: $15,000

Surprised? Don't be. Because this type of an event is fairly easy to create and can make anywhere from $10,000 to $40,000 in one day.

> This type of an event is fairly easy to create and can make anywhere from $10,000 to $40,000 in one day.

For more information on this topic, visit our Web site at www.businesstown.com

Corporate Donations: Learn the Rules, Reap the Benefits

Topics covered in this chapter:

- **Why corporations give donations**
- **How to begin your request campaign**
- **Making your pitch for support**

Some nonprofit organizations seem to reap the rewards of corporate gifts year after year while others continue to receive polite rejection letters. It is not lady luck. The secret to winning corporate support is to keep your request simple and to approach a company according to its own guidelines. Learn the rules, reap the benefits.

Why Corporations Give

Thirty years ago a corporation would make a contribution to a local nonprofit agency because it was "the right thing to do." These days, however, it is usually customary for that same corporation to have its own agenda. In other words, if you can answer its question, "What's in it for me?" then you have a good shot at getting corporate support.

According to the Conference Board, an organization that conducts research on business activities, traditional corporate philanthropy is being replaced with strategic investments that businesses hope will yield measurable returns.

Indeed, many corporate contributions officers are feeling more pressure these days to integrate a company's donations with its business goals. The ultimate goal is to create a win-win situation in terms of corporate image, employee morale, and customer loyalty. The strategies include:

> The ultimate goal is to create a win-win situation in terms of corporate image, employee morale, and customer loyalty.

- Creating programs to allow the greater use of company employees as volunteers
- Forming partnerships between the company's marketing, public relations, and advertising departments and a local nonprofit agency
- Promoting other noncash forms of support, including donations of both surplus and new materials, as well as assisting in service related activities
- Discovering ways to increase the company's own bottom line, while at the same time lending a hand in the community where it will have the greatest impact

- Making smaller grants to many organizations rather than one or two large grants to only a select group of nonprofit agencies
- Developing a plan where the company "adopts" a particular nonprofit agency for up to three years, providing it with contributions of cash, materials, services, and employee volunteers.

Create Your Own Corporate Information Files

The first rule in the hunt for corporate donations is to compile a list of corporations in your area. You can use a variety of sources. Try to get the current directory or membership list of the chamber of commerce. Some chapters charge a fee if you are not a member, but a copy of the list is likely on the shelf at the local library.

The Yellow Pages is an often-overlooked resource that is a gold mine of information. Many communities also publish a "business-to-business" edition that will be even more useful.

The Many Ways to Spell Help

There are many types of corporate support. One type growing in popularity is the matching gift. Many corporations will match the contributions of their employees. Some match dollar for dollar while others match at a ratio of two to one or even three to one. Remind everyone who donates to your organization to check with employers about matching gift programs.

A second type is the gift-in-kind. Some companies look for year-end tax breaks. Donating products from their inventory is not the only type of in-kind gift available. Donations of office furniture, copier paper, and other office supplies can usually be obtained from local businesses. Get to know the managers in the purchasing department and send them your monthly wish list.

A third type is the cash gift. American corporations give away more than $6 billion every year. While this represents only about 5 percent of the total dollar amount donated, it is an important source of revenue for many agencies. Some companies prefer to make a large number of small gifts within their community, while others still support larger dollar grant requests.

A fourth type is the loaned executive. In this kind of program an employee is released to work full- or part-time with a nonprofit agency for a specified period of time (up to one year) while receiving full pay and benefits from his or her corporation. Your local United Way office should have a list of corporations participating in this program.

In your community's daily newspaper are reports of record profits and losses, quarterly earnings, and other important information about local corporations. Clip relevant articles and add them to your files.

Many community foundations publish a directory of local grant makers. In Delaware, for example, the Delaware Community Foundation has put together an indispensable resource for any nonprofit organization seeking foundation or corporate support in that state. Such directories usually contain detailed information that will assist you in making grant requests.

Go to the local library and look for the following books: *Million Dollar Directory, Ward's Directory of U.S. Private and Public Companies,* and *Directory of Corporate Affiliations.* These books offer details on corporations throughout the country. Other helpful titles include *Dun & Bradstreet Regional Business Directories* and *Dun's Directory of Service Companies.*

After you have put together your list of prospective corporate donors, the next step is to research the giving policies of each corporation. Determine submission requirements, deadlines, and the name of the contact person. If you haven't uncovered all of this information as you compiled your list, a telephone call to each corporation will get you the information you need to complete the grant request.

Plot Your Strategy

By now your corporate information files should contain the necessary data for you to initiate your request. Many corporate contributions officers do not require a site visit or even a personal visit by a representative of your nonprofit agency. The list of these prospects becomes your *A* list. The corporations that require a site visit or a personal visit from you become your *B* list.

Personal Contacts Make a Difference

Before embarking on a corporate fund-raising drive, find out who on your staff and board has personal contacts at the various corporations. Are any of your board members shareholders? Is anyone on staff a relative of an employee, a former employee, or a known customer of a particular business in your community? Who on your staff or board sits on boards with corporate leaders? A personal contact at any corporation is always helpful.

Begin Your Corporate Contribution Request Campaign

By now, you hold the necessary information to obtain contributions. Since your *A*-list prospects will require nothing more than written requests, set aside the necessary time to get the job done. Even if your schedule is so packed that you can write only three letters a day, make sure to send out those three letters. At the end of two weeks you will have thirty corporate grant request letters in the mail.

Many of the *A*-list corporate grant amounts will range from $500 to $5,000, but nonprofit agencies have reported receiving anywhere from $20,000 to $35,000 using this method of corporate fundraising. Not a bad return on your investment of a few days of research and a few dollars for postage.

Next, it is time to tackle the *B* list. Call the corporate contact and ask to set up a convenient time to meet and discuss your project. When it is time for the meeting, take along a one- or two-page summary of the project, along with any brochures describing your nonprofit agency. Be brief and enthusiastic, and maintain a positive attitude.

Don't Take "No" for an Answer

While some people find this rule hard to swallow, more than 95 percent of nonprofit agencies who reported using this method successfully received a corporate gift by not taking "no" for an answer.

Here's an example: An agency sends a request for a $3,000 donation to a local corporation. A few weeks later they receive a rejection letter. The same day the agency sends another letter to the corporation, which reads something like this: "Thank you for taking the time to consider our grant request. We understand that not all requests can be honored. However, if your company could send a smaller donation of $500 or less, it would be extremely helpful. Or, if a cash donation is not possible at this time, perhaps you could supply an item or two from our enclosed Wish List."

Remember, the corporation that gives you $500 today may give you a much larger contribution in the years to come.

Keep in Touch

When you receive a corporate contribution, make sure to send an official thank-you letter the same day you receive the check. While this sounds like common sense, many corporations report that after issuing a check they never hear from the nonprofit agency again (until they want another contribution).

But don't stop there. Keep in touch by sending newsletters, progress reports, personal notes, and even photographs of the project or event. This ongoing contact is all part of the process of cultivating donors.

Raising Operating Funds: Difficult but Not Impossible

There comes a time in the life or every organization when they must seek the elusive "operating support" portion of their budget. Sure, everyone wants to give money to your new building project or to purchase a new van or to even buy the latest high-tech computer equipment. But just hint to a funding source that what you really need are operating funds and suddenly your request for funding is rejected. Why? Because most corporations prefer to earmark their contributions for specific programs.

Your fund-raising mission should include seeking out sources that do provide operating support, while at the same time rallying support for the various programs your nonprofit agency provides. Many managers of nonprofit organizations don't think about corporate donations, which is unfortunate because those local corporations want to be good community partners and will make contributions when asked.

Some nonprofit agencies have developed creative ways to get corporations to pay for basic operating expenses. A nonprofit agency in Kentucky asked a local tire company to pay its monthly telephone bill, which cost nearly $5,000 a year. The tire company said yes, which prompted that same nonprofit to ask another company to pay the electric bill for a year. They were again successful in their request.

Why would a company do such a thing? Most local businesses want to help but many are reluctant to have their money "sent into a dark hole," which is what many businesses equate operating funding requests to be. The nonprofit in Kentucky just sent its monthly telephone statement to the business that had agreed to foot the bill. That freed money in the agency's operating budget and it was able to concentrate on providing more programs and services to its clients, which is something that nonprofit managers must be able to do.

What do you have in your operating budget that you can ask a local business or corporation to provide? Printing services? Check the Yellow Pages and start calling printers. You will probably find one or more who will be willing to donate a project or two. Many of the largest nonprofit agencies in the country receive almost half of

> Your fund-raising mission should include seeking out sources that do provide operating support, while at the same time rallying support for the various programs your nonprofit agency provides.

their operating budget as noncash gifts or in-kind donations. What have you got to lose?

How to Make Your Pitch for Support

Although the competition for corporate funds is fierce, as long as you approach your task with professionalism you should be able to compete effectively. Take the time to put together a corporate solicitation kit that includes the following information:

A current list of the board of directors—The list should reflect what businesses the directors are associated with, how long they have been serving on the board, and what committees or offices they currently hold.

Mission statement—It can be as simple as a three-sentence paragraph, but make sure the mission statement accurately reflects the work your nonprofit is trying to accomplish.

Budget information—Ideally you should include a one-page summary of your budget for the current year, along with any projections for the upcoming year. Be prepared to explain any major differences in expenses or income from one year to the next. In other words, if your line item for transportation has increased substantially because you are now serving double the number of clients, point that out.

Audit information—For just a straightforward corporate donation request, audited information is not usually required. Some major corporations, however, do require that you provide a copy of last year's audit. So be prepared; have adequate copies on hand. Don't let a corporate contribution slip out of your hands because someone forgot to order extra copies of the agency's audit.

Purpose of funding request—You don't need ten pages of narrative when asking for a $2,000 corporate contribution. Keep your request short and easy to read and understand.

Looking for Mr./Ms. Right

In some corporations one person has the authority to approve a donation request up to a certain dollar amount. When a request for a contribution is above the dollar amount they can approve, it is sent to a committee for approval. For example, many corporations will allow that employee to approve an amount ranging from $500 to $5,000, without checking with a full committee.

Want to increase your chances of success? Then find out the name of the person who has the authority to approve corporate contributions and the dollar amount they are authorized to approve. Then send your request to that person, and don't ask for an amount higher than his or her approval level.

Getting ten corporations to send you a $1,000 check is a lot easier than getting one corporation to approve a $10,000 request. Chances are that request will be shot down at committee level, and it is no slight to your agency. It simply means the company does not have enough money to go around for everyone who asks.

Cause-related Marketing

The origins of cause-related marketing can be traced to an innovative New York City candy vendor who donated a percentage of his profits to a local orphanage. American Express is credited with bringing the concept into the modern era in 1983 when it raised $1.7 million for the Statue of Liberty Ellis Island restoration fund.

More and more forward thinking companies are making commitments to public-private partnerships because they know that in addition to helping a worthy cause, they can attract new business, generate positive publicity, improve their corporate image, and motivate their employees. In short, cause-related marketing is a win-win situation for everyone involved.

When consumers were surveyed nearly 70 percent said they would switch brands to support a cause they care about if price and quality were equal. It's no wonder that more and more corporations are taking note of cause-related marketing opportunities.

While many caused-related marketing promotions are conducted a nationally, it is possible to partner with local businesses. Some examples might include a car dealership making a $50 donation to a local nonprofit agency for each person who stops by to test drive a new car; a restaurant donating a percentage of daily sales to a local food bank or soup kitchen; or a department store donating a percentage of sales to a local homeless shelter.

Today, the public-private marketing partnership is an evolving marketing strategy with a wide variety of possible strategic alliances and promotions. Make sure you are taking advantage of any cause-related marketing opportunities in your community.

Signing Up for the Cause

A good example of corporate cause-related marketing occurred when Nabisco donated five cents per box from each special edition of Barnum's Animal Crackers. A total of $100,000 was made to the World Wildlife Fund. The company made it clear that the intention of the limited edition box of animal crackers was to build awareness for endangered animals and, through the donation, to help the World Wildlife Fund save them and their habitats.

Other examples include Red Lobster's donating a percentage of each lobster meal sold to the Special Olympics and Target department stores' contributing more than $1.5 million to Habitat for Humanity, along with other corporate partners such as VISA, Hanes, Keebler, and the National Football League.

For more information on this topic, visit our Web site at www.businesstown.com

Chapter 10

Direct Mail

Topics covered in this chapter:

- **Finding creative ways to use direct mail campaigns**

- **Creating a good direct mail letter**

- **Including a premium with your letter**

- **Finding the right direct mail service provider**

D irect mail can be a valuable way to raise funds for your non-profit agency. Many successful direct-mail campaigns are put together on a shoestring budget and bring in outstanding results.

What many people commonly refer to as "junk mail" can make the difference between success and failure to many managers of nonprofits, which is probably why direct-mail fundraising has grown in popularity over the past few years. Talk to any executive director or development director who has had a successful mail campaign and you will no doubt hear the praises of direct mail as a way to raise money.

But talk to a nonprofit manager whose direct-mail campaign has failed and you'll get less than a stellar response about its benefits.

Using certain techniques can increase your chances for success. You will go nowhere, for example, without developing a plan that will work for your own organization. Just because another local or even national nonprofit agency has had success with a direct-mail fund-raising letter does not mean that you will have the same success. Develop a plan that incorporates your mission statement and an appeal that will convince donors that yours is indeed a worthy cause.

Next, decide how often to mail your appeal. Some nonprofit agencies send out direct-mail fund-raising letters twice a year while others are satisfied with an annual campaign.

Look for creative ways of using direct-mail campaigns. Don't just slap together a we-need-your-money letter and hope for the best. Donors and prospective donors find those appeals in their mailboxes each and every week. What can you and your fund-raising committee do to make your appeal creative? What can you do to make your direct-mail appeal stand out above the crowd?

Remember to send a thank-you note. You would be surprised at the number of nonprofit managers who confess that sending a thank-you note is not a high priority. If you want to keep your donors as friends and supporters, make sure that someone on your fund-raising committee is sending a personal thank-you note on the same day that a check is received.

> Look for creative ways of using direct-mail campaigns.

Creative Direct-Mail Appeals That Worked: "No Go, No Show"

When I was development director at the Delaware Adolescent Program in Wilmington, Delaware, about ten years ago I needed to come up with a low-cost, high-return fund-raising idea. While I had some experience in special events fundraising, I knew that there wasn't time to put together a special event; the agency needed a quick boost of cash. As I scanned some fund-raising idea books, I noticed that several nonprofit agencies on the West Coast had some success in sending out a direct-mail appeal. The appeal invited donors to dinner, but the dinner would be held at their own home. The idea was that donors could send a check to the nonprofit agency and enjoy dinner in the comfort of their homes.

That got me thinking of ways I could turn that idea into something spectacular for my nonprofit agency. I grabbed a pencil and began jotting down one-word ideas on a plain piece of paper, and developed the idea for a local "No Go, No Show" fund-raising dinner.

I thought about creating an invitation with a humorous cartoon on the cover and the copy on the inside. Since I had this idea in September, I thought about how to make this fund-raising effort a real moneymaker by the end of the year. I wanted to take advantage of the spirit of the holiday fund-raising season that was just around the corner. (The time of the year around Christmas and New Year's can be quite profitable; people are in a giving mode and you want to make sure you get your share of donations that take place during that time.)

I brought my No Go, No Show idea to the fund-raising committee, and the members loved it. They thought it would be a success and make some money for the agency. A few days later I designed a card that invited people not to attend a special New Year's Eve party. The cover of the card had a funny cartoon. The first one showed a woman dressed in an evening gown, trying to drag her tuxedo-clad husband to the party. (Other years we showed a ballroom with New Year's Eve decorations but with no people.) Over the years I discovered that the cartoons were a big success; people wrote in saying they enjoyed them and thought we were being very creative.

> The time of the year around Christmas and New Year's can be quite profitable; people are in a giving mode and you want to make sure you get your share of donations that take place during that time.

The copy on the inside listed five humorous reasons why the donor should stay at home on New Year's Eve while making a contribution to our nonprofit agency. Some examples we used included, "You can alphabetize your New Year's Eve resolutions" and "You can sing *Auld Lang Syne* in the comfort of your living room."

The donor also received an RSVP card along with a return address, but no stamp (donors told us they did not mind springing for postage). The RSVP card had a space for the donors' name, address, and other contact info along with the five reasons we had given as alternate choices for their New Year's Eve plans. The donors were asked to check which activity they would be doing. (As a joke I started keeping statistics on how many people were doing crazy activities on New Year's Eve. The second year I incorporated those statistics into the new No Go appeal, and it made the second mailing even more successful.

We kept the No Go, No Show invitation small in size. A standard wedding invitation or thank-you note size worked fine for us. Each person's name was handwritten on the outside of the envelope, with no return address stamped anywhere on the envelope. We also used a first class stamp instead of bulk mail. And here was another clever way we used to mail the pieces: the date they were dropped in the mail was the Wednesday before Thanksgiving. As people received them over the Thanksgiving holiday, they were excited and thought they were receiving the first holiday card of the season. They thought they were opening a greeting from a friend or a relative. Instead, they were greeted with a funny cartoon and some hilarious ways to spend New Year's Eve.

Our direct-mail efforts were a success because getting a donor to open your appeal is half the challenge. When you receive a fund-raising appeal letter in the mail with the name of the agency as the return address, and a bulk mail stamp, don't you usually toss it into the trash?

What added to our success in this direct-mail fund-raising campaign were the personal notes that we included in each of the cards. To accomplish this task, I came up with the idea for a "list party." We conducted several list parties to which we invited staff, volunteers, board members, friends, vendors—basically, everyone we could

> What added to our success in this direct-mail fund-raising campaign were the personal notes that we included in each of the cards.

think of. We asked each person to bring his or her own mailing list, which could consist of friends, family members, business associates, doctors, and dry cleaners. People were asked to write a personal note on the inside of the No Go, No Show fund-raising invitation. The idea was that donors would respond to the humor and also to a handwritten appeal from someone they knew or were associated with. Everyone who attended our list parties was receptive to including a personal note to people they were sending an appeal to. They knew that our agency stood a higher chance of success with their personal signature inside of the invitations.

And we were right. People started sending in their donations right away. We started receiving checks and RSVP cards on the Monday after Thanksgiving. Obviously, local people who had received the appeal in the mail on the Friday after Thanksgiving had written a check and mailed it the same day. We were overwhelmed by the success of this simple effort. In addition to checks, we received notes from donors. One woman wrote, "Only because of your clever and innovative fundraising idea am I sending you this check." Another one wrote, "What a delightfully clever idea!" Comments poured in every week, along with contributions from people who were friends of our friends.

To make the appeal a newsworthy event, I looked in the local newspaper to see which celebrities were appearing in Atlantic City casinos (Wilmington is about ninety minutes from Atlantic City). I gambled on five famous people and sent each a No Go, No Show invitation. I still hand addressed a plain white envelope, with no return address and a first class stamp. I simply addressed it to the celebrities, care of the casinos at which they were scheduled to appear over the Thanksgiving holiday weekend.

My gambling efforts paid off. One of the celebrities I sent an invitation to, Phyllis Diller, responded with a check for $100. She sent her contribution on her personal check so I had an address to send her a personal thank-you note. Ms. Diller wrote back and asked for more information on our nonprofit agency. She then became a regular contributor over the next few years.

In the middle of December I sent press releases to all of the local media outlets, outlining what we had done and how much suc-

> One woman wrote, "Only because of your clever and innovative fundraising idea am I sending you this check." Another one wrote, "What a delightfully clever idea!"

cess we achieved almost immediately. And of course I included the celebrity angle (newspapers love to write about celebrities), which helped turn our press release into a story on page one.

I used the No Go, No Show fund-raising idea for the next five years. After I left the Delaware Adolescent Program and took a job with Family Services of Cecil County, I was happy to see that my old agency continued sending out those appeals every Thanksgiving. I started the entire process all over again at Family Services; they too received new donations and plenty of publicity.

Creative Direct-Mail Appeals That Worked: Fund Time at a Mother's Day Tea Party

When I began working as the development director at Family Services of Cecil County in Elkton, Maryland, one of the first things I did was to create a new version of the No Go, No Show fund-raising appeal. It was a success for that agency as well.

Sometime around Valentine's Day I was looking through a fund-raising publication when I came across a short news article about the Leukemia Society's annual direct-mail fund-raising event in the spring. For their Mother's Day Tea Party, they sent a formal invitation to prospective donors, suggesting they take a few moments on Mother's Day to have a cup of tea. The Society included a tea bag with each invitation. After enjoying the cup of tea, the donor was supposed to write a check to the Leukemia Society and mail it back in the return envelope that was enclosed.

I obtained a sample of the Leukemia Society's direct-mail piece, and it was indeed a first-class job. The printing and graphics were superb, and it was a cute and appealing idea. So I tried to think of how I can apply the society's idea to create something unusual for Family Services of Cecil County.

After a few hours of brainstorming, I developed a plan for our own version of the Mother's Day Tea Party. Instead of just sending a formal invitation asking donors to enjoy a cup of tea and send us a check, I decided to include a Mother's Day poem, written by a local student, on the theme "Why Mothers Are Special." I contacted all of

Bankable Excuses

Here are several of the humorous excuses we used in our No Go, No Show appeal:

- You won't miss the final showing of *It's a Wonderful Life* (colorized version) on cable TV

- Yet another chance for a year-end tax deduction

- You can sing *Auld Lang Syne* in the comfort of your living room

- You won't miss *Dick Clark's New Year's Rockin' Eve*

- No need to worry about waking up with a hangover

- A chance to rest before watching twelve hours of football games on New Year's Day

- No rubber chicken dinner

the elementary schools in our area, and asked them if they would participate in a poetry contest. The contest would be open to all elementary students in grades one through four. The winning poem, reproduced with the child's own handwriting, would then be printed inside of our Mother's Day Tea Party invitation.

The schools loved the idea. A simple flier that spelled out the rules of the contest was printed and each child took one home. Local printers donated copies of the fliers, so it did not cost the schools or our agency any money. A local pharmacy donated a brand new bicycle that was to be the prize for writing the winning poem. We even recruited the lieutenant governor of Maryland to be our Honorary Chairperson. Kathleen Kennedy-Townsend took the time out of her busy schedule to have photographs taken and to issue a press release inviting children to participate in the contest. A local limousine company donated the use of a driver and car to take the child and his or her family to the State capital for official photos and greeting with the lieutenant governor. Local newspapers and radio stations started writing and talking about the event. Excitement was building and within a few weeks entries started pouring into our agency.

Little did we realize how many students would enter the contest. Out of 5,500 eligible students, more than 1,000 sent in entries. We were amazed at the interest and the talent of the elementary students who had taken the time to write a poem.

We quickly formed a panel of judges made up of local business people and volunteers from our agency. I sat with them as they read many of the entries. Some of the poems were so funny they were "laugh out loud" while others were so sad there were tears flowing around the room. Then I realized what an opportunity I was sitting on.

I knew that somehow I would have to find a way to get all of the poems printed into a booklet for people to read and enjoy. I contacted the Thiokol Corporation, a local company, who agreed to handle the printing of the booklet at no cost. The booklet turned out to have more than sixty pages of poems, and of course we include some information about our agency. I asked Thiokol if they wouldn't mind adding a few more pages of ads from local businesses. They agreed, and then I was able to sell ad space to local merchants.

> A simple flier that spelled out the rules of the contest was printed and each child took one home.

When the booklet was finished, we decided to have it ready for sale by Mother's Day. We charged only $4 for each one. After all, the printing was donated and we even made money with the ad sales. The cost was kept low enough so that people could buy an inexpensive gift for Mother's Day. What child could resist buying a copy of a booklet that had a poem they had written for his or her own mother?

A first grader from Conowingo Elementary School wrote the winning entry. Here is what Gary Wienlenbeck wrote about "Why Mother's Are Special."

> *My mommy gives me hugs*
> *And a can to catch bugs.*
> *She takes me places*
> *And makes funny faces.*
> *Mommy makes me laugh*
> *And she helps me get a bath.*
> *She washes my dirty clothes*
> *And squirts me with a hose.*
> *My mommy loves me*
> *And I love mommy.*

The poem was reproduced in Gary's handwriting, exactly how he had written it. It was included in our Mother's Day Tea Party invitation that was being mailed to a growing list of people who wanted a card.

So the next time you read about another nonprofit agency having a successful direct-mail appeal, think of how you can spin off your own success story.

What Makes a Good Direct-Mail Letter?

What if your nonprofit agency wants to send out a traditional direct-mail appeal, instead of a No Go, No Show or a Mother's Day Tea Party invitation? There's nothing wrong with that idea; direct-mail letters have been raising millions of dollars for nonprofit agencies for a long time.

The Financial Report

The simple idea of the Mother's Day Tea Party that was based on an existing idea from another nonprofit agency brought the agency money in several ways:

- It received money from the sale of the booklets.

- It received donations from people who received the invitation and mailed in a check.

- It received money from ad sales in the booklets.

On top of everything, there were no expenses involved in this fund-raising effort. Everything was donated: printing, postage, design services, graphics, even the tea bags included in the invitation. All it took was a few telephone calls to local businesses and associations, and we had all of our expenses covered.

When I first started out working in the fund-raising field I would spend hours researching information at the University of Delaware library. I was excited when I found a lot of information about direct-mail fund-raising appeals, but I was confused by all of the advice concerning the issue. Here's a sampling of the advice I found on the topic:

- Write long letters. Write short letters.
- Don't include a premium. Include a premium.
- Use a fancy envelope. Use a plain envelope.
- Include return postage. Don't include return postage.
- Don't print your return address on the envelope. Print your return address on the envelope.
- Send your direct-mail letter via bulk mail. Don't send your direct-mail letter via bulk mail.
- Don't accept credit cards for donations. Accept credit cards for donations.
- Send direct-mail fund-raising letters in February only occasionally. Never send any direct-mail fund-raising letters in February.
- Rent a mailing list. Don't rent a mailing list.
- Don't exchange mailing lists with other nonprofit agencies. Exchange mailing lists with other nonprofit agencies.

After finding all of that advice I was confused. Everywhere I turned I read conflicting advice. Then it hit me. Every nonprofit agency is unique, and so every fund-raising direct-mail appeal needs to be unique as well.

I have found that the following advice applies to most situations. The first paragraph is your chance to introduce yourself and your agency. Briefly explain who you are and what your mission statement is.

Use the problem-solution format. State the problem in a few short sentences, then talk about how your nonprofit agency is able to fix those problems. Use statistics to show how you are solving a local community problem.

The Ingredients of a Tantalizing Letter

Keep these tips in mind when drafting your appeal letter:

- Always include a P.S. in your letter. People sometimes will scan down to the P.S. and read that information first.

- Make your letter upbeat and positive. People want to hear good news.

- Use a one-line paragraph that is underlined to emphasize any special points.

- Personalize each letter; no one wants to respond to a "dear occupant" or "dear friend" letter anymore.

- Use a combination of short and long paragraphs.

- Keep your letter short and to the point. If people are still wondering why you wrote to them by the third paragraph they may stop reading your letter.

- Make sure your letter conveys a sense of urgency.

- Don't make your letter a "if you don't give we'll be out of business" one. No one wants to send money to a nonprofit that is about ready to go out of business.

Use at least a twelve-point typeface for your letters. If your audience consists of many senior citizens, consider using a larger size.

Keep your letter focused on the issue at hand. Don't address more than one issue at a time.

Find a way to involve readers. Have them pick up a pen and fill out a survey card, for example.

Make your request for funds direct. Don't beat around the bush; if you are asking for a donation of $25 or more, say so.

Challenge people to move to the next level of funding, if they can afford to do so. Remind them just how much more you can provide for an additional $10 contribution.

Long Versus Short Letter

Entire books have been written on the subject of direct-mail fund-raising letters. For every ten success stories from nonprofit agencies who have used a short letter, you will find ten who had that same success using a long letter. So what are you supposed to do?

Twenty years ago, it was not uncommon to find a four- to six-page direct-mail appeal letter. These days, however, the average direct-mail appeal letter is between two and four pages. But I can't stress enough that you must do what is best for your nonprofit agency. You know your audience, and you know your mission statement.

When to Make the Plea

Do you know where you should be asking for the contribution in your direct-mail appeal letter? Most agencies struggle with this issue, but the average placement of the "gift request" comes in the third or fourth paragraph.

Should You Include a Premium?

How do you feel when you receive a premium—return address stickers, pens, or key chains—or a gift that arrives after you've made your donation? Some people enjoy receiving a premium with their letter, while others think it is a waste of money. Those people who feel that

> For every ten success stories from nonprofit agencies who have used a short letter, you will find ten who had that same success using a long letter.

a premium is a waste of money will most likely not send in a contribution, but those who like getting them often won't contribute unless you include one or promise one if they donate. So, what's a manager of a nonprofit organization to do? How can you decide if a premium or gift is right for your particular agency? This section gives you some ideas.

Match the Premium to the Values of Your Organization

If your organization promotes healthy nutrition as a way of reducing cancer, don't send candy as a premium. Instead, send a refrigerator magnet with a checklist of healthy foods that recipients can stick on the refrigerator—and, incidentally, see the name of your organization several times a day. Other examples follow:

- *Child-advocacy group*—Year-long, laminated school calendar, listing school-related activities, a list of shops and malls that offer safe Halloween trick-or-treating alternatives, or a booklet for teachers identifying signs and symptoms of child abuse
- *Friends of the local library*—Attractive bookmark
- *A cancer foundation*—Booklet of healthy cooking ideas or a plastic card that attaches to showerhead showing the how to complete a monthly skin or breast self-exam
- *Guide dog organization or local humane society*—$5.00 off local veterinary services, water dish, or booklet with tips for raising a healthy puppy
- *Environmental organization*—Free bulbs or seedlings, sample of fruit and vegetable washing solution, booklet listing local companies that recycle or sell organic produce, booklet listing of vehicles with the highest miles per gallon
- *Local housing/remodeling organization*—Tape measure
- *Local public radio station*—Offer free or discounted tickets to local cultural programs, flyer or booklet featuring a guide to local and national programs on that station

If your organization promotes healthy nutrition as a way of reducing cancer, don't send candy as a premium.

The point is to make the premium relevant. Getting a large cloth bag from your local humane society might see odd, but getting it from your local environmental organization, which might be advocating using cloth bags instead of plastic or paper, might be the perfect fit. Make sure the premium meshes with your mission and values. (See Chapter 2.)

Identify Yourself Through the Premium

Whatever premium you choose, make sure your organization's name is prominent, along with a Web site address, phone number, or other way of getting in touch with you. You want this premium to generate income, either now or later. If you run a lobbying organization that encourages the public to write to their senators, by all means, send a pen as a premium, but be sure your organization's name and contact information is on that pen!

Choose a Premium That Can Be Used Again and Again

Although no premium can possibly last forever, send the longest-lasting premium you can come up with. This way, your organization's name is in front of your potential donor for as long as possible. Calendars are popular for this reason—but before you send a calendar, make sure it's useful. If it's just a generic calendar that's also rather ugly, you can bet it'll end up in the trash instead of in a prominent place.

Whatever you do, don't send food as a premium: It'll be used up quickly and never remembered. At least a certificate for an event or a service will leave the potential donor with memories—food won't even do that!

Choose a Useful Premium

Choosing a useful premium can be difficult to do, because "useful" is really in the eye of the beholder. Refrigerator magnets may be useful to some people, but if you're going to go that route, include

> Whatever premium you choose, make sure your organization's name is prominent, along with a Web site address, phone number, or other way of getting in touch with you.

more than just your organization's name. Include some useful information on that magnet that potential donors can use when they are in the kitchen. Sticky-backed notes are often useful, but make sure they're large enough to have enough room to write in while still, of course, displaying your organization's name, logo, and contact information.

Whatever you do, don't send a gift that's completely useless, even if it's really cute and you got it at a great price.

Make Sure the Premium Is Neither too Chintzy nor Too Expensive

If you're thinking of sending some trinket, consider what you would do with such an object. If you can't think of a single use for it, choose something else. Yet while you don't want to send anything really cheap, you also don't want potential donors to think you're in the habit of wasting money with expensive premiums. If you want to send expensive premiums, send it as a donation gift. (See the following section.)

Consider a Donation Gift Instead

Instead of a premium that comes in a direct mailing, many non-profits offer a gift to donors that they receive after their check is received. The direct mailing often includes a flyer or brochure that describes the gift in detail, and then offers that gift at a fairly high "price." The Crystal Cathedral in Garden Grove, California, is a perfect example of how this system works. Viewers of the Sunday morning advertising-free church service are invited to join the Eagles Club, either by sending $600 or by pledging $50 per month for a year. In return, they receive a statue of an eagle, and because a new one is designed every year by a famous sculptor, Eagle's Club members add to their collection. If you like collectibles, the Eagle's Club donation gift is something to look forward to each year and is a reminder of the church it is supporting.

Give Recipients the Option to Decline the Gift

For donors who would rather see their money spent on services instead of gifts, be sure to give them the option to decline the gift.

> If you're thinking of sending some trinket, consider what you would do with such an object.

Make it easy! They shouldn't have to write you a letter or make a call asking how to return a gift. Include a checkbox on the form they send with their donation that allows them to decline the gift.

When donors decline a gift, you both win. The donor doesn't have to receive something he or she doesn't want, and you don't have to pay for and ship a gift when that money could go toward services.

Honor Recipients in Nonmaterial Ways

In lieu of premiums or gifts, have donors join "clubs" at various dollar-levels of giving, and then publish those lists, making a big fuss over all donors, but especially those at the top level. This great payback for donors is practically free for you.

Don't forget to let donors opt out, though. Some would prefer to remain anonymous.

Poll Your Loyal Gift Givers

The best way is determine what the recipients of your direct mail want is to experiment by sending out some letters with a premium and some without. On those letters that you include a premium with, ask potential donors how they feel about getting a premium. Do they feel good and more likely to send in a check, or do they feel the money should be spent on programs instead? Pay close attention to the responses you do get, and then decide for yourself.

How Do You Handle Mailing Lists?

Your nonprofit agency has made the decision to send out a direct-mail appeal. You've spent plenty of time drafting your award-winning letter and have a really great looking envelope. Now you need to know whom to send the appeal to. Sometimes having a great letter can be useless unless you have a great mailing list to go along with it.

List management is becoming a big business in the United States. Dozens of Web sites offer mailing lists for sale and rent. In addition to finding list management firms on the Internet you can

> In lieu of premiums or gifts, have donors join "clubs" at various dollar-levels of giving, and then publish those lists, making a big fuss over all donors, but especially those at the top level.

find some companies listed in fund-raising publications, such as *The Chronicle of Philanthropy* and *The Nonprofit Times.* If you have never rented a mailing list before, ask for some basic information: how much it costs to rent or buy, what you get for your money, and how many names you will receive.

If your nonprofit agency will be using thousands of names for a direct-mail campaign, it is a good idea to look into software that will keep track of everything you are doing. You want to create a way to keep track of your donors and their personal information, and to make sure they receive timely thank-you notes.

How to Select the Right Direct-Mail Service Provider

Just as there are all kinds and sizes of generalized advertising agencies offering access to all kinds of media, direct-mail specialists come in many varieties, and can further zero in on the best way to reach your perfect donor.

Browse direct-mail specialist listings on the Web, in the Yellow Pages, and the direct-mail trade publications. Call a few specialists who seem right for your project, tell them you're getting started on budgeting, and ask for rate sheets.

The specialist can put together the entire package or you can assemble a direct marketing team yourself, doing some work in-house and hiring out the other parts.

The team consists of the following:

> *The creative contributors of both artwork and writing*–These people can include the designers of the overall campaign.

> *The list developers*–They assemble names as general as all residents living in specific zip codes or as "enhanced" as all men living in a specific zip codes who have signed up for a gym class in the last six months. The more enhanced a list, the more it costs because it has been compiled from cross-referencing numerous lists and checked for dupli-

Do Not Disturb

It is no surprise that some people deeply resent receiving unsolicited mail. What's the point of going to the expense of sending a direct-mail piece to people who will, by reflex, toss your unopened letter in the trash?

Did you know that the Direct Marketing Association (DMA) maintains a do-not-mail list of people who have asked to be taken off mailing lists? Before you rent or buy any mailing lists, make sure that the list has been checked against that do-not-mail list.

cates and names on the Direct Marketing Association's do-not-mail list.

The printer and the mailing house–They assemble the mailing package and attach the labels. The mailing house also performs the vital job of sorting and bundling according to Post Office regulations.

The U.S. Post Office–Always check with your post office or log on to *www.usps.gov/busctr* to get in touch with your local Bulk Mail Office. An official will not only give you current postal rate sheets, but also translate the complicated rates into what you need to know for your market. Sign up for a free newsletter on mail piece design, inexpensive list cleanup and zip confirmation services, and all kinds of insights on how to save money on a direct-mail campaign.

A "combo" service–Under Mailing Services in the Yellow Pages, you will find numerous businesses that combine printing, label affixing, sorting, and bundling. Sometimes these companies also offer inbound telemarketing services to answer orders and even add fulfillment warehouse and shipping services to further help streamline your operation.

Sign up for a free newsletter on mail piece design, inexpensive list cleanup and zip confirmation services, and all kinds of insights on how to save money on a direct-mail campaign.

For more information on this topic, visit our Web site at www.businesstown.com

Chapter 11

Understanding Foundations and Endowments

Topics covered in this chapter:

- **What is a foundation**
- **Different types of foundations**
- **How to form an endowment**

Public foundations exist to give money away, so the more you know about them, the more your nonprofit stands to benefit. But getting money from an existing foundation isn't the only way a foundation can have a role in your nonprofit. Within your existing organization, you can start a foundation in the name of your biggest donor(s). And you can also start an endowment that can, if managed effectively, make your organization self-sufficient, so that you never having to fundraise or apply for grants ever again!

What Foundations Are

Foundations, which range from private, family-run organizations to groups formed with the blessing of and funds from a major corporation, are unique nonprofits. People usually give to foundations (or set them up themselves) because they want to see their money fill a particular need or serve a particular constituency. If you listen to National Public Radio, you often hear the names of foundations that fund programs that cover particular information, such as the "Annie E. Casey Foundation, working to build better futures for disadvantaged children and their families" or the "William T. Grant Foundation, helping the nation value young people." These foundations have identified a niche that they wish to serve and faithfully serve that constituency.

In general, foundations are good at accounting for funds received and used and evaluating the impact of the money they distribute. This accountability may appeal to people who are unsure of how their donation dollars are being spent at nonfoundation charities. Many foundations—especially community foundations—tend to be small, so donors can talk to the board of directors, staff members, and volunteers, and most donors to foundations like that control. On the other hand, many donors couldn't begin to tell you the difference between donating to a foundation and donating directly to a nonprofit organization that provides services.

Some foundations exist solely to provide funds for a particular charity (for example, a certain women's center or youth athletic organization) or for an institution (for example, a scholarship fund, the

> People usually give to foundations (or set them up themselves) because they want to see their money fill a particular need or serve a particular constituency.

salary of a gifted professor, or the expenses of a particular college or office at a large university). These foundations do not serve any other function except to collect money for and distribute money to that particular cause.

Other foundations, however, exist to fill a particular need or serve a certain geographic area but haven't determined at the outset exactly who will receive the funds. These foundations review a large number of applications (from organizations like yours) to determine exactly where and how their money should be spent. To obtain funds from such a foundation, you must submit a grant proposal. (See Chapter 12.)

Understanding the Types of Foundations

Foundations can be private, public, or corporate. This section fills you in on the details of each.

Private Foundations

Private foundations, also called family foundations, are usually started by individuals or families who want to give large amounts of money away, but control how that money is dispersed. Many of these trusts are named in memory of loved ones who have passed away and honor them by keeping their names in the public eye. Family members often operate these foundations. A foundation also acts as a buffer between the giver and the receiver, which can be more anonymous and more comfortable than direct giving.

Private foundations, however, are usually only for the wealthy, or at least moderately wealthy people. One generally accepted guideline is that unless you're willing to donate at least $25,000 per year, setting up a foundation probably isn't a very good idea, although smaller foundations have been formed and run successfully. Many private foundations do not accept grant proposals; instead, they seek out worthy organizations on their own or have already chosen one or two and aren't seeking any more. If you can get a wealthy donor to start a private foundation that supports your nonprofit, though, you've done something very right, my friend!

Mining the 990-PF

By law, every foundation in the United States is required to file an annual tax return using a form known as 990-PF. (See Chapter 6.) The form provides an excellent source of information on foundations and what agencies they make grants to.

The good news is that the Internal Revenue Service posts all of the 990s on its Web site. The next time you are searching for good, solid information about foundations, visit the IRS Web site at *www.irs.gov* and follow the links to the listings of the foundation annual tax returns. (It usually takes about eighteen months before a 990 is posted.)

One way for individuals to start a smaller individual foundation is to create a support foundation or named fund that's part of a larger nonprofit. Under this arrangement, the nonprofit manages the private foundation, freeing the individual from administrative nightmares. The named donor (who can remain anonymous) can give an unrestricted gift, which can be used by your organization in any way. Other times, the donor recommends where his or her money is to be spent but does not have final discretion over how the money is used. Sometimes, however, the fund is designated specifically to serve a particular constituency or be used for a particular need in a field-of-interest fund. You might consider having large donors start a support foundation or named fund within your own organization: It often encourages high-dollar, regular giving from your higher-income donors.

Corporate Foundations

Corporate foundations are like private foundations, but are linked to a corporation instead of an individual or family. A corporate foundation normally receives a set percentage of the corporation's profits. These foundations are often run by the CEO of the corporation or by a committee, and corporate officers and staff members are usually heavily involved. Most corporate foundations make grants to nonprofit agencies in the communities in which they operate—contact the corporate foundation directly for grant-proposal information.

Government Foundations

Government foundations are created by Congress and funded by the Treasury. The National Science Foundation (NSF) is a good example. The NSF promotes science and engineering by granting money to individuals and teams who are engaged in research or education related to science and engineering. It's a government agency, which means that it is financed by the federal government, but it's also a grant making foundation. The government is able to justify this foundation's being funded by taxpayers because the NSF promotes scientific discovery, advances health care for Americans, and secures the national defense—all of which strengthen the nation.

Using the Web to Find Foundations

Some small foundations may not appear in the various directories that are for sale to nonprofit organizations, but you can still track them down on the Internet.

Use a variety of search engines, such as Google, Dogpile, and others that give you good results. You may be surprised at the number of foundations that you discover using the Internet.

Public Foundations

Public foundations are nonprofits that generate and distribute money to other nonprofits or to individuals, usually in the form of grants, which means that your organization can apply to them for funding. There is no legal or IRS definition of a public foundation, but they are generally described as "not private foundations, not corporate foundations, and not government foundations." How's that for a straightforward definition?

Community Foundations

Community foundations can be either public or private foundations. Members of a small geographic area, usually a community, give small donations to a foundation that distributes money to community residents or small nonprofits in the community who demonstrate a particular need. The money is often held in an endowment (see the next section). For more information on a community foundation in your hometown, refer to Appendix D of this book. Community foundations should be one of your first places to look for sources of local funds.

Forming an Endowment

An endowment is a large fund that that you don't spend. You invest the money or principal and use only the interest from your investment for a specific purpose, such as paying for your organization's operating expenses.

Many nonprofits have started forming endowments to reduce or eliminate their need to raise funds or to ensure that a particular need in the community will always be met by the foundation. If, for example, your operating expenses are $100,000 per year, you can either raise $100,000 per year or you can raise $1.5 million one time and use the interest from the investment of that money to run your organization indefinitely. Or, if some of your constituents would be greatly at risk if your nonprofit were unable to raise enough funds or was dissolved—say, a small clinic for HIV-infected babies—you could

The Foundation Center

The Foundation Center should be your first stop when you are getting ready to research information about foundations in the United States. The Foundation Center collects, organizes, analyzes, and disseminates information about foundations, corporate giving, and related subjects by maintaining an electronic database, publishing dozens of guides, offering seminars, and conducting research. In short, it is one-stop shopping for foundation information.

The Foundation Center also operates libraries in New York City, Washington, D.C., Atlanta, Cleveland, and San Francisco. Center libraries provide access to a unique collection of materials on philanthropy and are open to the public free of charge. Free training sessions are also available at each of the five library locations.

start an endowment that would ensure the support of that portion of your organization for many years to come.

The catch is that raising $1.5 million is much more difficult than raising $100,000. And while you're raising money for your endowment, you still need support for your everyday expenses. Many universities, churches, and even high-school organizations are attempting to start endowments but often find that donors divert their annual support into the endowments, leaving the nonprofit in dire financial straits because the funds in the endowment cannot be touched (only the interest can be).

One of the best ways to start an endowment is to encourage your best donors to will their estates to your organization upon their deaths. If an estate is worth, say, a million dollars, you're quite a long way toward reaching your endowment goal. But even small nonprofits can create endowments. A small nonprofit that gives an annual scholarship to a high-school student, for example, could put half of its donations toward an endowment from the outset. Although during the first years of operation the scholarship awards would be smaller than they would have been if the endowment hadn't been formed, after a few years, the endowment would be large enough to fund the scholarship without new donations.

Most nonprofits starting an endowment conduct a separate public relations campaign for the endowment, asking people to donate both to the organization and to the new endowment in order to ensure both the current and future success of the organization.

> One of the best ways to start an endowment is to encourage your best donors to will their estates to your organization upon their deaths.

For more information on this topic, visit our Web site at www.businesstown.com

Chapter 12

Obtaining Grants

Topics covered in this chapter:

- **Applying for a grant**
- **Parts of a proposal**
- **Basic rules for grant proposals**

For a manager of a nonprofit organization, one of the biggest thrills is to receive a grant as the result of a large donation. Writing the grant itself, however, may be much less thrilling. This chapter helps you establish a system for writing grant proposals (also called grant applications), one that you can customize for each proposal you write.

Getting Ready to Apply for a Grant

Don't make the mistake of diving right in to the grant proposal process. Instead, prepare yourself for the task at hand: (1) develop a clear picture of what you want, (2) match your project with the best possible funding agency, (3) find out what the funding agency expects in your proposal, and (4) develop a detailed plan for the grant proposal process. The following discussion will show you how.

Develop a Clear Picture of What You Want

Before you begin applying for any grants, establish exactly what you will accomplish with this grant money or other resources. Consider brainstorming with colleagues about the vision you have for this grant. Start with a statement such as, "If we got that grant, we could . . . ." and write down all of the responses. Sort through the answers, looking for the most specific ones. For example, a request for funds to "change the world" isn't going to get you a grant, but requests to, "fund our free health clinic for one year," "place 150 homeless puppies in good homes," "provide 1,000 meals from November to April," or "offer a low-cost summer day camp for the children of Clarksville" are specific enough to get you started. But even they need more specificity. To develop a really clear picture, brainstorm answers to the following:

- Is this project necessary? Why?
- How is our organization uniquely qualified to meet this need?
- What specific objective do we want to accomplish?
- How will we know whether we have achieved those goals?

> Before you begin applying for any grants, establish exactly what you will accomplish with this grant money or other resources.

- What group of people will we serve?
- How will they benefit from this program?
- How will we let them know that our program is available?
- How will we spend each dime of the grant money, exactly?
- Who will be in charge of the project and budget?
- Who will assist that person?
- Who will we hire, if anyone?
- When will we start?
- When will the project end (or will it continue indefinitely)?

You may want to write a mission statement for this project, just as you will or have done for your entire organization. (See Chapter 2.) A mission statement takes your vision for this project and puts it in writing, as if it is already fact. For example, "The mission of the Homes for Puppies Project is to vaccinate and neuter the expected 150 puppies who will be euthanized in Bedford County this year, place them for adoption with families in the county, and have each adopter take a basic puppy care and training course with the new puppy." Of course, this project won't be possible if the grant money doesn't arrive, but the mission statement is written as if the money were already on its way.

After you have a mission statement, write down specific goals and objectives for the project, as in the following:

1. Save 150 puppies from euthanization.
2. Ensure that all new owners are dog lovers who have the time and space for their new puppies (and the grown dogs).
3. Teach new puppy owners how to care for their pets.

From there, develop a project task list, as in the following:

1. Develop a brochure explaining the large number of euthanized puppies in the county each year and the Homes for Puppies Project.
2. Kick off the Homes for Puppies Project at the 4th Annual Humane Society 5K Dog Trot and begin signing up prospective adopters at that event.
3. Assign Nancy Spellman to chair the project. Hire half-time employee to take over some of Nancy's existing duties.

> After you have a mission statement, write down specific goals and objectives for the project.

4. Visit churches, schools, businesses, and local media outlets to ask for their assistance in widening the list of potential adopters.
5. Purchase vaccines, surgical supplies, medication, and collars.
6. Develop list of on-call veterinarians to perform the surgeries.
7. Develop screening process for potential adopters, including questionnaire and home visits. Be sure to match the type of dog to the personality of the new owner as closely as possible.
8. Develop puppy care and training classes that all adopters will take with their new puppies and begin offering it semi-monthly. Train Nancy to teach this class. Also consider opening this class to others in the community for a fee.

Now attach timelines and deadlines to each of the tasks. Now you are at a good starting point for selecting potential funding agencies, writing the grant proposal, and creating a budget.

Match Your Project with the Best Possible Funding Agency

If you're crystal clear on exactly what you're trying to accomplish, you can find a funding agency (sometimes called a grant maker) that wants to fund projects like yours. The surest way to have your grant proposal turned down is to submit it to the wrong funding agency. If you're in the business of finding a cure for a terminal disease, don't ask the National Endowment for the Arts for a grant! Instead, go to the Internet or your local library and search for "medical research grants" to find close matches. Also ask your staff, colleagues, and board members to brainstorm potential funding agencies for your project.

When you think you've identified a potential match, make sure your mission is consistent with the funding agency's mission. Contact someone at the agency, identify yourself and your project, and ask for as much information as possible, keeping in mind that your relationship with this person could ultimately determine whether you receive this grant. Look at the types of projects the agency has previously funded. Make sure it is currently offering grants at the funding level you plan to request. If the agency does not offer grants large enough to cover

> The surest way to have your grant proposal turned down is to submit it to the wrong funding agency.

your expenses, find out whether the funding agency will provide partial funding and allow another agency (or agencies) to partially fund it. Ask whether the agency offers assistance in writing grant proposals. Find out who reviews the proposals and the criteria used to approve or deny the grant.

Find Out What the Funding Agency Expects in Your Proposal

Some funding agencies have such detailed submission guidelines that they tell you what weight of paper and what font size you should use when you print your proposal. Others offer only a deadline and an address. Whatever the conventions of your funding agency, find out precisely what it wants and follow the guidelines to the letter. Be sure you know what format they want, including the following:

- Number of pages (minimum and maximum)
- Margin widths, font sizes, and paragraph spacing
- Binding (whether it should be professionally bound or held together with a paper clip or staple)
- Cover letter requirements (if any)
- Required sections or other components
- Number of appendices or other supporting materials (or whether they're even allowed)
- Number of copies of the proposal
- Deadlines
- Submission requirements (mail, registered mail or delivery service, hand delivered, and so on)

Remember that even the above list may not include every detail that a funding agency can specify. Whatever they ask for, do! Don't waste time grumbling about how silly it is. If you receive the grant, all the silliness will have been worthwhile.

Look for More Than Money

Don't forget that corporate support can come in forms other than money. An architectural firm could provide the plans for a drug rehabilitation center or a local bus company could offer transportation.

Develop a Detailed Plan for the Grant Proposal Process

Before you dive in to writing the proposal, be sure that you can make your deadline. Determine who is going to oversee the proposal process, what other project he or she may have that will be affected, who may be available to help that person, who will read and evaluate the proposal before it's sent out, how much time it will take, and what final and intermediate deadlines the person or group must meet.

If this is your first grant proposal experience, determine how much time you think the process will take and double it. The first grant proposal *always* takes twice as long as anyone expects. Later, as you and your staff gather experience, the process will take less time.

Sections of a Grant Proposal

Although each grant proposal is arranged slightly differently, all grants have similar sections. Every organization will want your proposal to have these sections, so in the text that follows, you find out about each section and get tips on how to complete each one. Note that each heading lists the sections by the various names they may be called.

Cover Letter/Project Overview/Introduction

This one-page section identifies your proposed project (sometimes called a program or activity), the amount you're requesting and what you intend to do with that money, and how the project ties in with the funding agency's mission and goals. This is generally printed on your organization's letterhead, written as a letter to a person at the funding agency, and signed by the highest-ranking employee at your organization.

Note that while this section may contain signatures from the project or organization manager, in some cases the funding agency may provide a special form or ask for a special section with authorized signatures.

Cover Sheet/Summary

Write your cover sheet after you've written the entire proposal and think of it as an outline. Include the name of your organization and a one-sentence (or less) statement of the following (each is discussed in the following sections):

- Qualifications
- Statement of need
- Project or program objectives
- Approach or methods
- Total cost and amount requested

The cover sheet generally runs about half a page and is often centered on the page with a lot of white space around it.

Organizational Information/Qualifications of the Organization/Credentials

This section, which usually runs one or two pages, tells the funding agency how your organization is uniquely qualified to be responsible for this project. Here's where you talk about your organization: your mission, service area, constituency, history, track record, successes, and so on. Also include information about your organization's overall goals and how those goals have been met to date. Whenever possible, give statistics or other evidence of your accomplishments, but don't dwell too much on this section. The highlight of the proposal is the need for your project and the means by which you will address those needs, so let those sections shine.

Also talk about your staff, board of directors, and volunteers. Include the credentials and experience of the individual(s) who will lead the project, and perhaps the credentials of your organization's manager or other executive (that's you!) and the board of directors. The funding agency wants to ensure that this project will be successful, so show that the individuals involved have had success in similar projects and/or have the training, education, experience, or personality to guarantee that this new venture will succeed.

Problem Statement/Statement of Need/Needs Assessment/Situation Analysis

Although it goes by many names, this section answers the question, "Why are we doing this?" or "Why is this so important?" You're

> ### Cover Letter *and* Cover Sheet?
>
> Including both may seem like a bit much, and some funding agencies want you to combine these two sections into one document. Simply write the cover letter as described, but add in the information that would normally go on a cover sheet.

establishing a specific need for this project in your community (or larger area, if applicable), and you want the funding agency to feel that yours is such a worthwhile and useful project that they couldn't possibly refuse it. Provide as much information and evidence as you can in this section, which usually runs from three to four pages (additional statistics, tables, and charts can go in an appendix), but don't always use statistics—use case studies and personal stories, too.

Whenever possible, provide third-party evidence stressing the overwhelming need for this project, but don't embellish, lie, or exaggerate. After all, if there isn't much need for the project, why are you doing it? On the other hand, if there's an overwhelming need for help and your project barely scratches the surface, you probably won't get the grant. Be sure the need is expressed as extremely important and be addressed by your project.

Don't assume the funding agency understands your needs. *Prove* that the need exists and that the grant money will be used to address the need with statistics, case studies, and so on. But don't use a lot of jargon and expect the funding agency to understand. Write about the problem in a way that any layperson can grasp quickly. Also, don't use circular logic—that a need exists because your project hasn't been funded.

Project Goals and Objectives

This section, which also has a multitude of names, answers the question, "What do we hope to accomplish?" and "If this project is funded, how, specifically, will the world be a better place?" You describe the goal(s) of the project, the scope, and the activities associated with it in one or two pages. You're not telling the funding agency how you plan to meet the goals, you're simply outlining what you plan to achieve through this project. List the number of constituents you plan to serve, the activities you will complete or offer, the people involved, the location(s), and so on.

Although you don't need to attach a specific timeline to this section, always state your goals in terms of time. For example, "In the next twelve months, we're going to discuss the benefits of breast-feeding with all new mothers at Bickford Community Hospitals and provide ongoing assistance to these mothers for four months after they're released."

Don't be general. Instead, be extremely specific, stating *measurable* results. Say, for example, that you plan to deliver 1,000 meals per month to the elderly, and if you do so, you will reduce illness and early death among that population by 25 percent over the next five years. The number of meals and the resulting increase in quality of life for the population you're serving over a certain amount of time are tangible and measurable, which is what the funding agency wants to see. (Of course, your proposal will also include information in the other sections that establishes a need among an elderly population for healthy meals in order to combat illness and early death.)

Although finding measures can be difficult, you'll ultimately have an easier time managing this project if you know precisely what you need to achieve—and your funding agency will have an easier time deciding whether your project is worthy. If you want to get a grant, find hard and fast ways to measure your success or failure.

Methodology/Specific Activities/ Work Plan/Approach

This section, which often runs from four to ten pages, answers the question, "How do we hope to accomplish our goals?" You list the specific, concrete actions you'll use to reach your objectives. (See the sample tasks listed in the "Develop a Clear Picture of What You Want" section earlier in this chapter for an example of what to include in this section.) You restate the need(s) and goal(s), and then clearly describe each of the activities involved and who will organize and operate those activities.

Also be sure to include a timeline. (Some proposals have a separate section called "Timeline"). Show when the project will start and end, of course, but also list target deadlines for each step in the project.

Evaluation/Impact of Activities

In the one or two pages of this section, you're looking into the future, helping the funding agency see the positive change that will come from this project and how both you and they will know

---

Reeling Them In

By knowing the goals and values of the funding agency, you can tie their goals to those of your project. In fact, don't be shy about using one or two of the same words in the agency's mission statement in your statement of needs. If the agency's mission statement says it "provides relief to victims of disaster," as does the mission statement of The American Red Cross (see Chapter 2), you could say in your grant proposal that you "intend to provide relief to victims of Hurricane Humbard."

whether this project has been successful. This section discusses who and how evaluations will be done, including how data will be gathered, who will be responsible for the evaluations, what timeline will be used for the evaluations, what reports will show this evaluation, and so on. The funding agency wants to make sure you have a plan in place—even a low-tech one—for determining whether you're meeting your stated goals.

Budget

Your budget tells the funding agency both *how* and *how well* you plan to spend the money they give you. This section will be of great interest to them, because they want to know that their money will be used efficiently. They also want to make sure that you're obtaining enough money to cover your expenses so that your project will not fail.

In this section, show the funding agency how you're going to spend the money, that the project can actually be accomplished for that amount of money, that your estimations are reasonable (and, if your project is long-term, that they allow for increases in costs down the road), and that you're not wasting the money in any way.

Don't be vague here: The funding agency wants to know where every nickel and dime is going to go and doesn't want to see "miscellaneous" as a category in a budget. And be sure to include *all* costs, including operating expenses (lease, utilities, and such), salary/benefit costs, supplies, equipment, insurance, taxes, and so on. If some supplies or salaries will be donated (by volunteers), include this information as well so that the funding agency doesn't think you've overlooked these expenses. You may also want to include a timeline of when expenses will be incurred.

In addition to this section, some funding agencies provide budgeting worksheets that must accompany the proposal.

Other Funding/Current Funding

This section describes where else you plan to get funding for the project (or where you have already have gotten funding, if the project is already in existence and you're applying for funds to keep

> Your budget tells the funding agency both *how* and *how well* you plan to spend the money they give you.

it going). This section may include other grant proposals, proposed funding from memberships or individual donations, proposed entrance fees, and so on.

Note that most funding agencies don't want information on prior funding for your project (that is, funding that has now expired) unless they specifically ask for it.

Future Funding

In this section, you tell the funding agency how you plan to fund the project in the future, beyond the scope of this particular grant. Tell them how you'll meet all future expenses, from salaries to maintaining equipment. If the goal of the project is to be self-sufficient in the future, describe in detail how this process will work. Or if you plan to continue to apply for grants (from other sources) indefinitely, be specific about which grants and which funding agencies you'll apply to.

Be specific in your future plans: The funding agency wants to make sure that this project won't abruptly end, even when their part in the funding does.

Appendices/Supplementary Materials/ Supporting Materials/Attachments

Supporting materials range from tables and charts to verification of tax-exempt status to biographies of staff members associated with the project. Don't be surprised if the funding agency wants information that extends beyond the scope of the project for which you're requesting a grant. They may want to see a list of credentials for your board of directors, the bylaws of your organization, financial statements and budgets for your entire organization, and other information that may not seem especially relevant.

Following Up

Find out from the funding agency how quickly you'll receive an answer and whether you can contact the funding agency for an update on the status of your proposal.

Should You Hire a Grant Writer?

Professional grant writers are experienced freelancers who write grants for a living, and many are so experienced that they could write grants in their sleep. If you plan to hire one, however, you won't be able to wash your hands of the project entirely. You'll still have to take all the steps to prepare yourself to write a grant, even if someone else is doing the actual writing. In addition, if you plan to apply for many grants in the future (and what nonprofit doesn't?), you'll have to hire this person again and again.

One option is to hire a professional grant writer to teach specific in-house personnel how to write grant proposals. Plan to pay well for this service and keep the grant writer close by to check the progress of the first few grant proposals your staff writes. By using a grant writer this way, however, you'll soon have the in-house capability to write successful grant proposals without his or her help.

Whether your proposal is accepted or rejected, follow up with a thank-you note to your primary contact at the funding agency. You never know when you may need to apply for a grant from that agency in the future. In addition, if your proposal is rejected, call and ask whether you can get feedback as to the weaknesses of the proposal or what you can do to be more successful next time. While some funding agencies are too busy to give this feedback, yours may not be, and you'll get critical information.

Don't be afraid to apply again in the future if you still see a match between your project and the funding agency.

Which Way to Government Coffers?

The government—federal, state, and local—offers an almost overwhelming number of grants. A great deal of information about federal funding programs is available on the Internet, but call or e-mail the agency in question before applying in order to obtain the most up-to-date information. By contrast, information on state and municipal grants is harder to pin down, so check with local officials and congressional offices. The following is a list of Web sites and publications that are useful for those seeking government funding:

FirstGov *(www.firstgov.gov)* is the first government Web site to provide one-stop access to all online federal government resources, including information on grants.

The Catalog of Federal Domestic Assistance *(www.cfda.gov)* is a searchable database of information about federal assistance programs.

National Endowment for the Arts *(http://arts.endow.gov)* supports learning in all areas of the arts. Appendix D of this book uses the NEA as an example of the number and scope of federal grants that are available.

National Endowment for the Humanities *(www.neh.fed.us)* supports learning in all areas of the humanities.

Preliminary Funding Proposals

Sometimes, a funding agency will want to see a preliminary proposal from your organization to save you the time and hassle of preparing the full proposal. If they aren't interested, you can set your sights elsewhere. If they are, they'll ask for the full proposal.

Preliminary proposals usually run two or three pages and include a paragraph on each of the following:

- Overview of your organization
- Reason for and amount of funding requested
- Needs assessment
- Project description
- Other funding

ScienceWise *(www.sciencewise.com)* offers a series of searchable databases of federal funding opportunities. These databases include FEDIX (for grant information to educational and research organizations from participating federal agencies) and MOLIS (or the Minority On-Line Information Service, for information on minority institutions and minority targeted opportunities). You can also sign up for ScienceWise Alert, a funding opportunity e-mail service.

The Nonprofit Gateway *(www.nonprofit.gov)* includes links to federal Web sites and information about grant programs, organized by Cabinet department and federal agency. Visitors can also search Notices of Funding Availability from the Federal Register, prepared each business day by the federal government.

Community of Science Funded Research Database *(http://login.cos.com)* allows you to search grants given by the National Institutes of Health, National Science Foundation, United States Department of Agriculture, Small Business Innovation Research, and the Medical Research Council in a variety of ways. You can search grants by keyword, geography, institutional recipient, award amount, date, agency, investigator, departments, and more. Free registration is required.

A handy reference is the annual *Government Assistance Almanac*, published by Omnigraphics, Inc.

> ## Basic Rules of Grant Proposals
>
> Consider the following basic rules of proposal writing:
>
> - Don't ask for more than you need.
> - Take your time writing the proposal.
> - Never lie.
> - Never use the same proposal twice.
> - Be upfront about asking for money.
> - Don't waste time getting to the point.

Note that federal funders generally prefer projects that serve as prototypes or models for others to replicate, while local government funders require strong evidence of community support for a project. Although a fair number of individual awards exist, the majority of government grants are awarded to eligible nonprofit organizations, not to individuals. Government grants nearly always have stiff reporting requirements; careful record keeping is a must, because an audit is always a possibility.

Chapter 13

The Board's Role in Fundraising

Topics covered in this chapter:

- **How to recruit fund raisers**
- **Conquering fund raising fears**
- **Encouraging your board members**

Would you like to see board members squirm in their seats? Tell them they have to participate in the next fund-raising event. Many board members are reluctant to become involved in the fund-raising process because they do not understand the basics of fundraising. Once you orient the board about your agency's fund-raising policies and procedures, it will be easier for them to want to participate in fund-raising activities.

> "The board members are responsible for the organization's financial condition."

Are All Board Members Responsible for Fundraising?

How is that question answered at your nonprofit agency? And why has it become such a controversial question for some people? According to Millie DeAnda, executive director of the Greater Dallas Crime Commission, it is an important issue at her agency.

"The board members are responsible for the organization's financial condition," she says. "Most board members think they have to ask for money personally, but there are other ways to help. In an ideal world, it would be great if each board member asked for money. However, most people don't like to ask for money and it is incumbent upon the executive director to be creative and find other ways for the board member to participate in fundraising."

What other ways would that be? DeAnda suggests that a board member can provide a list of potential donors and contacts. A development committee can be organized of board members who enjoy this type of activity. "You must remind them that people won't give unless they are asked to give," says DeAnda. "Make sure the board members are well informed regarding the organization or specific project before they solicit donors for money."

To what degree a board is involved in fundraising depends upon the individual nonprofit agency and its internal rules and regulations. In defining your own board's role in fun raising, a good place to start is to encourage each board member to make an annual contribution. How can you expect other donors to give if the board isn't doing so? It doesn't have to be a large amount but enough that you can tell everyone that 100 percent of your board supports your non-profit agency financially.

In addition to making a personal financial contribution, each board member should be encouraged to donate a few hours to volunteer service, which will help each one become more involved in the agency's mission and to better see how the agency operates on a day-to-day basis.

Ask the board to create its own fund-raising policy; that way, each and every board member will know what the policy calls for and how he or she is supposed to participate. Even better is to encourage board members to come up with their own fund-raising ideas. There's nothing like the excitement at the board level to create a spark in a fund-raising campaign.

Finally, recruit board members who enjoy fundraising. While this may sound like a difficult task, plenty of people are comfortable participating in fundraising if their roles are clearly defined. Make sure your board nominating committee is aware of this requirement.

Evaluate every fund-raising effort at the board level. After a board fund-raising campaign, stop and evaluate the results. Were they successful? Were board members happy with the outcome?

How to Help Board Members Conquer a Fear of Fundraising

Fundraising. The very word strikes fear into many people, and board members are not immune. But it's not just board members who are afraid of fundraising. Sometimes the fear of asking for money can be overpowering.

How do you help board members conquer their fear of fundraising?

For one thing, you can help alleviate fears that no one wants to donate money. Many board members report being fearful of asking people to donate money because they did not think people wanted to donate anymore. Remind them that according to the AAFRC Trust for Philanthropy, charitable contributions in the United States reached $204.45 billion for the year 2000.

Why Board Members Fear Fundraising

The biggest fear board members have about asking for donations is that they will be rejected, or that the prospect will yell at them. But many have other concerns as well.

- They are afraid the person will ask them questions about the organization they do not feel qualified to answer.

- They are afraid the person they are asking really cannot afford to make a donation.

- They are afraid they are imposing on a friendship.

- They are afraid that the person will make a contribution, then turn around and solicit them for a donation for a cause they are representing.

Help alleviate fears that it is bad form to talk about money. Many board members do not feel that they should be discussing the agency's financial situation outside of the boardroom. To that, respond, "Hey, it's okay!"

Have board members practice asking people for money. Asking a person for money takes practice, so pencil in some training for the board. If necessary, hire a fund-raising consultant to handle the training.

And on the subject of training, teach board members to feel good about fund raising. Once they conquer their fear of asking people for money, they will begin to feel good about themselves and the entire fund-raising process.

How to Encourage Board Participation in Fundraising

While every executive director of a nonprofit organization feels it's only his or her own board that is lukewarm about fundraising, it is not the reality. In truth, many board members feel they should be exempt from any fund-raising activities. They rationalize that their volunteer time on the board is their contribution. Why get involved in fundraising? Someone else will take care of it, they figure.

It is your job to convince them that *they* are a part of *everyone else*. It is not an easy task but one that can be completed with a little effort on your part. Before blaming board members for not jumping for joy about fundraising, ask yourself, Are their job descriptions spelled out for them? If so, do those job descriptions include any mention of fundraising?

It is imperative that everyone on the board is involved in the agency's fund-raising process. While each board member does not have to have the same level of responsibility, they all need to be a part of the process if it is to succeed. Goals, objectives, and plans must be discussed and debated at the board level if any serious fundraising is to take place at all. Board members should learn as much as they can about the agency's history of fundraising. They should study the strengths and weaknesses of the agency, and take steps to increase those strengths while chipping away at the weaknesses.

Have Some, It's Good for You

There are a number of commandments—ways of thinking, really—that you must convince board members to adopt. Board members, for example, need to accept fundraising as good, not evil.

They need to make the donor feel good about giving.

They need to support every fund-raising effort at every level and participate in all fund-raising training offered.

Raising the Roof While Raising Money

Just because a person is a board member doesn't mean that he or she can't have fun and raise some money at the same time. Board members, however, can be at a loss when it comes to brainstorming new, creative, and exciting fund-raising ideas. Consider throwing the following ideas on the table.

Hold a wine and cheese party at your home. This is a favorite fund-raising idea for board members who love to entertain at home. Once people realize that they are being invited to a wine and cheese fund-raising party, they won't mind opening their checkbooks at the end of the evening.

Ask board members to ask ten of their closest friends to donate $1,000 to the cause.

Encourage board members to see if the company they are working for has a matching gift program. Many corporations have such a program in place; when an employee makes a contribution to a 501-C3 charitable organization, the company he or she works for will double or sometimes even triple the amount.

Suggest they sell any unused frequent flyer miles they have accumulated and donate the money to their nonprofit agency. Check with the various airlines on the rules and regulations.

Hold a service auction. Have board members recruit friends and business associates, and host a party to auction off their services to the highest bidder.

Host a murder mystery fund-raising dinner just before Halloween. Encourage visitors to dress in theme costumes.

If your board members belong to local churches, have them check and see if their churches have programs where they make donations to local nonprofit agencies. Perhaps a church has a special collection at one of its services.

Start a monthly dinner party. Invite board members, their spouses, family members, friends, and business associates, and charge each person $20 to come (in addition to the cost of their dinner).

Ways to Encourage Board Members to Raise Funds

Often the best ways to encourage board members to become involved in fundraising is to offer a list of activities and objectives. Take a look at the following examples:

- Ask board members to serve on a fund-raising committee or to suggest ideas for a board fund-raising activity.

- Make sure they know the fund-raising goals and objectives and how much money the agency needs to raise in the next fiscal year.

- Have them develop a list of prospective donors and key corporate contacts they have in the community and then have them brainstorm to see how to turn those contacts in contributions.

- Suggest that they visit local foundations.

- Discuss how they should embrace fundraising as part of their individual mission and contribution to your nonprofit agency.

Board Fund-raising Manual: Does Your Nonprofit Have One?

While few nonprofit organizations have a fund-raising manual for their boards, those that do are learning just how useful it can be. A board fund-raising manual can actually be one part of the board's general orientation manual. Even if you only have a few pages that address the board members' responsibilities regarding fundraising, it will be worth the effort.

At the beginning, a board fund-raising manual should lay out the basic policy, which will set the tone for the rest of the agency when it comes time to raise funds.

It should list the history of board fund-raising activities so that new board members can have that historical context. The list should include fund-raising initiatives that were not successful.

The manual can provide list of fund-raising publications, those the agency subscribes to as well as other publications and Web sites. Individual board members may choose to subscribe on their own. The more informed your board is about fundraising, the better your chances of fund-raising success.

The manual should also indicate what training opportunities are available, such as board fund-raising workshops or seminars. The many fund-raising consultants, both independent and full-service agencies, usually offer effective training programs.

Have your board develop the best possible manual for its own use and everyone will feel good about the fund-raising activities that your agency takes on. With a little effort and a lot of excitement, everyone on your board will soon get over their fear of fundraising and look forward to discussing fund-raising options at their next meeting.

By the Book

If your nonprofit agency does not have a board fund-raising manual, check with your local United Way office to see if it has any samples available. Sometimes collecting examples of board fund-raising manuals of other agencies will help you to create the perfect one for your own nonprofit.

For more information on this topic, visit our Web site at www.businesstown.com

Marketing, Public Relations, and the Internet

In this section you find out how to market your nonprofit agency to make it a success. You will also learn why marketing is important for nonprofit agencies and how it differs from marketing in the for-profit world. Included are plenty of tips on how to create a public relations plan on a shoestring budget and ten ways your nonprofit agency can get free publicity. You will also be given examples of advertisements from a variety of nonprofit agencies and find out how the Internet can be a powerful marketing and public relations tool.

Why Market Your Nonprofit?

Topics covered in this chapter:

- How to determine your marketing needs
- Understanding the competition
- The six Ps of marketing

Marketing can help you and your organization in a variety of ways. It defines your unique niche in the marketplace and ensures that you posses the right services to meet the needs of your donors and consumers. With marketing initiatives you reach the audiences you want with a message that motivates people to respond. You stand out from the crowd and attract the kind of attention, support, and enthusiasm you need and deserve. Marketing will give your organization a greater impact on the social welfare agenda in your community and beyond.

> Marketing will give your organization a greater impact on the social welfare agenda in your community and beyond.

Fighting Marketing Resistance

You may, however, run into resistance from your board or employees. Have you ever heard (or thought) any of the following?

- Marketing for nonprofit agencies is a waste of time.
- Nonprofit agencies don't need a marketing plan.
- An executive director shouldn't waste time marketing a nonprofit agency.
- A logo is a complete waste of time and effort for a nonprofit agency.
- Nonprofit agencies can never market themselves with newsletters.

Let's take a closer look at each statement.

Myth #1: Marketing for nonprofit agencies is a waste of time.

An effective nonprofit manager knows the value of marketing his or her agency. Some people believe marketing has no place in a nonprofit agency. They are wrong. Ever wonder why some nonprofit agencies succeed and others don't? The flourishing nonprofit is the one with marketing as a top priority.

Myth #2: Nonprofit agencies don't need a marketing plan.

Without a marketing plan, how can you expect to take your nonprofit agency to the next level of excellence? You can hunt and peck your way around town, but without that all-important marketing plan, your job will be immeasurably more difficult. Why not take the necessary steps to create a marketing plan that will work for your nonprofit agency?

Myth #3: An executive director shouldn't waste time marketing his or her nonprofit agency.

If you agree with that statement, it is time to rethink your career choice. Any good executive director or nonprofit manager knows it is not a waste of time and energy to market his or her agency. Marketing will let the community know who you are, what your mission is, and how others can assist you in your efforts to fulfill that mission.

Myth #4: A logo is a complete waste of time and effort for a nonprofit agency.

A good logo is inviting to potential donors: It helps them remember your organization and instantly establishes a feel for what you do. Remember that a picture is worth a thousand words, so a well-designed logo is a must. A poorly designed logo, on the other hand, will only detract from your organization, so hire a professional designer for your logo. Logo designers generally don't cost a fortune and are worth every penny.

> Marketing will let the community know who you are, what your mission is, and how others can assist you in your efforts to fulfill that mission.

Myth #5: Nonprofit agencies can never market themselves with newsletters.

A newsletter, whether it's a print or electronic edition, can do wonders for the marketing of your nonprofit agency. Effective newsletters increase donations from current supporters and educate prospects about your nonprofit agency. A newsletter helps establish expertise and credibility. Many news organizations do not hesitate to quote a nonprofit from one of its newsletters. Newsletters are always passed on to friends and associates, so it has the ability to reach out and spread the good word about your organization to many new people in the community.

How Marketing Differs in the Nonprofit World

Nearly all for-profit companies market their products and services. Nonprofits, however, rarely think they need to market their services and certainly don't use marketing as the powerful tool that for-profits think it is.

Marketing is really about figuring out what a customer—in this case, a donor or a constituent (someone who uses your services)—wants and giving it to him or her. It's not necessarily selling or advertising (or doing anything else that makes you uncomfortable)—it's helping donors and constituents find out about your organization and have an easy way to donate funds or use your services. If you do this well, the "selling" takes care of itself.

Now, in order to get the word out, you may choose to use advertising (see Chapter 15) or public relations (see Chapter 16).

Determining Your Marketing Needs

As do for-profits, you want to understand your marketing needs before you spend any money on marketing. Knowing your needs helps you identify where and when you need to spend your marketing dollars and makes sure that you're focused on the donors and constituents you want to target. Although it's not always easy to determine your needs, developing a strong marketing initiative without knowing what you want to get out of it is almost impossible. And in the nonprofit world, you can't afford to make mistakes with your marketing dollars.

The purpose of this section is to help you develop a sense of what you hope to gain from a marketing effort, how this effort ties in with your organization's overall goals, whom you're trying to target, and knowing how much you can spend.

Buffing Your Professional Image

Does your nonprofit agency present a professional image in everything that it does? Or is the attitude, "Hey, we're a poor, struggling nonprofit that doesn't have to worry about our image."

Everything you do is part of your marketing package—your sign in front of the building, your attitude, and the materials that you print. Make sure that you consider your organization's image before you make a decision.

If you want to produce a marketing plan that you can include in a grant proposal or application for a bank loan, consider getting help writing an official marketing plan, which includes lots of charts and graphs and technical jargon. In this section, you find out only how to put your marketing needs on paper so that you have them available to help you make future decisions.

And do put it on paper—don't just think about these questions and concerns. Make your marketing needs a written document that you can refer to when you're unsure of how to proceed.

Know Your Mission Statement

Mission statements are covered in depth in Chapter 2. But if you're thinking, "I don't need a mission statement, those are useless," just remember that a good mission statement isn't maudlin or sappy—it's just a few sentences describing what your organization does. A great mission statement is one you can use every time someone asks where you work and what, exactly, your nonprofit does. Knowing what it is you do helps you focus your marketing plan to further your organization's goals.

Know Why You're Marketing

You need to decide what you want to gain from marketing it in the first place. Are you trying to increase the geographic region you serve, attract more members or donors, or serve a larger number of constituents? If so, you must put these goals on paper, being very specific about the geographic region you now want to serve, how many more members or donors you want to attract, and which (or how many) new constituents you want to serve.

You probably already know what these goals are and can put them into words without much help. What if, however, your goals are harder to quantify. What if your organization's former manager was involved in a well-publicized scandal, and your main marketing goal is to get the public to realize that your organize is still a good place to donate their money and use your services? Well, that may be a taller order, but restoring your agency's reputation is a reasonable goal for a marketing plan.

> A great mission statement is one you can use every time someone asks where you work and what, exactly, your nonprofit does.

Know What You Do and Don't Do

Be clear about what services you do and don't offer. You may serve a wide range of constituents and have many different initiatives, but you don't do everything. If you train guide dogs for the seeing and hearing impaired, you are not in the business of helping children get properly immunized—that's obvious. But clarify where you draw lines. Do you place guide dogs with good adoptive families? Perhaps you don't intend to, but if puppies don't make the grade or guide dogs lose their owners and are too old to be retrained, you may provide that service. If you don't provide that service, you need to be clear on how you handle that situation, whether you euthanize the dogs or have another organization take over the adoption role.

Know Whom You're Serving (Your Target Market)

Although this may seem obvious, make sure you know your constituents. Do you have any research showing who uses your services? If not, why not? You're going to have an awfully tough time serving your constituents' needs if you don't really know whom they are and what they need. And remember that marketing is all about finding out people's needs and serving them.

Know Who's Giving You Money

Who are your donors, including individuals, corporations, foundations, and so on? Do you know why they give to you? Do you know what they expect from you? Do you know what they hope you'll be doing in the future? If not, find out. If you know what they want from you, you can give it to them and vastly increase your donations in the process.

Know How Much You Can Spend

Earmark a certain amount for marketing and stick to that amount. Even with just a few dollars, you can market your organization and its services in some small way, so don't think that a strict budget means you can't market your nonprofit adequately. You'll have to make tougher decisions than someone at a for-profit with

> You're going to have an awfully tough time serving your constituents' needs if you don't really know whom they are and what they need.

deep pockets, but knowing your budget and sticking to it can make you more discerning about your marketing plan.

Even the smallest nonprofit organization with limited resources for marketing and promotion can find ways to spread the word about its organization. The following are just some examples of how to use free media and volunteer resources:

- Send out news releases regularly to media representatives and other key people on your mailing list.
- Cultivate relationships with local media representatives. These people can be of great assistance in placing feature material, calendar information, and coverage of press conferences and events.
- Write articles for local media or professional journals and newsletters that describe the benefits of your services.
- Periodically stage public relations events that volunteers can plan and execute. Any means of creating broader interest in your community or constituency, and the resulting publicity, will help the image of your organization.
- Send out a newsletter periodically to your list of supporters. If different groups of people would be better served by different messages, create separate newsletters.
- Build relationships with local schools. Identify functions and initiatives the students are learning that would benefit your organization.
- Participate in trade shows at the local, regional, or national level.

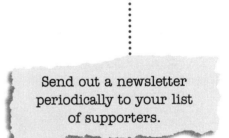

Send out a newsletter periodically to your list of supporters.

Understand the Competition

"Competition" may seem an uncomfortable word to use for the other nonprofits that serve similar needs in your area, but they are competing with you for donations and grant monies. With this in mind, paint a clear picture of your competition and analyze what they offer that you don't, and vice versa.

Study the marketing initiatives of your competition. Look at their Web sites, brochures, posters, radio campaigns, special events, fundraisers, and so on.

Also look at their services. Take a tour of their service locations and form business friendships with the managers of those nonprofits. They really aren't competitors in the true sense of the word, and you may ultimately be able to help each other by producing joint marketing campaigns.

The Six Ps of Marketing

For the nonprofit world, software experts Campagne and Associates have designated six "Ps" to consider when developing your marketing strategy: product, publics, price, place, production, and promotion. They are summarized here:

- *Product*—Let the public know that the programs and services you offer are of the highest quality.
- *Publics*—This group includes your board members, constituents, potential donors, foundations from which you may obtain grants, and so on. Know exactly who they are and what they want from you.
- *Price*—Price can be an important element in the marketing mix. If you offer your services for free or for a very low cost, you have a great marketing opportunity.
- *Place*—The geographic location were you provide services. If you're a small, community-based nonprofit, you can leverage your location much more effectively in a marketing campaign than can a large, national nonprofit.
- *Production*—Not as in creating widgets, but as in how well you serve the needs of your constituents. If you operate a soup kitchen, but you have enough food for 100 people and can fit only five in your facility, your production isn't very good. Think about the areas in which you provide excellent services and capitalize on this in your marketing strategy.

Evaluate Continuously

Never spend any money on marketing without knowing whether it's effective. Always get feedback on any marketing campaign, no matter how small. If you spend $6,000 on a direct-mail campaign and don't get one response, you don't ever want to use that same campaign again. You need to either change it or find another way to reach your audience. It is important to evaluate your progress and results regularly as well as to be flexible and responsive. Follow-through is paramount. As you go along, things will change; challenges and opportunities both will arise. If your marketing or promotional plan needs adjustment, do it.

- *Promotion*—Many nonprofits don't promote themselves or their services, but clearly, you need to get the word out for your constituents and potential donors. People need to know who you are before they'll give you money, offer you a grant, or use your services.

Going Forward with Your Marketing Initiative

So now what? You know what you're trying to get out of your marketing initiative, to whom you're trying to target, and what you want to spend. But you still don't know *what* to do next. You can choose one of several options: hiring a marketing consultant, hiring an in-house marketing professional, putting together a team within your organization that will do the work of a marketing professional, or using interns or volunteers to manage your marketing campaign. (And don't forget to read the next three chapters for more information on advertising, public relations, and the Internet.)

Hiring a Marketing Consultant

While this option seems the easiest route, it isn't. Hiring a marketing consultant costs money—sometimes lots of money—and you still have to work closely with this company or individual to communicate your needs and give feedback. However, a marketing consultant is a professional, and one who is experienced in marketing nonprofits can ultimately save you time and money.

A marketing consultant is a professional, and one who is experienced in marketing nonprofits can ultimately save you time and money.

Hire an In-House Marketing Pro

A paid staff member who is adept at guiding nonprofit marketing initiatives will be expensive, too, but can be extremely valuable, especially if he or she can also lead an internal marketing team of inexperienced staff members or volunteers who are enthusiastic and willing to give of their time.

Consider hiring a professional in a part-time capacity. More and more professionals are looking for balance in their lives by working less than full-time while still using their skills and experience.

Forming an Internal Marketing Team

Forming an internal marketing team is initially cheaper than hiring a professional, but remember that those staff members have job functions that they won't be able to spend as much time on, and that will cost you in the long run. Also, your staff, which is likely not made up of marketing professionals, will have a learning curve—perhaps a long one—that may not be efficient. They may initially produce more mistakes than successes, and if they leave your organization, their new-found expertise goes with them.

Using Interns

If you live near a college or university that offers a marketing major, consider starting a semester-long internship program that will give two or three students valuable experience and will give you a free staff of enthusiastic semiprofessionals. Similar to using an internal team, you may get a lot of false starts and other missteps, but you're likely to have so much enthusiasm from interns that they keep at it until they succeed.

If you live near a college or university that offers a marketing major, consider starting a semester-long internship program that will give two or three students valuable experience and will give you a free staff of enthusiastic semiprofessionals.

For more information on this topic, visit our Web site at www.businesstown.com

Chapter 15

Using Advertising

Topics covered in this chapter:

- **Realizing when you need to advertise**
- **Planning public service announcements**
- **Finding free advertisement**

How much time and energy do you devote to advertising your nonprofit agency? Unless you are with a large, cash-rich agency, you probably don't even have a budget for advertising. But as a nonprofit agency, sometimes you will need to spend money on advertising or find low-cost or no-cost ways to advertise. This chapter shows you how.

Knowing When to Use Advertising

Most nonprofit agencies advertise when the following needs arise:

- You need to place an advertisement to hire a new staff member. When you are ready to place an employment ad, ask your local newspaper if they have a special rate for nonprofit organizations (most do but won't give it to you unless you ask for it).
- You need to advertise a fund-raising special event. Again, make sure you ask for the rate for nonprofits.
- You need to advertise for volunteers.
- You need to place a public service announcement. (See the following section.) When you submit a public service announcement, otherwise known as a PSA, media will usually run them at no cost to your nonprofit agency.

Preparing Public Service Announcements

Public service announcements (PSAs) allow your nonprofit to get its message—usually a simple, clear call to action—out over the airwaves, on radio and television, in newspapers and magazines (often in their unsold advertising space), and on bulletin boards and posters. PSAs can also be used on stadium signs, ad banners on Internet sites—you name it!

PSAs you may have seen on TV range from encouraging parents to read to their kids, showing the effects of drug use, giving kids reasons to stay in school, highlighting the tragedy of drunk-driving accidents, touting the benefits of breastfeeding and childhood

---

Start a Clipping File

You might not be thinking about your advertising needs today, but it is a good idea to create a clipping file in which you can place samples of advertisements from other nonprofit agencies.

When you attend other nonprofit events and see samples of their ads, add them to your clipping file. The same goes for ads by nonprofits in newspapers, newsletters, and magazines.

Ask board members and other volunteers to do the same. That way whenever you are ready to create an ad you will have an abundant supply of samples from which to draw.

immunizations, supporting the notion of volunteerism, and so on. These PSAs on TV are often tied to nationwide poster campaigns, radio spots, and magazine ads. PSAs on network stations are generally funded by federal agencies or national nonprofits, but cable stations and local news shows are increasingly a great source for community-based nonprofits.

Television stations require that you send a high-quality PSA of thirty or sixty seconds that's ready to broadcast. If you don't have the means or expertise to produce such a PSA and you have an upcoming event you want to promote, find out whether your local TV station(s) offers a community calendar of nonprofit events, usually as part of their noon news broadcast. Competition for these "spots" is tight, however, so call, write, or fax months in advance of your event and be prepared to explain why your event is important enough to air. Make your event easy for the station to choose from the pile of applicants by writing a short, snappy, broadcast-quality announcement. Be sure to label it "public service announcement" and put the words "community calendar" on your letter.

Radio stations, unlike TV stations, may help you produce your PSA if you have a quality script. Radio PSAs are similar to press releases, although they are usually shorter in length—fifteen, thirty, or sixty seconds long when read by a professional announcer. Most music-only radio stations have limited time for PSAs, though, so target only those stations that have news shows, community calendars, and so on. Do use radio stations for other marketing, though, such as broadcasting live from your event or otherwise sponsoring and promoting your special event.

Newspapers may also help you with the layout of your PSA, or they may require camera-ready layout and art. They may also have staff members that can help design posters, banners, and other types of PSAs, but you'll likely have to pay for that service.

If you want expert help with your PSA—no matter what form it may take—contact the Ad Council, a nonprofit that is devoted to creating PSA campaigns. They charge for their services, but they are one of the largest advertisers in the United States, all using donated media time and space.

> Make your event easy for the station to choose from the pile of applicants by writing a short, snappy, broadcast-quality announcement.

If you've seen PSAs aired at unusual times of the day and night, it's because the media use PSAs as fillers in their schedules, so you're at their mercy as far as scheduling is concerned. However, if your event is seasonal or high profile, odds are the media will give it a better time slot. Plus, you can always ask the TV station or newspaper to cover your preparations for the event (one or two days before the event itself), and your local radio station may broadcast live from the event, if asked. You'll want to ask for this sort of coverage several months in advance, however, so that you get on their calendar.

Most media outlets are more than happy to work with local non-profit agencies to help spread the word about their activities and calls to action. Check with your TV and radio stations and newspapers and local magazines to determine their PSA requirements and find out the name of the person in charge of coordinating PSAs. Get to know this person so that he or she eventually knows you by name. When you send or fax your letter attempting to get air time or space, be sure to use the words "public service announcement," not "press release." Press releases can be about anything–from a company's new widget to an announcement of a new minister at a local church–but PSAs have to pertain to issues and events that serve the public good.

Advertising Strategies: How to Find Free Expertise and Ad Space

When you need professional advertising help, don't hesitate to contact the experts. Look in the Yellow Pages for the names and telephone numbers of local advertising agencies. Call them and ask if they would consider providing pro bono help in preparing an advertisement. Many will respond positively.

You can also check with your local chamber of commerce to see what advertising, marketing, or public relations firms are members. That is another good way of networking with those professionals who can really help your nonprofit agency when you need advertising help and expertise.

If you are looking for free and inexpensive ways to advertise your next event, or even if you are recruiting volunteers or hiring

---

What Is Your Ad Trying to Accomplish?

Before you spend a lot of time and money creating an advertisement for your nonprofit agency, spend time thinking about what your ad is trying to accomplish.

For example, if you are going to place an ad in the newspaper to get publicity for an upcoming special event, make sure it gives as much information as possible. Also, make sure your ad contains a telephone number or a Web site address where people can go for additional information about the event and your nonprofit agency in general.

staff, check in your local community to see what businesses and professional organizations have Web sites. See if they will allow you to place your ad on their site.

Bulletin boards in local supermarkets, drugstores, and community areas inside shopping malls usually will have a section or two reserved exclusively for use by local nonprofit agencies. Make use of them.

Virtually every town has weekly "shoppers' guides" that offer inexpensive classified ads. Check and see if they offer free or discount rates for local nonprofit agencies.

And don't forget to contact local corporations to ask if they will run your advertisement for free. Most will be glad to do so because they want to be good corporate and community neighbors.

> Virtually every town has weekly "shoppers' guides" that offer inexpensive classified ads. Check and see if they offer free or discount rates for local nonprofit agencies.

For more information on this topic, visit our Web site at www.businesstown.com

Chapter 16

Public Relations

Topics covered in this chapter:

- Creating a Public Relations Office
- Ten ways to find free publicity
- Making connections with the media

Good public relations, quite simply, is priceless. Without public relations, a nonprofit agency cannot communicate with its local community or with local corporations and businesses. Without pubic relations, a nonprofit agency cannot communicate with potential donors. It is an absolutely critical component of a successful fund-raising event. Many a nonprofit agency has spent months behind closed doors, planning a gala event, only to find out that no one shows up because organizers failed to take advantage of public relations opportunities in community.

How to Create a PR Office on a Shoestring Budget

Any nonprofit agency can create a public relations office with very little money. But too many nonprofit agencies fail to grasp the importance of having a dedicated public relations office. They either don't bother with one or leave those duties to a secretary or someone else who does not have the authority to handle public relations issues.

You can create a PR office on a shoestring budget. Contact your local office of the Public Relations Society of America (PRSA). They are experts with a wealth of information, and can provide mentors, printed information, samples, and everything else you need to set up shop. Officials at your local United Way office may also offer public relations training and support.

Keep an electronic file of all of your media contacts. If you are not sure how to create an e-mail mailing list for media contacts, ask someone to help you. Getting the word out to the media via e-mail will help your PR efforts.

Make sure you have a current media list at all times. The local chamber of commerce, United Way, and other organizations usually publish a media list several times a year.

Community Groups Can Help Your PR Efforts

Managers of nonprofit agencies should consider offering their services as speakers at meetings of local community groups. By placing themselves in the spotlight, they reach a captive audience and have the opportunity to turn everyone who is within listening range into a potential donor or volunteer.

Check the Yellow Pages for a listing of service organizations (such as the American Legion, Lions Club, or Rotary Club) or local chamber of commerce for contacts.

Ten Ways Your Nonprofit Can Get Free Publicity

Here are ten resourceful ways for you to wave the flag of your non-profit organization.

1. Take advantage of Public Service Announcement (PSA) opportunities with local media. PSAs are great ways to spread the word about your organization. (See Chapter 15.)
2. Look for community calendars that are published in your town. They usually allow nonprofit agencies to send in information to be included in their calendar of events.
3. Contact area advertising and public relations agencies and ask for help. You will usually find one or more companies that are ready to provide you with expert help.
4. Contact local colleges and universities. Their community service organizations are always looking for ways to serve local nonprofit agencies.
5. Ask local businesses to post flyers and posters about your next special event in their windows.
6. Ask local businesses that have Web sites to include a banner advertisement with a link to your Web site.
7. Send press releases and other media information to local corporations and businesses. Most will have company newsletter editors who are always looking for local news to include in every issue.
8. Get a free Web page and use it to promote events at your agency.
9. Keep a clipping file of other nonprofit agencies and their PR efforts. Review it often and make sure you are taking advantage of every media outlet they are using.
10. Make sure your board members carry information about your nonprofit agency—mission statement, brochures, and business cards—with them at all times.

Contact local colleges and universities. Their community service organizations are always looking for ways to serve local nonprofit agencies.

Developing Relationships with the Media

One of the best ways to get press coverage is to have an ongoing relationship with the media. You want the media to know that you're the best possible person to call whenever a news event touches—even slightly—on your organization's area of expertise.

You'll establish your organization as an expert in your nonprofit field, which can ultimately lead to more donations, more volunteers, and more constituents.

Start by contacting all local newspapers, the chamber of commerce, and (if one exists), the tourism board in your area. Also contact the magazines, TV stations, and radio stations of the largest city near you.

You may want to contact city, county, state, and federal officials in your area, arts councils, foundations, and professional associations and civic groups. These organizations may be contacted by the media and, if they are aware of your organization's mission, may direct those calls to you.

Send all of these groups information about your organization, then periodically send information about your special events, new programs or services, new employees and promotions, grants received, annual fundraising campaign, and so on. But don't send every press release to every media outlet every time. Instead, target the information. Your local newspaper may be more interested in one event, while the TV station that's thirty miles away may be interested in quite a different one (one that, perhaps, translates better to TV). Also, send the information about a month in advance—sometimes longer for monthly or bimonthly publications—not a few days before, or you'll miss an opportunity for free PR.

Although initially you may not know the names of every reporter and editor, learn them as you go so that you can target your press releases not only to certain media but also to particular contacts at each media outlet.

Make sure you "market" the press release, too. Besides telling the media what, when, and where your events are being held, let them know why this event is going to interest their audience.

> You may want to contact city, county, state, and federal officials in your area, arts councils, foundations, and professional associations and civic groups.

Once a year (or more often), evaluate how your media relations are going. Is your organization getting in the news? Are donations increasing? Are more people using your services?

Priming Your Staff for PR and Media Coverage

Everyone at your organization—from volunteers to the board of directors to the person who answers the phone—should know who is responsible for public relations and should direct those questions and requests for interviews to that person. Make sure that person is always accessible—perhaps with a cell phone or pager—or has a backup and a backup backup! You never want the media to call or visit and not have your top communicators available.

Finding Out More

Public relations principles work both for nonprofits and for-profit companies, so check out the many public relations books written for corporate executives and staff members. You may have to tweak the information a little, but the basic ideas are the same. Whenever you hear a good PR idea from the for-profit world, see whether you can apply it to your own organization.

For more information on this topic, visit our Web site at www.businesstown.com

Chapter 17

Making the Most of the Internet

Topics covered in this chapter:

- **Building your Web site**
- **How to maintain your Web page**
- **Saving money with e-mail**

Web sites and e-mail are relatively inexpensive marketing tools that you can put to work for your nonprofit right away. Although the best sites and e-mails are usually designed by professionals, you can teach yourself to be a pretty sophisticated designer without getting a Ph.D. in Internet-ology.

Building a Nonprofit Home on the Web

Nearly every national and international nonprofit has a Web site, and your organization can take advantage of this powerful promotional tool, too. A few years ago, having a Web site wasn't even close to a necessity. In fact, potential donors may have thought you were wasting precious resources by developing such a site.

How times have changed! While some people still wait to receive direct mail from nonprofits or donate only to organizations they can see in their own communities, millions of potential donors are surfing the Web right now, using search engines to locate "environmental charities" or "churches in Los Angeles" or "cancer research organizations." If you don't have a Web site, how will these high-tech potential donors find you?

The Internet can be used as a brochure for your organization, an online store, a listing of your services and locations, or a place for donors to pledge. Or it can be all of those things.

Getting Started on the Web

Your first step in starting an Internet site is securing a domain name, which is what comes after the "www." and before the ".org." To find out whether your potential name is taken, go to *www.register.com* and follow the instructions on the screen. If the name is available, secure it by paying for it for one or two years, usually at about $35 per year.

Creating a Web Site

With a little study, you can create a Web site for your organization. Simply purchase a copy of Microsoft FrontPage, Adobe GoLive,

---

Make Sure It's an Org

You want your nonprofit to end in .org and nothing else. Using a .com for your nonprofit is sure to confuse visitors to your site, who won't know whether you're a for-profit operation or a nonprofit.

Also, avoid securing a name that is the same as a .com or .net name. The possible resulting confusion may cause headaches down the road. If you want to be sure that your domain name will clearly belong only to your organization, secure the .com, .net, and .org versions, and then use only the .org for your site.

or some other simple Web design software, load it into your computer, read the manual that came with the software, take the computer tour, and start trying it out. Beware: Developing a Web site can take entire chunks of your life away from you before you've even noticed what has happened. I'm not kidding. You can easily spend hundreds of hours developing a site, and then not be very happy with the results. Unless you're pretty savvy with technology already, hire an experienced Web designer—and don't forget that this might be a sixteen-year-old!—to design your site for you.

Make It Searchable

Be sure that your Web site will pop up when potential visitors type in certain words on their search engine. This process isn't always as easy as it seems, because you have to identify which key words your audience will use. In addition, search engines can take as long as eighteen months to get your site incorporated into theirs. Check with your Web designer for tips on how to make your site come out on top in a Web search.

Hosting the Site

Securing the domain name and creating a Web site using a software package is not the end of the story. You still have to pay someone to host the site or buy very expensive servers and host the site yourself (which you don't want to do). Web site hosting ranges from about $20 to about $5,000, depending on what you want your site to be able to do. When you sign up for your domain name, you'll be deluged with e-mails and direct-mail pieces that describe hosting services. You can also search on the Web for "Web hosting" to find out more.

The good news is that many companies offer free Web hosting, as long as you aren't selling anything online. If you want an informational site only and don't want donors to be able to pledge online, free Web hosting might be right for you.

> ### Make Your Mission Statement Visible
>
> You mission statement (see Chapter 2) should have central stage on your Web site. As long as your statement is concise and up-to-date, it conveys better than anything else what your organization does.

Maintaining the Site

Nothing annoys savvy Web surfers as much as an out-of-date Web site. If you pay someone to develop the site, set up a schedule now for him or her to come back—monthly will probably work—to update the content, check for errors, and so on. If you design the site yourself (or have someone in-house design it), establish a monthly deadline for updating it.

Also set your home page on your computer to your site so that you can see what it looks like every day. Most Internet browsers (Microsoft Explorer and Netscape Navigator) allow you to change your home page with a few clicks of your mouse.

Using E-mail

You can use e-mail for nearly anything that you used to use regular mail for—sending monthly newsletters, direct mail, thanking donors for their support, notifying constituents of special events, kicking off an annual fund-raising drive, and so on. You'll have to gather e-mail addresses from your current mailing list, but you can do that easily by sending a direct mailing, asking recipients to fill out a questionnaire that asks them whether they prefer to be contacted by mail or e-mail. If they prefer e-mail, ask them to provide an e-mail address. And be sure to tout the cost savings of using the Internet!

Sending Newsletters

E-mail newsletters are so much less expensive than their snail mail counterparts that they are definitely worth investigating. The basic idea is that whatever you would have put into a printed newsletter—charming stories combined with a nice layout, including pictures and special fonts—you put in list form in an e-mail. (You can also post the newsletter, with all of its bells and whistles, to your Web site.) You simply insert the text into an e-mail and send it off. Well, not that simply. Keep the following in mind:

The Million Dollar Duck Race

The Million Dollar Duck Race in 2001 was the first time that the Internet has played an integral role in a fund-raising event for Special Olympics New York. For $5, donors could adopt a rubber duck by logging onto a special Web site. The organization's initial goal was for donors to adopt 5,000 ducks, but the number of entrants doubled by race day. The ducks, which were numbered, were then dropped into the East River under the Brooklyn Bridge and slowly bobbed to the finish line at the South Street Seaport. By melding traditional fundraising with online marketing, the organization reached a larger number of participants who contributed to a great cause.

- Give recipients the opportunity to get off your mailing list easily.
- Use the blind-send function so that every recipient (and there could be thousands) doesn't see the e-mail address of every other recipient.
- Don't use attachments—not everyone has the same software you do.
- Don't use special fonts or pictures. They take far too long to download.

Also make sure that the newsletter contains information that is useful to readers. Whatever you would have included in an old-fashioned newsletter and however often you would have sent it, do the same with your e-mail newsletter.

As with all marketing and PR tools, evaluate your e-mail newsletter process to make sure it meshes with your organization's vision and is an efficient use of your organization's time and resources.

Direct Mail

You can use e-mail much like you do regular mail. If you were going to send out a glossy brochure, just imagine the cost savings of sending mass e-mails. You'll have to find a way to make them look attractive—and may want to hire a professional writer or Web designer to do that—but with what you save in printing and mailing costs, the price should be well worth it.

Acknowledging Donors

If donors agree, you may be able to save both the paper and mailing costs of acknowledging donations. A well-written thank-you note sent via e-mail will arrive faster, can be just as charming, and will certainly save your organization a lot of money.

Announcing Special Events

Although you probably want to announce your special events well in advance of their event dates on your Web site and in your

What Should a Newsletter Include?

Consider these topics for your newsletter:

- Recent accomplishments by your organization
- Upcoming special events
- Fund drive kickoff
- Additions or improvements to your Web site
- Grants received
- New programs or projects
- New employees and promotions
- Legislative alerts and calls to action

printed or e-mail newsletter, you can use e-mail to remind recipients of the event just a day or two before. Think of how the dentist's office always calls the day before to remind you of your appointment. They do this so that you'll show up, helping them make money and efficiently serve all of their customers. You can do the same thing with your special events. Remind people of the upcoming event so that they come out in droves.

Remind people of the upcoming event so that they come out in droves.

For more information on this topic, visit our Web site at www.businesstown.com

SECTION V

Appendices

Nonprofit Board
Assessment Tools

Appendix A

This appendix contains tools that you can use to assess the strengths and weaknesses of your board of directors. Besides this appendix, however, check with your local United Way office to see if it has any board assessment tools that you can use. Other sources include the Internet and board members themselves. Also, a board member may have served on the board of another nonprofit agency that had assessment tools that are worth looking into.

Reviewing Assessment Tools

The California Assembly of Local Arts Agencies (CALAA), a nonprofit membership organization representing the state's 250 local arts agencies, has posted resources on its Web site that can help nonprofit boards take an honest look at themselves and examine how well members believe they are doing. CALAA's template is reprinted here with the organization's permission.

Organizational Assessment

An assessment of an organization is a brief internal review that reveals the organization's strengths and weaknesses at the time the assessment is conducted. An assessment enables you to compile somewhat subjective information regarding individual perceptions and levels of knowledge of the individuals completing the assessment of board members. The results also provide you with indicators of organizational performance.

Organizational assessment forms are usually designed for use by the board of directors. A sample form is included in this section. Decide whether it is appropriate for your board, or adapt it to suit your organization.

This exercise can be used as part of an evaluation and planning process or as just a quick check up on management practices. The responses will assist you to:

- Look at strengths and identify what makes those areas strong.
- Develop strategies to address identified weaknesses.

> An assessment of an organization is a brief internal review that reveals the organization's strengths and weaknesses at the time the assessment is conducted.

- Identify areas where you need additional information or training.
- Examine areas that have mixed responses, which may indicate a lack of understanding or effective communication.

Assessment Worksheet

(Answer Yes/No/Don't Know to the following questions)

I. Board of Directors

1. Board meetings are well attended.
2. A board orientation session is held for new board members.
3. Our board members understand the mission of our organization and how our programs help achieve it.
4. Our board members understand the basic organizational responsibilities that go along with our not-for-profit (tax-exempt) status.
5. Board members understand their individual responsibilities.

II. Effective Meetings

1. An agenda for each board meeting is distributed ahead of time.
2. A procedure exists to add an item to the printed agenda (or "Other Business" is written at the end of the agenda).
3. The agenda is followed during the meeting.
4. Important agenda items receive sufficient time during meetings.
5. The meeting starts on time and concludes within a reasonable period of time.
6. The person presiding keeps the meeting under control.
7. Minutes are kept and distributed following a board meeting.
8. Board members come to meetings prepared.
9. The location is comfortable and suitable for a business meeting.

> Our board members understand the basic organizational responsibilities that go along with our not-for-profit (tax-exempt) status.

III. Planning

1. Our organization produces an annual work plan that informs staff, board, and volunteers about our activities.
2. Most of our activities and events are scheduled at least six months in advance.
3. Our organization regularly evaluates programs.
4. We hold an annual planning meeting.
5. Our organization has a long-range plan (three to five years).
6. Our city has a community plan.

IV. Program Development

1. The entire board participates in the programming decision-making process.
2. We regularly make an effort to discover what kinds of programs the community is interested in.
3. We make an effort to present programs about a variety of cultures.
4. We are familiar with the resources available concerning artists and arts programs.

V. Financial Management

1. We prepare an annual budget and operate within its guidelines.
2. A treasurer's report is regularly presented at board meetings.
3. The treasurer's report includes information on how closely we are following the budget.
4. An income statement and balance sheet are presented as part of the treasurer's report.
5. Project chairpersons understand how much money they must earn and how much money they can spend.
6. I understand how to read and interpret financial statements.

VI. Fund-raising Planning

1. Our membership chair is provided with a dollar goal for the annual drive.
2. Fund-raising needs are clearly stated in the budget.

> We regularly make an effort to discover what kinds of programs the community is interested in.

3. More than one board member or staff person is proficient at grant writing.
4. Every board member makes a personal donation to the organization.
5. We receive income form a variety of sources including donations, ticket sales or admissions, and grants.

VII. Audience Development

1. We try to reach different segments of the community through our marketing efforts.
2. We encourage audience members to return through follow-up contact and targeted marketing.
3. We include funds for publicity costs in our budget.
4. We have a capable individual responsible for planning publicity.
5. We have a capable individual responsible for designing publicity.

VIII. Volunteers

1. We have written job descriptions for our volunteers.
2. We maintain volunteer profile records on our volunteers.
3. We actively recruit new volunteers each year.
4. We provide orientation and training for our volunteers.
5. We regularly recognize and/or reward our volunteers.

IX. Community Partners

1. I am familiar with the organizations that work as our partners.
2. We actively engage in partnerships/collaborations when appropriate and feasible.
3. We engage in a variety of partnership relationships ranging from simple communication to cosponsoring events.
4. We explore the full range of partnership benefits including sharing/exchange of material, human, and financial resources.

> We actively recruit new volunteers each year.

X. Services

1. We circulate flyers, newsletters, brochures, etc. from state and national organizations as appropriate.
2. We belong to one or more service organizations that I am aware of.
3. Someone from our organization attends at least one workshop, conference, or meeting each year.

XI. Evaluation

1. The board of directors regularly evaluates the director, programs, and activities of the organization.
2. When possible, we ask audience members to evaluate the programs they attend.
3. Committees are regularly involved in evaluation.
4. Staff (if applicable) provides evaluation to the board.

> The board of directors regularly evaluates the director, programs, and activities of the organization.

Sample Board Documents

CALAA has also prepared examples of board documents that encourage member involvement. The documents were contributed by a variety of CALAA agencies and are reprinted here with permission.

Commitment to Serve

In recognizing the important responsibility I am undertaking in serving as a Member of the Board of Directors of the Humboldt Arts Council, I hereby personally pledge to carry out in a trustworthy and diligent manner all the duties and obligations inherent in my role as a trustee of the organization. I acknowledge that my role as a trustee is primarily:

1. To contribute to defining the organization's mission and the fulfillment of that mission and
2. To carry out the functions of the Board of Directors that are specified in the organization's bylaws and governance policies.

I will exercise the duties of this role with integrity, collegiality and due care. I Pledge to:

1. Establish as a high priority my attendance at all meetings of the board and committees on which I serve.
2. Come prepared to contribute to the discussion of issues and business to be addressed at scheduled meetings, having read the agenda and all background support material.
3. Represent the organization in a positive and supportive manner at all times and in all places.
4. Refrain from intruding in administrative issues that are the responsibility of management, except to monitor the results and prohibit methods not in congruity with board policy.
5. Make every effort to learn the job of being a Board member and seek methods to help me function better as part of the Board team.

If, for any reason, I find myself unable to serve in the capacity outlined above, I agree to communicate promptly to the appropriate officer to remedy this situation.

Signature, Date

> Come prepared to contribute to the discussion of issues and business to be addressed at scheduled meetings, having read the agenda and all background support material.

Advisory Board: Purpose

Advisory Board, Humboldt Arts Council
Purpose of Advisory Board

To provide professional input and assistance to the Executive Committee on particular Humboldt Arts Council projects and programs.

To ensure the program's quality, thoughtfulness, and responsiveness to the cultural community by assisting the Executive Committee with planning, evaluation, problem solving, marketing, and community assessments.

To act in an advisory capacity to monitor the continuity of the Executive Committee, as guided by the goals and objectives specified in the Arts Council Mission Statement. The Advisory Board does not make decisions.

Advisory Board's Responsibilities

To meet semi-annually with the Executive Committee for problem solving and/or brainstorming.

To be available to provide advice on an ad hoc basis.

To inform the Executive Committee of problems and opportunities in the larger community.

Code of Ethics

Humboldt Arts Council
A Code of Ethics for Board Members
As a member of the board I will:

1. Consider myself a trustee of the organization and do my best to ensure that the agency is well maintained, financially secure, growing, and operating in the best interests of our constituents.
2. Participate fully in board meetings and actions.
3. Respect the other members of the board and the constituents I serve.
4. Keep well informed of developments that are relevant to issues that may come before the board.
5. Recognize that all authority is vested in the board when it meets in legal session and not with individual board members.
6. Refer constituent or staff issues to the proper officer or committee.
7. Recognize that the board member's job is to ensure that the agency is well managed, not to manage the agency.
8. Declare any conflicts of interest between my personal life and my position on the board, and to avoid voting on issues that are a conflict of interest.
9. Do my best to continue to grow personally and professionally in order to best serve the organization.

> Keep well informed of developments that are relevant to issues that may come before the board.

As a member of the board I will not:

1. Be critical of fellow board members.
2. Use the organization for my personal advantage.
3. Discuss the confidential proceedings of the board outside board meetings.
4. Interfere with the duties of the administrator or undermine the administrator's authority.

Standards of Conduct

Standards of Conduct for Nonprofit Board Members
(reprinted from "The Legal Obligation of Nonprofit Boards")

A nonprofit board may wish to adopt a formal statement of conduct for members. Here are some issues that such a statement should address. Note that grants or contracts may contain conditions that require the organization to enforce certain standards of conduct in administering the grant or contract, such as antinepotism rules.

FINANCIAL INTERESTS: Statement of circumstances under which board members must disclose business and family relationships that create a potential conflict of interest; the extent to which a board member may participate in board decisions in which the member has a personal financial or other interest; and policy for retaining board members to provide services to the organization, such as accounting or legal services.

BOARD MEMBER COMPENSATION: Policy covering reimbursement of board members' direct expenses incurred participating in board activities (e.g., travel, meals) and indirect expenses (e.g., lost wages) and provisions for any direct compensation or honoraria for board members' services.

GIFTS AND GRATUITIES: Statement of policy concerning whether board members may accept gifts or gratuities from persons or organizations doing business with the

> A nonprofit board may wish to adopt a formal statement of conduct for members.

nonprofit and any limitations on such policy (e.g., gifts of token value).

POLITICAL ACTIVITIES: Policy statement requiring board members to disassociate the organization from any personal political activities and prohibiting using the organization's name, property, or facilities in connection with any political activity.

HIRING OR CONTRACTING WITH RELATIVES (NEPOTISM): A statement of circumstances under which the organization will or will not hire persons related to board members.

VIOLATIONS: A statement of consequences for violating any of the board member standards of conduct (dismissal from the board, termination of a contract, etc.) and procedures for resolving disputed cases.

Board Member Commitment and Evaluation

Name: _____

Date: _____

Term covered by this commitment: from_____to_____

My board partner is: _____

My committee assignments are: _____

My officer or committee chair assignment is: _____

I commit to: Attend all board meetings

　　　　　　Attend events: _____ All _____ 1–2 _____ 3–4 _____ 5+

　　　　　　Recommend at least _____ names for board membership or committee service

　　　　　　Be a partner to a fellow board member

　　　　　　Donate the following professional services:

　　　　　　Join as an individual member at the $ _____ level, with payment by:

　　　　　　Lump sum payment of $ _____ payable by this date:

　　　　　　Monthly payments of $ _____ for a total of $ _____

　　　　　　Solicit the membership of _____ other individuals, organizations, and/or businesses.

　　　　　　Support the organization's fund-raising by participating with staff and/or other board members in at least _____ fund-raising and/or membership solicitations.

I understand that the nominating committee will evaluate my adherence to this commitment, and present its evaluation to the board.

Signature date: _____

Manual/Handbook Sample Outline

Once an individual has agreed to become a member of your board, the following information should be provided in a handbook, which can be given out during the orientation session:

- Brief History of the Organization
- Statement of Purpose (mission)
- Long-range Plan
- Bylaws
- Articles of Incorporation
- Policies (Personnel, Conflict of Interest, etc.)
- Board of Directors Roster with Biographical Information
- Board Responsibilities: General and Specific
- Committee Composition and Job Descriptions
- Organizational Chart
- Minutes
- Budget and Recent Financial Statements
- Meeting Dates
- Program Description
- Membership List
- List of Major Funders
- Calendar of Events
- Other relevant information

> Once an individual has agreed to become a member of your board, the following information should be provided in a handbook.

For more information on this topic, visit our Web site at www.businesstown.com

Sample Bylaws

Appendix B

The following set of bylaws is for a nonprofit organization based in Montana.

BYLAWS OF
GALLATIN COMMUNITY CLINIC, INC.

ARTICLE I. OFFICES

Section 1.1 - Business Office

The corporation's principal office shall be located either within or outside of Montana. The corporation's most current Annual Report, filed with the Montana Secretary of State, shall identify the location of the principal office. The corporation may have other offices, either within or outside of Montana. The board of directors may designate the location of these other offices. The secretary of the corporation shall maintain a copy of the records required by section 2.1 of Article II at the principal office.

Section 1.2 - Registered Office

The corporation's registered office shall be located within Montana at the address of the corporation's registered agent. The location of the registered office may be, but need not be, identical with that of the principal office if the latter is located within Montana. The board of directors may change the registered agent and the address of the registered office from time to time, upon filing the appropriate statement with the Secretary of State.

ARTICLE II. RECORDS

Section 2.1 - Corporate Records

(a) **Minutes and Accounting Records**. The corporation shall keep a permanent record of the minutes of all meetings of its board of directors, a record of all actions taken by the board of directors without a meeting, and a record of all actions taken by a committee of the board of directors acting in place of the board and on behalf of the corporation. The corporation shall maintain appropriate accounting records.

> The corporation's principal office shall be located either within or outside of Montana.

(b) **Form.** The corporation shall maintain its records in written form or in another form capable of conversion into written form within a reasonable time.

(c) **Other Records.** The corporation shall keep a copy of the following records at its principal office or at a location from which the records may be recovered within two (2) business days:

    (1) its articles or restated articles of incorporation and all amendments to them currently in effect;

    (2) its bylaws or restated bylaws and all amendments to them currently in effect;

    (3) resolutions adopted by its board of directors;

    (4) the financial statement furnished for the past three (3) years to the board of directors;

    (5) a list of the names and business addresses of its current directors and officers; and,

    (6) its most recent annual report delivered to the Secretary of State.

ARTICLE III. BOARD OF DIRECTORS

Section 3.1 - General Powers

All corporate powers shall be exercised by or under the authority of the board of directors. The business and affairs of the corporation shall be managed under the direction of the board of directors.

Section 3.2 - Number, Tenure, and Qualifications of Directors

The authorized number of directors shall be not less than seven (7) or more than thirteen (13), until changed by a duly adopted amendment to these bylaws. Each director shall have one vote on any matter that comes before the board. Directors shall serve staggered three (3) year terms, determined by lot, and shall be elected at the annual business meeting of the board of directors. Each director shall hold office for their specified term, or until removed in accordance with section 3.3. However, if the director's term expires, the director shall continue to serve until the board of directors has elected and qualified a successor or until there is a decrease in the number of directors. Directors need not be residents of Montana.

> The business and affairs of the corporation shall be managed under the direction of the board of directors.

If a director resigns effective at a specific later date, the directors may fill the vacancy, before the vacancy occurs, but the new director may not take office until the vacancy actually occurs.

Section 3.3 - Removal of Directors

A director may be removed, with or without cause, if a majority of the directors present at a duly constituted meeting votes for the removal. Removal is effective only if it occurs at a meeting called for that purpose. Notice must be sent to all directors that a purpose of the meeting is removal.

Section 3.4 - Board of Director Vacancies

If a vacancy occurs on the board of directors, including a vacancy resulting from an increase in the number of directors, the directors shall fill the vacancy.

If the directors remaining in office constitute fewer than a quorum of the board, they shall fill the vacancy by the affirmative vote of a majority of all the directors remaining in office.

If a director resigns effective at a specific later date, the directors may fill the vacancy, before the vacancy occurs, but the new director may not take office until the vacancy actually occurs.

Section 3.5 - Ex-officio Members of the Board

The officers and executive directors or managers of the corporation shall serve as non-voting, ex-officio members of the board. They are members by virtue of their office. Each ex-officio member officer or director may attend board meetings and participate in discussion; however, each ex-officio member shall be entitled to one vote only if the individual is a regularly elected or appointed board member.

Section 3.6 - Regular Meetings of the Board of Directors

The board of directors shall hold a regular meeting at least once per quarter. One of these quarterly meetings shall be designated as the board's annual business meeting, for the purpose of electing directors. The board of directors may provide, by resolution, the date, time and place (which shall be within the county where the company's principal office is located) of additional regular meetings. Regular board of director meetings may be held by conference telephone, if convened in accordance with section 3.8.

Section 3.7 - Special Meetings of the Board of Directors

The presiding officer of the board, the president, or 20 percent of the directors then in office may call and give notice of special meetings of the board of directors. Those authorized to call special board meetings may fix any place within the county where the corporation has its principal office as the special meeting place. Special board of director meetings may be held by conference telephone, if convened in accordance with section 3.8.

Section 3.8 - Board of Director Meetings by Conference Telephone

If authorized by the board of directors, the board of directors or any designated committee of the corporation may participate in a board or committee meeting by means of a conference telephone or similar communications equipment, provided all persons entitled to participate in the meeting received proper notice of the telephone meeting (see section 3.9), and provided all persons participating in the meeting can hear each other at the same time. A director participating in a conference telephone meeting is deemed present in person at the meeting. The chairperson of the meeting may establish reasonable rules as to conducting the meeting by phone.

Section 3.9 - Notice of, and Waiver of Notice for, Special Director Meetings

(a) **Notice.** The corporation's secretary shall give either oral or written notice of any special director meeting at least five (5) business days before the meeting. The notice shall include the meeting place, day and hour. If the meeting is to be held by conference telephone, (regardless of whether it is regular or special), the secretary must provide instructions for participating in the telephone meeting.

(b) **Effective Date.** If mailed, notice of any director meeting shall be deemed to be effective at the earlier of:

  (1) five (5) days after deposited in the United States mail, addressed to the director's business office, with postage prepaid; or

> A director participating in a conference telephone meeting is deemed present in person at the meeting.

(2) the date shown on the return receipt (if sent by registered or certified mail, return receipt requested, and the receipt is signed by or on behalf of the director); or

(3) the date when received.

(c) **Waiver of Notice.** Any director may waive notice of any meeting. The waiver must be in writing, signed by the director entitled to the notice, and filed with the minutes or corporate records.

A director's attendance at a meeting waives the director's right to object to lack of notice or defective notice of the meeting; this shall be true unless the director, at the beginning of the meeting (or promptly upon arrival), objects to holding the meeting or transacting business at the meeting, and does not vote for or assent to action taken at the meeting.

Neither the secretary nor director needs to specify in the notice or waiver of notice the business to be transacted at, or the purpose of, any special board meeting.

> A director's attendance at a meeting waives the director's right to object to lack of notice or defective notice of the meeting.

Section 3.10 - Director Quorum

A majority of the number of directors shall constitute a quorum for the transaction of business at any board of director meeting.

Absent board members may give their proxy to a board member in attendance at a board of director meeting. Such proxy can be counted in determining a quorum.

Section 3.11 - Directors, Manner of Acting

(a) **Required Number to Constitute Act.** The act of a majority of the directors present at a meeting at which a quorum is present (when the vote is taken) shall be the act of the board of directors. If no quorum is present at a meeting of directors, the directors may not take action on any board matter other than to adjourn the meeting to a later date.

(b) **Director Approval.** The corporation shall deem a director to have approved of an action taken if the director is present at a meeting of the board unless:

(1) the director objects at the beginning of the meeting (or promptly upon arrival) to holding it or transacting business at the meeting; or

(2) the director's dissent or abstention from the action taken is entered in the minutes of the meeting; or

(3) the director delivers written notice of dissent or abstention to the presiding officer of the meeting before its adjournment or to the corporation immediately after adjournment of the meeting. The right of dissent or abstention is not available to a director who votes in favor of the action taken.

Section 3.12 - Conduct of Board of Director Meetings

The president, or in the president's absence, the vice president, or in their absence, any person chosen by the directors present shall call the meeting of the directors to order and shall act as the chairperson of the meeting. The chairperson, or the chairperson's designee, shall establish rules of the meeting that will freely facilitate debate and decision making. The chairperson will indicate who may speak when and when a vote will be taken. The secretary of the corporation shall act as the secretary of all meetings of the directors, but in the secretary's absence, the presiding officer may appoint any other person to act as the secretary of the meeting.

Section 3.13 - Director Action Without a Meeting

The directors may act on any matter generally required or permitted at a board meeting, without actually meeting, if: all the directors take the action, each one signs a written consent describing the action taken, and the directors file all the consent with the records of the corporation. Action taken by consent is effective when the last director signs the consent, unless the consent specifies a different effective date. A signed consent has the effect of a meeting vote and may be referred to as a meeting vote in any document.

Section 3.14 - Director Committees

(a) **Creation of Committees.** The board of directors may create one or more committees and appoint members of the board

> The chairperson, or the chairperson's designee, shall establish rules of the meeting that will freely facilitate debate and decision making.

to serve on them. Each committee must have one (1) or more directors, who serves at the pleasure of the board of directors. Volunteers from the community may serve on these committees when appropriate.

(b) **Selection of Members.** To create a committee and appoint members to it, the board must acquire approval by the majority of all the existing directors when the action is taken.

(c) **Required Procedures.** Sections 3.6, 3.7, 3.8, 3.9, 3.10, 3.11, 3.12, and 3.13 of this Article III, which govern meetings, notice and waiver of notice, quorum and voting requirements, conduct of the board of directors, and action without meetings apply to committees and their members. In addition, the committees shall keep regular minutes of their proceedings and report the same to the board of directors. The committees are subject to all the procedural rules governing the operation of the board itself.

(d) **Authority.** Each committee may exercise the specific board authority which the board of directors confers upon the committee in the resolution creating the committee. Provided, however, a committee may not:

> Each committee may exercise the specific board authority which the board of directors confers upon the committee in the resolution creating the committee.

(1) approve the dissolution, merger, or the sale, pledge, or transfer of all or substantially all of the corporation's assets;

(2) elect, appoint, or remove directors or fill vacancies on the board of directors or on any of its committees; or

(3) adopt, amend, or repeal the articles or bylaws.

Section 3.15 - Compensation, Loans to, or Guarantees for Directors

(a) **Director Compensation.** The board of directors may, upon approval of the majority of that board, pay each director expenses, if any, of attendance at each board meeting or committee meeting of the board. The directors shall not be paid a salary or fee for attending the meeting. A director may not serve the corporation as an employee and receive compensation.

(b) **Loans to or Guaranties for Directors.** The corporation may not lend money to or guarantee the obligation of a director of the corporation.

Section 3.16 - Board Member Service at the Clinic

Board members are expected to serve as a volunteer at the Gallatin Community Clinic a minimum of six times during the calendar year.

ARTICLE IV. OFFICERS

Section 4.1 - Number of Officers

The officers of the corporation shall be a president, a vice president, a secretary, and a treasurer. The board of directors shall appoint each of these officers. The board may appoint other officers and assistant officers if it deems it necessary. If the board of directors specifically authorizes an officer to appoint one or more officers or assistant officers, the officer may do so. The same individual may simultaneously hold more than one office in the corporation.

Section 4.2 - Appointment and Term of Office

The board of directors shall appoint officers of the corporation for a term that the board determines. If the board does not specify a term, the officers shall hold office for one year or, within that year, until they resign, die or are removed in a manner provided in section 4.3 of Article IV.

A designation of a specified term does not grant to the officer any contract rights, and the board can remove the officer at any time prior to the termination of the designated term.

Section 4.3 - Removal of Officers

The board of directors may remove any officer or agent any time, with or without cause. The removal shall be without prejudice to the contract rights, if any, of the person removed. A board's appointment of an officer or agent shall not of itself create contract rights.

> The officers of the corporation shall be a president, a vice president, a secretary, and a treasurer.

> The vice president shall perform, in good faith, the president's duties if the president is absent, dies, is unable, or refuses to act.

Section 4.4 - President

The president shall be the principal executive officer of the corporation. The president shall be subject to the control of the board of directors, and shall in general oversee, in good faith, the affairs of the corporation. The president shall, when present, preside at all meetings of the members and of the board of directors. The president may sign, with the secretary or any other proper officer of the corporation that the board has authorized, corporation deeds, mortgages, bonds, contracts, or other board authorized instruments.

Section 4.5 - The Vice President

The vice president shall perform, in good faith, the president's duties if the president is absent, dies, is unable, or refuses to act. If the vice president acts in the absence of the president, the vice president shall have all presidential powers and be subject to all the restrictions upon the president. (If the vice president is unable or refuses to act, then the secretary shall perform the presidential duties.) The vice president shall perform any other duties that the president or board may assign to the vice president.

Section 4.6 - The Secretary

The secretary shall in good faith: (1) create and maintain one or more books for the minutes of the proceedings of the board of directors; (2) provide that all notices are served in accordance with these bylaws or as required by law; (3) be custodian of the corporate records; (4) when requested or required, authenticate any records of the corporation; (5) keep a current register of the post office address of each director; and (6) in general perform all duties incident to the office of secretary and any other duties that the president or the board may assign to the secretary.

Section 4.7 - The Treasurer

The treasurer shall: (1) have charge and custody of and be responsible for all funds and securities of the corporation; (2) receive and give receipts for moneys due and payable to the corporation from any source, and deposit all moneys in the corporation's name in banks, trust companies, or other depositories that the board shall select; (3) submit the books and records to a Certified Public Accountant or other accountant for annual audit or review; and (4) in general perform all of the duties incident to the office of treasurer and any other duties that the president or board may assign to the treasurer. If required by the board of directors, the treasurer shall give a bond for the faithful performance of the treasurer's duties and as insurance against the misappropriation of funds. If a bond is required, it shall be in a sum and with the surety or sureties that the board of directors shall determine.

Section 4.8 - Loans to or Guarantees for Officers

The corporation may not lend money to or guarantee the obligation of an officer of the corporation.

ARTICLE V. NOTIFICATION OF ATTORNEY GENERAL

Section 5.1 - Notification of Attorney General

The secretary of the corporation shall notify the attorney general of the State of Montana when dissolution, indemnification, merger, removal of directors, and the sale of assets (as defined in the Montana Nonprofit Corporation Act) occur. The secretary shall deliver notice in the manner required by each event and cooperate with the Attorney General in providing necessary information.

(a) **Dissolution.**

   (1)   In the event of dissolution, the secretary shall give the Attorney General written notice that the corporation intends to dissolve at or before the time the secretary delivers articles of dissolution to the secretary of state. The notice must include a copy or summary of the plan of dissolution.

   (2)   The corporation shall not transfer or convey assets as part of the dissolution process until twenty (20) days after the secretary has given the written notice required by section 5.1(1)(i) to the Attorney General or until the Attorney General has consented in writing to the dissolution or indicated that the Attorney General will not

> The secretary shall deliver notice in the manner required by each event and cooperate with the Attorney General in providing necessary information.

take action in respect to transfer or conveyance, whichever is earlier.

(3) When the corporation has transferred or conveyed all or substantially all of its assets following approval of dissolution, the board shall deliver to the Attorney General a list showing those, other than creditors, to whom the corporation transferred or conveyed assets. The list must indicate the address of each person, other than creditors, who received assets and an indication of what assets each received.

(b) **Indemnification.** The secretary of the corporation must give the Attorney General written notice of its proposed indemnification of a director. The corporation may not indemnify a director until twenty (20) days after the effective date of the written notice.

(c) **Merger.** The secretary of the corporation must give the Attorney General written notice of a proposed merger of the corporation, and include with the notice a copy of the proposed plan of merger, at least twenty (20) days before consummation of any merger.

(d) **Removal of Directors.** The secretary of the corporation must give written notice to the Attorney General if the corporation commences a proceeding to remove any director by judicial proceeding.

(e) **Sale of assets.** The secretary of the corporation must give written notice to the Attorney General twenty (20) days before it sells, leases, exchanges, or otherwise disposes of all or substantially all of its property if the transaction is not in the usual and regular course of its activities, unless the Attorney General has given the corporation a written waiver of this subsection.

ARTICLE VI. INDEMNIFICATION OF DIRECTORS, OFFICERS AGENTS, AND EMPLOYEES

Section 6.1 - Indemnification of Directors

(a) **General.** An individual made a party to a proceeding because the individual is or was a director of the corporation may be indemnified against liability incurred in the proceeding, but only if the indemnification is both:

  (1) determined permissible and
  (2) authorized, as defined in subsection (b) of this section 6.1 (The indemnification is further subject to the limitation specified in subsection (d) of section 6.1.)

(b) **Determination and Authorization.** The corporation shall not indemnify a director under section 6.1 of Article VI unless:

  (1) *Determination.* Determination has been made in accordance with procedures set forth in the Montana Nonprofit Corporation Act that the director met the standard of conduct set forth in subsection (c) below, and
  (2) *Authorization.* Payment has been authorized in accordance with procedures listed in the Montana Nonprofit Corporation Act based on a conclusion that the expenses are reasonable, the corporation has the financial ability to make the payment, and the financial resources of the corporation should be devoted to this use rather than some other use by the corporation.

(c) **Standard of Conduct.** The individual shall demonstrate that:

  (1) the individual acted in good faith; and
  (2) the individual reasonably believed:
    (i) in acting in an official capacity with the corporation, that the individuals conduct was in the corporation's best interests;

> Determination has been made in accordance with procedures set forth in the Montana Nonprofit Corporation Act that the director met the standard of conduct set forth in subsection (c) below.

(ii) in all other cases, that the individuals conduct was at least not opposed to the corporation's best interests; and

(iii) in the case of any criminal proceeding, that the individual had no reasonable cause to believe that the conduct was unlawful.

A director's conduct with respect to an employee benefit plan for a purpose the director reasonably believed to be in the interests of the participants in or beneficiaries of the plan is conduct that satisfies the requirement of subsection (c)(2)(ii).

The termination of a proceeding by judgment, order, settlement, conviction, or upon a plea of nolo contender or its equivalent, is not, of itself, a determination that the director did not meet the standard of conduct described in this section.

(d) **No Indemnification Permitted in Certain Circumstances.** The corporation shall not indemnify a director under section 6.1 of Article VI if:

(1) the director was adjudged liable to the corporation in a proceeding by or in the right of the corporation; or

(2) the director was adjudged liable in any other proceeding charging that the director improperly received personal benefit, whether or not the individual acted in an official capacity.

(e) **Indemnification Limited.** Indemnification permitted under section 6.1 of Article VI in connection with a proceeding by the corporation or in the right of the corporation is limited to the reasonable expenses incurred in connection with the proceeding.

Section 6.2 - Advance Expenses for Directors

The company may pay for or reimburse, in advance of final disposition of the proceeding, the reasonable expenses incurred by a director who is a party to a proceeding if:

> The termination of a proceeding by judgment, order, settlement, conviction, or upon a plea of nolo contender or its equivalent, is not, of itself, a determination that the director did not meet the standard of conduct described in this section.

(1) by following the procedures of the Montana Nonprofit Corporation Act the board of directors determined that the director met requirements (3)–(5) listed below; and

(2) the board of directors authorized an advance payment to a director; and

(3) the director has furnished the corporation with a written affirmation of the director's good faith belief that the director has met the standard of conduct described in section 6.1 of Article VI; and

(4) the director has provided the corporation with a written undertaking, executed personally or on the director's behalf, to repay the advance if it is ultimately determined that the director did not meet the standard of conduct; the director's undertaking must be an unlimited general obligation, but need not be secured, and the corporation may accept the undertaking without reference to financial ability to make repayment; and

(5) the board of directors determines that the facts then known to it would not preclude indemnification under section 6.1 of this Article VI or the Montana Nonprofit Corporation Act.

Section 6.3 - Indemnification of Officers, Agents and Employees

The board of directors may choose to indemnify and advance expenses to any officer, employee, or agent of the corporation applying those standards described in sections 6.1 and 6.2 of Article VI.

Section 6.4 - Mandatory Indemnification

Notwithstanding any other provisions of these bylaws, the corporation shall indemnify a director or officer, who was wholly successful, on the merits or otherwise, in the defense of any proceeding to which the director or officer was a party because he or she is or was a director or officer of the corporation, against expenses incurred by the director or officer in connection with the proceeding.

> The director has provided the corporation with a written undertaking, executed personally or on the director's behalf, to repay the advance if it is ultimately determined that the director did not meet the standard of conduct.

ARTICLE VII. CONTRACTS, LOANS,
CHECKS AND DEPOSITS; SPECIAL CORPORATE ACTS

Section 7.1 - Contracts

The board of directors may authorize any officer or officers, agent or agents, to enter into any contract or execute or deliver any instruments in the name of and on behalf of the corporation and such authorization may be general or confined to specific instruments.

Section 7.2 - Loans

The corporation shall not allow anyone to contract on behalf of it for indebtedness for borrowed money unless the board of directors authorizes such a contract by resolution. The corporation shall not allow anyone to issue evidence of the corporation's indebtedness unless the board of directors authorizes the issuance by resolution. The authorization may be general or specific.

Section 7.3 - Checks, Drafts, etc.

The board of directors shall authorize by resolution which officer(s) or agent(s) may sign and issue all corporation checks, drafts or other orders for payment of money, and notes or other evidence of indebtedness. The board of directors shall also determine by resolution the manner in which these documents will be signed and issued.

Section 7.4 - Deposits

The treasurer of the corporation shall oversee the deposit of all funds of the corporation, in banks and other depositories; the board of directors shall authorize by board resolution the exact location of the banks and depositories.

ARTICLE VIII. PROHIBITED TRANSACTIONS

Section 8.1 - Prohibited Transactions

(a) **Prohibition Against Sharing in Corporation Earnings.** No director, officer, employee, committee member, or person connected with the corporation shall receive at any time any of the net earnings or pecuniary profit from the operations of the corporation; provided that this shall not prevent the corporation's payment to any person of reasonable compen-

> The corporation shall not allow anyone to issue evidence of the corporation's indebtedness unless the board of directors authorizes the issuance by resolution.

sation for services rendered to or for the corporation in effecting any of its purposes as determined by the board of directors.

(b) **Other Prohibitions.** Neither the corporation, nor its directors, nor its officers have any power to cause the corporation to do any of the following with Related Parties:

(1) make any substantial purchase of securities or other property, for more than adequate consideration in money or money's worth;

(2) sell any substantial part of its assets or other property, for less than an adequate consideration in money or money's worth.

For the purpose of this subsection, Related Parties means any person who has made a substantial contribution to the corporation, or with a brother, sister, spouse, ancestor, or lineal descendant of the person giving, or with a corporation directly or indirectly controlled by the person giving.

Section 8.2 - Prohibited Activities.

Notwithstanding any other provisions of these bylaws, no director, officer, employee, or representative of this corporation shall take any action or carry on any activity by or on behalf of the corporation not permitted to be taken or carried on by an exempt organization under section 501(c)(3) of the Internal Revenue Code of 1986 and its regulations as they now exist or as they may later be amended, or by an organization, contributions to which are deductible under section 170(d)(2) of the Internal Revenue Code of 1986 and regulations as they now exist or as they may later be amended.

Section 8.3 - Corporate Funds Used For Indemnification.

Corporate funds may be used to benefit officers and directors by way of indemnification, but only if such indemnification is authorized by Article VI of these bylaws.

> Corporate funds may be used to benefit officers and directors by way of indemnification, but only if such indemnification is authorized by Article VI of these bylaws.

ARTICLE IX. AMENDMENTS

Section 9.1 - Amendments

These bylaws may be amended, altered, repealed or enhanced by an affirmative vote of a simple majority of the entire board of directors.

These bylaws were adopted by the unanimous consent of the board of directors on May 20, 1996.

These bylaws may be amended, altered, repealed or enhanced by an affirmative vote of a simple majority of the entire board of directors.

For more information on this topic, visit our Web site at www.businesstown.com

Sample Grant Proposal

The following is a partial sample of a grant proposal, reprinted with permission from The Gill Foundation. If this were being sent to a funding agency, it would also include full budgeting and funding information.

If this were being sent to a funding agency, it would also include full budgeting and funding information.

September 29, 1998

Ms. Katherine Pease
Executive Director
The Gill Foundation
8 South Nevada Ave
Colorado Springs, CO 80903

Dear Katherine:

Please find enclosed Servicemembers Legal Defense Network's grant proposal requesting support from the Gill Foundation for 1999 and 2000.

Last week, there was a disappointing loss in Able vs. United States, the most prominent federal case challenging the constitutionality of "Don't Ask, Don't Tell, Don't Pursue." With this development, the outlook for victory in the courts has sadly dimmed. Our communities also face a hostile Congress that is not likely to overturn the law any time soon.

There is no quick fix. Even if the outlook in the courts and Congress were brighter, it would still be necessary to reform military culture in order to truly end discrimination. As the largest employer in the United States, what the military says about and how it treats gay men, lesbians, and bisexuals matters.

Now more than ever, SLDN is committed to staying its course. A course that attacks the pillars on which this law stands. A course that protects and saves the lives and careers of service members serving under "Don't Ask, Don't Tell, Don't Pursue." A course that undermines the rationale of the ban by making it possible for service members who are gay, lesbian, and bisexuals to serve along side their heterosexual counterparts.

It is a course that has yielded significant results to date. Step by step, SLDN is changing hearts and minds to hasten the day when this anti-gay law is overturned. And when it is, the military as an institution will have been so relentlessly challenged and so fundamentally affected that its standard practices will discourage rather than foster discrimination and intolerance toward gay men, lesbians, and bisexuals.

Financial and moral support from the Gill Foundation has played a crucial role in SLDN's ability to stay its course and achieve tremendous results. We respectfully request a grant of $50,000/year in 1999 and 2000 for general operating purposes. On behalf of the men and women we serve, thank you.

Sincerely,

Michelle M. Benecke
Co-Executive Director

Organization: Servicemembers Legal Defense Network (SLDN)
Person Submitting Proposal: Mary H. Ester, Director of Development
Lead Contact and Title: Michelle M. Benecke, Co-Executive Director
Address: PO Box 65301, Washington DC 20035-5301
Phone: (202) 328-3244
Fax: (202) 797-1635
E-mail: sldn@sldn.org
Web: *www.sldn.org*
Dollar Amount Requested: $50,000 per year, 1999 and 2000
1998 Operating Budget: $788,982

SLDN is spotlighting twin national disgraces: the policy that destroys the military careers of anyone found to be gay and the Pentagon's failure to end the anti-gay witch hunts, harassment, and snooping outlawed by "Don't Ask, Don't Tell." . . . SLDN has repeatedly forced the Pentagon not just to take notice but to change.
                                        —Deb Price, *The Detroit News*, April 25, 1998

It is nothing short of astonishing that a five-year-old organization has produced such dramatic results in the military, an institution known for its intransigence to change. The significance of Servicemembers Legal Defense Network's ability to spotlight the military's "disgraces" and force the military to change cannot be underestimated. With three million members on active duty and in the reserves, the military is the largest employer in the United States. The military socializes more of America's young people than any institution except the public school system.

The military is the only entity that destroys careers and derails educational opportunities under sanction of law. The military's anti-gay policy sends an insidious message that gay men, lesbians, and bisexuals are second-class citizens. The message is even more devastating within the ranks. Young men and women, especially, are bombarded by, and are often victims of, firmly entrenched anti-gay attitudes and behavior, including violence.

Ridding society of "Don't Ask, Don't Tell, Don't Pursue" is critical to establishing equality for gay, lesbian, and bisexual Americans. Founded in October 1993, SLDN has developed strategies to empower individual service members and create institutional reform. With SLDN's help, service members are fighting back to save their lives and careers. With SLDN's sustained, well-calculated pressure, the pillars upholding the military's anti-gay policy are beginning to crumble.

I. RECENT ACCOMPLISHMENTS

SLDN's unique strategy combining watchdog and policy activities, outreach and education, and aggressive legal intervention has proven highly successful.

1. *Obtained Landmark Pentagon Policy Against Anti-Gay Harassment.*

In March 1997, SLDN obtained from the Department of Defense (DOD) an historic memorandum denouncing anti-gay harassment and lesbian-baiting. The memo instructs commanders to investigate perpetrators of harassment, not the sexual orientation of their

> With SLDN's sustained, well-calculated pressure, the pillars upholding the military's anti-gay policy are beginning to crumble.

victims. The memo from Undersecretary of Defense Edwin Dorn was issued in direct response to SLDN's casework and our Third Annual Report on the policy, which documented that service members cannot report death threats, hate crimes, or harassment without triggering investigations into their orientation. Women, especially, cannot report sexual harassment without facing retaliatory investigations. When implemented correctly, the Dorn memo will improve the safety of service members' daily lives and keep careers intact.

2. *Compelled Pentagon to Conduct Internal Review of Policy*

In April 1998, Secretary of Defense William S. Cohen made public a year-long study of "Don't Ask, Don't Tell, Don't Pursue," which he ordered as a direct result of SLDN's Third Annual Report. In its report, DOD officials adopted several groundbreaking SLDN recommendations, including:

> a. *Reissue Guidance on Anti-Gay Harassment and Lesbian-Baiting*

In the past year, SLDN documented that the services failed to distribute the aforementioned Dorn memo. The DOD report acknowledged this problem and recommended concrete steps to fix it. Further, the report clarified the memo and broadened its scope, as per SLDN's request. At least one service, the Navy, has already complied and sent the memo to the field.

> b. *Cease Use of Pretrial Agreements to Ferret Out Gays*

The DOD report included a new policy to end the use of pretrial agreements to cajole service members facing criminal penalties to turn in suspected gay, lesbian and bisexual service members in exchange for lenient treatment. One example of this practice is when Air Force prosecutors in Hawaii agreed to reduce an airman's life sentence for rape and other charges on the sole condition that he accuses other military

When implemented correctly, the Dorn memo will improve the safety of service members' daily lives and keep careers intact.

members of engaging in gay relationships. He accused seventeen men in all services. The five men named in the Air Force lost their careers. SLDN intervened and stopped the investigations that were underway in the Army, Navy, and Marine Corps, and then launched a two-year campaign using political and media strategies to outlaw pretrial agreements of this sort. As a result, one more door has been closed to the military to hunt down and destroy people's lives and careers. This project went hand-in-hand with our broader effort to close down the use of the criminal system, described below.

c. *End Criminal Prosecutions of Gay, Lesbian, and Bisexual People*

SLDN obtained strong language in the report to discourage criminal prosecutions of gay people for consenting adult relationships, a gain that reinforces our successes in several high-profile individual cases. Ending this punishment is necessary not only for the individuals targeted, who face a federal felony conviction and imprisonment, but also to undercut the military equating gay people with criminals, a pillar supporting the military's anti-gay policy.

d. *Clarify that Health Professionals Are Not Required to Turn in Gays*

For the first time, DOD stated that mental health care providers are not required to turn in gay people. This significant development furthers our goal of stopping the military from using private counseling sessions as a basis for investigation or discharge, and to create safe space for military members. Additionally, our aim is to dispel the stereotype that gay people are a threat to their units and the mistaken view that homosexuality is a sickness, both of which are inherent in the rationale for the military's policy. DOD's move is in response to SLDN cases, including that of former Marine Corporal Kevin Blaesing, who was turned in by his Navy psychiatrist for simply asking questions about homosexuality.

> For the first time, DOD stated that mental health care providers are not required to turn in gay people.

3. Obtained the First-ever Federal Court Ruling that the Military Violated "Don't Ask, Don't Tell, Don't Pursue"

In January 1998, our client, Master Chief Petty Officer Timothy R. McVeigh ("America Online-Navy case"), won his suit against the Navy, affirming the online privacy rights of millions of Americans, both military and civilian, and holding the military accountable for conducting a witch hunt—a first for the courts. SLDN assisted Tim for months in the military system and, when the Navy would not back down, we went to court with help from our cooperating attorneys at the firm of Proskauer Rose, LLP. As important, SLDN collaborated with privacy and technology groups to apply political pressure on Tim's behalf, and assisted Tim in channeling the enormous grassroots support he received into an effective media and political strategy. As a result of this pressure, the Navy agreed to drop its appeal and settle Tim's case on his terms, preserving the strong ruling he had received and his retirement benefits. SLDN has already used this ruling to stop other inquiries based on anonymous statements and allegations.

> SLDN has already used this ruling to stop other inquiries based on anonymous statements and allegations.

4. Obtained Revised Recruiting Forms that Stopped Asking

In its first two annual reports, SLDN revealed that recruiting forms still asked the question, "Are you homosexual or bisexual?" Working closely with Representative Patrick Kennedy's office, SLDN was able to secure an order from Secretary of Defense Cohen instructing the military to replace these recruiting forms. Based on our monitoring of recruiting stations, the old forms have indeed been replaced with a new form that does not ask about sexual orientation.

5. Published Survival Guide for Service Members and Their Allies

The military is not training people about what "Don't Ask, Don't Tell, Don't Pursue" means. Service members have no idea how to protect themselves or what to do if targeted by command abuses. SLDN published the Survival Guide, written in collaboration with the Military Law Task Force, to fill this void. Already, SLDN has mailed the *Survival Guide* to clients and to every base librarian and military defense attorney here in the U.S. and overseas. The results? Captain John Baker recently e-mailed SLDN: "I'm the senior defense counsel for Marine Corps Air Station Cherry Point, NC. I received your *Survival Guide* and wanted to thank you for providing me and my attorneys with this excellent source of information."

6. Obtained Recognition of Lesbian-baiting as Sexual Harassment

In 1997, both the Senate Armed Services Committee and the Army Senior Review Panel recognized lesbian-baiting as a problem and urged DOD leaders to take concrete steps to address it. This was a direct result of SLDN's extensive case documentation. These developments build on SLDN's success in obtaining the Dorn memo, and are part of our ongoing effort on this issue.

7. Continued Focusing Public Attention on the Plight of Service Members

A death threat. The loss of a career. A woman accused of being a lesbian because she reported sexual harassment. When the American public sees a face and hears a story, hearts and minds begin to change. And they are changing. Recent opinion polls, including several of military members, indicate opposition to gays, lesbians, and bisexuals serving in the military is dropping significantly. SLDN has exposed military abuses under the policy and has brought service members' stories to the public. Among others, they include: Kevin Blaesing in *The New York Times*, highlighting psychotherapist-patient confidentiality; Amy Barnes on CNN's Impact, highlighting lesbian-baiting; the "Hawaii 17" on ABC's Nightline, concerning pretrial agreements; and Sean Fucci on ABC's San Diego affiliate, putting the spotlight on death threats.

> Recent opinion polls, including several of military members, indicate opposition to gays, lesbians, and bisexuals serving in the military is dropping significantly.

II. SUMMARY OF MAJOR GOALS

1. Ensure that Recent DOD Report Recommendations Are Properly Implemented

If the DOD report recommendations are implemented properly, fewer careers will be derailed and service members will be safer. The pillars upholding this policy will be weakened. To that end, SLDN and, by our request, the Human Rights Campaign have already met with Undersecretary of Defense Rudy DeLeon and White House officials to make clear our expectations and our intent to grade the Pentagon on its progress as part of SLDN's upcoming Fifth Annual Report. Marking the policy's fifth anniversary, the report is expected to garner wide media attention. Other strategies include partnering with the American Psychiatric Association to press for guidance to mental health care professionals and to achieve the longer-term goals described below.

2. Ensure that Guidance on Limits to Gay Investigations Is Sent to the Field

Gay discharges soared to 997 in 1997, a 67 percent increase under the policy and the highest level of discharges since 1988. Every day last year, two to three service members were kicked out of the military under "Don't Ask, Don't Tell, Don't Pursue." The toll would not have been as high if commanders knew about the limits to gay investigations and the intent of "Don't Ask, Don't Tell, Don't Pursue" to respect service members' privacy. The Pentagon has failed to instruct commanders, some of whom are well-intentioned, on the policy in any meaningful way. Recently, SLDN called on Secretary Cohen to issue clear guidance on the policy. In the meantime, SLDN has produced its own memorandum explaining the limits to gay investigations and has launched a pilot project to distribute it to commanders at Norfolk Naval Base.

> Other strategies include partnering with the American Psychiatric Association to press for guidance to mental health care professionals and to achieve the longer-term goals described below.

3. *Full Distribution of SLDN* Survival Guide

In addition to our clients, librarians, and military defense attorneys, SLDN is distributing the *Survival Guide* over the Internet and to bookstores, houses of worship, community centers, grassroots organizations, and other venues near our top five "worst bases." Next year, SLDN would like to distribute the guide more widely, reaching the top twenty "worst bases."

4. *Force the Air Force to Stop Recoupment of Education Monies*

Losing one's livelihood, profession, and military family is devastating enough. The Air Force makes it nearly impossible for service members to start over in civilian life, too, by pursuing service members who they kick out under the gay policy for repayment of education monies and reenlistment bonuses. This occurs despite the fact that service members are willing to stay and fulfill their obligations. This violates a policy SLDN obtained in 1994 ending recoupment in most cases. SLDN has fought this battle before with the Army, Navy, and Marines, and we succeeded in bringing them into line. Now, SLDN and our political allies, including Members of Congress, are pressing Pentagon leaders to bring the Air Force, which we have isolated, into compliance to end the vindictive practice of recoupment once and for all.

5. *Keep the Spotlight on Service Members and Military Abuses*

Educating people about service members' experiences and focusing a bright spotlight on military practices is key to deterring future abuses. It makes life safer for service members and exposes the fallacies underpinning the policy itself.

III. OUTCOMES AND EVALUATION

We have set and reached significant, concrete goals over the last five years, using a unique strategy combining watchdog and policy activities, outreach and education, and aggressive legal interven-

> Now, SLDN and our political allies, including Members of Congress, are pressing Pentagon leaders to bring the Air Force, which we have isolated, into compliance to end the vindictive practice of recoupment once and for all.

tion. Our heavy case load from all fifty states and fifteen countries allows us to identify systemic problems and design specific strategies to target them.

1. Policy and Watchdog Activities

Ensure that Recent DOD Report Recommendations Are Properly Implemented.
Action Item: Obtain congressional letter requesting that Secretary Cohen brief key Members on the Pentagon's progress.
Timeline: Last quarter 1998 and first quarter 1999.
Action Item: Grade the Pentagon's progress in implementing the DOD report recommendations in SLDN's widely covered Fifth Annual Report.
Timeline: February 1999.
Action Item: Monitor progress, implement follow-on strategy as needed. Timeline: mid-1999 through 2000.
Press for Psychotherapist-Patient Confidentiality.
Action Item: Obtain a rule of confidentiality, or at the minimum a guarantee of privacy that prevents investigations based on confidences shared with mental health professionals.
Timeline: Fourth quarter of 1998 to solidify strategy with allies such as the American Psychiatric Association; 1999 to obtain actual rule.
Ensure that Guidance on Limits to Gay Investigations Is Sent to the Field.
Action Item: Meet with appropriate officials to press for the Pentagon to issue such guidance.
Timeline: Ongoing.
Action Item: Complete pilot project to distribute SLDN's memorandum on limits to commanders and investigators at Norfolk Naval Base, one of the largest in the world.
Timeline: Fourth quarter 1998.
Action Item: Be prepared to distribute SLDN memo to top ten bases, with top twenty bases to follow in the next year.
Timeline: 1999–2000.
Force the Air Force to Stop Recoupment of Education Monies.

Action Item: Monitor progress, implement follow-on strategy as needed. Timeline: mid-1999 through 2000.

Action Item: Meet with Undersecretary of Defense DeLeon, who is in charge of this issue, and organize key congressional members with affected constituents to do the same.

Timeline: 1999.

Stop Criminal Prosecutions for Consenting Gay Adult Relationships Once and for All.

Action Item: Monitor to ensure our progress is not reversed.

Timeline: Through 2000.

2. Legal Aid

Assist Service Members.

Action Item: Directly assist 200–250 service members each year. Provide effective legal assistance.

Timeline: Ongoing.

3. Outreach and Education

Survival Guide.

Action Item: Distribution to bookstores, houses of worship, community centers, grassroots organizations, Pride Festivals, etc.

Timeline: Top five "worst bases" by end of 1998; top ten by mid-1999; top 20 by end of 1999; ongoing to clients, at speaking engagements, etc.

Army Times, Navy Times, and Air Force Times.

Action Item: Place weekly classified ads to educate service members, reaching a million subscribers, plus base newsstands.

Timeline: Ongoing.

"Eyes and Ears" Tours.

Action Item: Conduct four in-depth service member trainings per year.

Timeline: In conjunction with Pride Festivals in second and third quarters of 1999 and 2000.

> Action Item: Directly assist 200–250 service members each year. Provide effective legal assistance.

> We cannot fully capitalize on potential policy changes that arise out of our cases without additional staff.

IV. GREATEST CHALLENGES/WEAKNESSES

1. Legal Work Assisting Clients.

For optimal representation, we need to staff one attorney per thirty cases. We currently staff one attorney per sixty cases. That is counting Michelle Benecke and Dixon Osburn as full-time staff attorneys, who have additional responsibilities for public policy, press, publications, fundraising, and grassroots organizing. We have a daily average of one hundred fifty cases.

Changing Policy. We cannot fully capitalize on potential policy changes that arise out of our cases without additional staff. Windows of opportunity are often short. We have identified opportunities that need more intense follow-up than we can currently provide. Initiatives include adoption of a psychotherapist-patient rule of confidentiality, ending once and for all the practice of criminally prosecuting gay people for consensual adult sex, and ensuring that recognition of lesbian-baiting as a form of sexual harassment filters down to the field.

2. Outreach and Education Training Service Members.

We have trained hundreds of service members and their families and friends over the past three years at major bases in San Diego, Colorado Springs, Norfolk, and elsewhere. However, caseload is so heavy, we have not been able to travel to all the major bases every year to ensure that the preventative lessons we teach take deep root.

Grassroots Organizing.
One of the most effective ways to ensure that our elected officials and other leaders help those harmed by witch hunts and other abuses of the current policy is to apply grassroots support and opposition as necessary. We have started a grassroots program, but there is no staff dedicated to ensure that the program develops in the most efficient manner.

Coordinating Media.
We have had hundreds of media stories in the last five years, every one of them favorable, including coverage by *The New York Times*, *The Washington Post*, CNN, CBS, NBC, ABC, and others. We

have achieved this without a person on staff specifically to field press calls, educate reporters, write press releases, and cultivate new press contacts. To date, these tasks have fallen exclusively on the Co-Executive Directors.

3. Development Conducting Donor Research.

In order to make fundraising as effective as possible, SLDN would like to know more about its donors. Strategic questions include: "What motivates donors to support SLDN?" and "What SLDN messages resonate?" The answers would allow us to highlight what is important to donors, making our fundraising more efficient. SLDN would also like to have the capacity to conduct sufficient research on major donors, foundations and corporations.

4. Administrative Support Staff.

An administrative weakness that we face is lack of support staff. There is one administrative support staff person, who serves as the receptionist and is also required to perform client "triage" during especially heavy case intake periods. To ensure that service members who need help do not fall through the cracks, and that each of our sections operates more efficiently, additional support personnel are needed.

> To ensure that service members who need help do not fall through the cracks, and that each of our sections operates more efficiently, additional support personnel are needed.

For more information on this topic, visit our Web site at www.businesstown.com

Government Grants

Appendix D

overnment grants aren't exactly easy to come by, but they are available to someone—why not your organization! This appendix lists the community foundations by state and also lists information about some of the larger grants.

Community Foundations by State

This section lists community foundations by state. Look up your state and see what grant money might be available for your nonprofit.

Alabama

Calhoun County Community Foundation
Central Alabama Community Foundation
The Community Foundation of Greater Birmingham
Community Foundation of South Alabama
Community Foundation of Southeast Alabama
Walker Area Community Foundation

Alaska

The Alaska Community Foundation
Alaska Conservation Fund

Arizona

The Arizona Community Foundation
Community Foundation for Southern Arizona
Women's Foundation of Southern Arizona

Arkansas

Arkansas Community Foundation
Northwest Arkansas Community Foundation
Union County Community Foundation, Inc.

California

Anaheim Community Foundation
Auburn Community Foundation
Berkeley Community Fund
California Community Foundation
The Claremont Community Foundation
Coastal Community Foundation
Community Foundation for Monterey County
Community Foundation of the Napa Valley
The Community Foundation of Santa Cruz County
The Community Foundation Serving Riverside and
    San Bernardino Counties
Community Foundation Silicon Valley
Crockett Community Foundation
East Bay Community Foundation
El Dorado Community Foundation
Fresno Regional Foundation
Glendale Community Foundation
The Humboldt Area Foundation
Kern County Community Foundation
Los Altos Community Foundation
Marin Community Foundation
Mendocino County Community Foundation
North Valley Community Foundation
Orange County Community Foundation
Paradise Community Foundation
Pasadena Foundation
Peninsula Community Foundation
Rancho Santa Fe Foundation
Sacramento Regional Foundation
The San Diego Foundation
The San Francisco Foundation
San Luis Obispo County Community
    Foundation, Inc.
Santa Barbara Foundation
Shasta Regional Community Foundation
The Sonoma County Community Foundation

Sonora Area Foundation
Streams in the Desert Foundation, Inc.
Truckee Tahoe Community Foundation
Ventura County Community Foundation

Colorado
The Aspen Valley Community Foundation
Broomfield Community Foundation
The Community Foundation Serving Boulder County
The Community Foundation Serving
    Greeley and Weld County
Community Foundation Serving
    Northern Colorado
Community Foundation Serving
    Southwest Colorado
The Denver Foundation
Mesa County Foundation
Pikes Peak Community Foundation
Rose Community Foundation
Southern Colorado Community Foundation
The Summit Foundation
Western Colorado Community Foundation
The Wright-Stuff Community Foundation
Yampa Valley Community Foundation

Connecticut
Berkshire Taconic Community Foundation
The Branford Community Foundation
The Community Foundation for Greater New Haven
The Community Foundation of Southeastern
    Connecticut
Eastern Connecticut Community Foundation
Fairfield County Community Foundation, Inc.
The Greater Bridgeport Area Foundation, Inc.
Greater Windham Community Foundation
Guilford Foundation

Hartford Foundation for Public Giving
Main Street Community Foundation
The Meriden Foundation
Middlesex County Community Foundation
New Britain Foundation for Public Giving
New Canaan Community Foundation, Inc.
Orange Foundation
Torrington Area Foundation for Public Giving
The Waterbury Foundation
The Watertown Foundation

Delaware
The Delaware Community Foundation

Florida
Community Foundation for Palm Beach and Martin
    Counties, Inc.
The Community Foundation in Jacksonville
Community Foundation of Brevard
Community Foundation of Broward
Community Foundation of Central Florida, Inc.
Community Foundation of Collier County
Community Foundation of North Florida
Community Foundation of Sarasota County, Inc.
Community Foundation of Tampa Bay, Inc.
Community Foundation of the Florida Keys
Coral Gables Community Foundation
Dade Community Foundation
The Gainesville Community Foundation
Manatee Community Foundation
Mount Dora Community Foundation
Pinellas County Community Foundation
South Lake County Community Foundation, Inc.
Southwest Florida Community Foundation, Inc.
The Venice Foundation

Georgia

Central Savannah Area River (CSRA) Community
  Foundation
Chattahoochee Valley Community Foundation
Community Foundation for Greater Atlanta, Inc.
Community Foundation of Central Georgia
Community Foundation of Northwest Georgia
Community Foundation of Southwest Georgia, Inc.
The Gwinnett Foundation, Inc.
North Georgia Community Foundation
The Savannah Foundation, Inc.

Hawaii

Hawaii Community Foundation

Idaho

Caldwell Community Foundation
Idaho Community Foundation

Illinois

The Aurora Foundation
Charleston Area Charitable Foundation
The Chicago Community Trust
Community Foundation of Champaign County
Community Foundation of Decatur/Macon County
DeKalb County Community Foundation
The DuPage Community Foundation
Evanston Community Foundation
Morris Community Foundation
Oak Park-River Forest Community Foundation
Peoria Area Community Foundation
Quincy Area Community Foundation
Rockford Community Foundation
Rock Island Community Foundation

Indiana

Adams County Community Foundation
Blackford County Community Foundation
Brown County Community Foundation
Central Indiana Community Foundation
Community Foundation Alliance, Inc.
Community Foundation of Bloomington &
  Monroe County
Community Foundation of Boone County
Community Foundation of Grant County,
  Indiana, Inc.
The Community Foundation of Howard
  County, Inc.
The Community Foundation of Jackson County
Community Foundation of Madison & Jefferson
  County, Inc.
Community Foundation of Morgan County
The Community Foundation of Muncie and Delaware
  County, Inc.
Community Foundation of Randolph County
Community Foundation of Southern Indiana
Community Foundation of St. Joseph County
Community Foundation of Switzerland
  County, Inc.
The Community Foundation of Wabash County
Covington Community Foundation, Inc.
Crown Point Community Foundation
Dearborn County Community Foundation
Decatur County Community Foundation, Inc.
DeKalb County Community Foundation Inc.
Dubois County Community Foundation, Inc.
Elkhart County Community Foundation, Inc.
Fayette County Foundation
Fort Wayne Community Foundation, Inc.
Franklin County Community Foundation
Greater Johnson County Community Foundation

Greater Lafayette Community Foundation
Greene County Foundation, Inc.
Hancock County Community Foundation, Inc.
Henry County Community Foundation Inc.
Heritage Fund of Bartholomew County, Inc.
Heritage Fund of Huntington County
The Huntingburg Foundation
The Indianapolis Foundation
Jasper Foundation Inc.
Jennings County Community Foundation, Inc.
Kosciusko County Foundation
Lagrange County Community Foundation, Inc.
Lawrence County Community Foundation
Legacy Foundation, Inc.
Legacy Fund of Hamilton County
Madison County Community Foundation
Marshall County Community Foundation, Inc.
Montgomery County Community Foundation
Noble County Community Foundation
Northern Indiana Community Foundation
Ohio County Community Foundation
Owen County Community Foundation Inc.
Parke County Community Foundation Inc.
The Portland Foundation
The Putnam County Foundation
Ripley County Community Foundation
Rush County Community Foundation, Inc.
South Madison Community Foundation
Steuben County Community Foundation
Tipton County Foundation, Inc.
Union County Foundation Inc.
The Unity Foundation of LaPorte County
Vermillion County Community Foundation Inc.
Wabash Valley Community Foundation
Washington County Community Foundation, Inc.
Wayne County Foundation
The Wells County Foundation, Inc.

The White Lick Heritage Community Foundation
Whitley County Community Foundation

Iowa
The Clarinda Foundation
Community Foundation of the Great River Bend
Community Foundation of Waterloo
    and Northeast Iowa
The Greater Cedar Rapids Community Foundation
Greater Decorah Area Community
    Foundation, Inc.
The Greater Des Moines Foundation
The Greater Jefferson County Foundation
Greater Poweshiek Community Foundation
Maquoketa Area Foundation
Pella Community Foundation
Siouxland Community Foundation
South Central Iowa Foundation
Waverly Community Foundation

Kansas
The Abilene Community Foundation, Inc.
Community Foundation of Southwest Kansas
The Greater Salina Community Foundation
Hutchinson Community Foundation
Legacy, A Regional Community Foundation
Newton Community & Healthcare Foundation
South Central Community Foundation
Topeka Community Foundation
Western Kansas Community Foundation
Wichita Community Foundation

Kentucky
The Blue Grass Community Foundation
The Community Foundation of Louisville

Foundation for the Tri-State Community, Inc.
Paducah Area Community Foundation

Louisiana
Baton Rouge Area Foundation
Central Louisiana Community Foundation
Community Foundation of Shreveport-Bossier
The Greater New Orleans Foundation
The Legacy Foundation of Acadiana

Maine
Maine Community Foundation
North Haven Foundation

Maryland
Baltimore Community Foundation
Chesapeake Community Foundation, Inc.
The Columbia Foundation
The Community Foundation of Frederick
    County, Inc.
Community Foundation of the Eastern Shore, Inc.
Community Foundation of Washington
    County, Maryland
Mid Shore Community Foundation Inc.
The Montgomery County Community Foundation
Prince George's Community Foundation, Inc.

Massachusetts
Berkshire Taconic Community Foundation
The Boston Foundation
Brookline Community Foundation
The Cambridge Community Foundation
Community Foundation of Cape Cod
Community Foundation of Southeastern
    Massachusetts

Community Foundation of Western Massachusetts
Crossroads Community Foundation
Essex County Community Foundation
Greater Lowell Community Foundation
Greater Worcester Community Foundation
Merrimack Valley Community Foundation
Old Colony Charitable Foundation
Permanent Endowment for Martha's Vineyard
Quogue Community Foundation
South Shore and Neponset Valley Community
    Foundation
The Woods Hole Foundation

Michigan
Albion Community Foundation
Alger Regional Community Foundation
Allegan County Community Foundation
Anchor Bay Community Foundation
Ann Arbor Area Community Foundation
Baraga County Community Foundation
Barry Community Foundation
Battle Creek Community Foundation
Bay Area Community Foundation
Berrien Community Foundation
Branch County Community Foundation
Cadillac Area Community Foundation
Canton Community Foundation
Capital Region Community Foundation
Central Montcalm Community Foundation
Charlevoix County Community Foundation
Community Foundation for Muskegon County
Community Foundation for Northeast Michigan
Community Foundation for Southeastern Michigan
Community Foundation of Delta County
Community Foundation of Greater Flint
Community Foundation of Greater Rochester

GOVERNMENT GRANTS

Community Foundation of Monroe County
Community Foundation of St. Clair County
Community Foundation of the
    Holland/Zeeland Area
Community Heritage Foundation of Eaton Rapids
Dickinson Area Community Foundation
Four County Community Foundation
The Fremont Area Foundation
Grand Haven Area Community Foundation, Inc.
The Grand Rapids Community Foundation
Grand Traverse Regional Community Foundation
Gratiot County Community Foundation
Greater Frankenmuth Area Community Foundation
Greenville Area Community Foundation
Grosse Pointe Farms Foundation
Hillsdale County Community Foundation
Huron County Community Foundation
The Jackson County Community Foundation
Kalamazoo Community Foundation
Keweenaw Community Foundation
Leelanau Township Foundation
Livonia Community Foundation
Ludington Area Foundation
M & M Area Community Foundation
Mackinac Island Community Foundation
Manistee County Foundation
Marquette Community Foundation
Marshall Community Foundation
Michigan Gateway Community Foundation
Midland Area Community Foundation
Mt. Pleasant Area Community Foundation
Northville Township Centennial Foundation
Oakland County Community Trust
Petoskey-Harbor Springs Area Community Foundation
Saginaw Community Foundation
Sanilac County Community Foundation
Sault Area Community Foundation

Schoolcraft County Community Foundation
Shelby Community Foundation
Shiawassee Foundation
Southfield Community Foundation
Sterling Heights Community Foundation
The Sturgis Foundation
Tecumseh Community Fund Foundation
Three Rivers Area Foundation
Troy Community Foundation
Tuscola County Community Foundation
Upper Peninsula Community Foundation Alliance

Minnesota
Central Minnesota Community Foundation
Duluth-Superior Area Community Foundation
Grand Rapids Area Community Foundation
Greater Winona Area Community Foundation
Headwaters Fund
Initiative Foundation
The Minneapolis Foundation
Northwest Minnesota Foundation
Redwood Area Communities Foundation
The Rochester Area Foundation
The Saint Paul Foundation
Southwest Minnesota Foundation

Mississippi
Community Foundation of East Mississippi
CREATE Foundation
Greater Jackson Foundation
Gulf Coast Community Foundation
Lowndes Community Foundation

Missouri
Community Foundation of the Ozarks

The Greater Kansas City Community Foundation
Independence Community Foundation
Sedalia Area Community Foundation
St. Louis Community Foundation

Montana
The Community Foundation of the Lower Flathead
    Valley
Montana Community Foundation

Nebraska
Fremont Area Community Foundation
Grand Island Community Foundation, Inc.
Hamilton Community Foundation
Hartington Community Foundation
Hastings Community Foundation, Inc.
Kearney Area Community Foundation
La Vista Community Foundation
Lexington Community Foundation
Lincoln Community Foundation
Merrick Foundation, Inc.
Mid-Nebraska Community Foundation, Inc.
Nebraska Community Foundation
Omaha Community Foundation
Oregon Trail Community Foundation
Phelps County Community Foundation

Nevada
Community Foundation of Western Nevada
Lake Tahoe Community Trust
Nevada Community Foundation
The Parasol Foundation of Incline Village

New Hampshire
Dublin Community Foundation

New Hampshire Charitable Foundation

New Jersey
Community Foundation of New Jersey
Princeton Area Community Foundation
The Summit Area Community Foundation
The Westfield Foundation, Inc.

New Mexico
Albuquerque Community Foundation
Carlsbad Foundation
New Mexico Community Foundation
The Santa Fe Community Foundation
Southern New Mexico Community Foundation
Taos Community Foundation, Inc.

New York
Adirondack Community Trust
Bethesda Foundation
Central New York Community Foundation
Chautauqua Region Community Foundation, Inc.
Community Foundation for Greater Buffalo
Community Foundation for the Capital Region
Community Foundation of Dutchess County
The Community Foundation of Herkimer and Oneida
    Counties
Community Foundation of Orange County, Inc.
The Community Foundation of the Elmira-Corning
    Area, Inc.
Cooperstown Community Foundation
The Glens Falls Foundation
The Greater Broome Community Foundation, Inc.
Long Island Community Foundation
New York Community Trust
Northeastern New York Community Trust

Northern Chautauqua Community
    Foundation, Inc.
Northern New York Community Foundation, Inc.
Rochester Area Community Foundation
The Schenectady Foundation
The Westchester Community Foundation

North Carolina
Cape Fear Community Foundation, Inc.
Community Foundation of Gaston County, Inc.
Community Foundation of Greater Greensboro
Community Foundation of Henderson County, Inc.
The Community Foundation of Western North
    Carolina
Cumberland Community Foundation
Elizabeth City Foundation
Foundation for the Carolinas
Lenoir Community Foundation
North Carolina Community Foundation, Inc.
Outer Banks Community Foundation
Polk County Community Foundation, Inc.
Salisbury Community Foundation, Inc.
Thomasville Community Foundation
Triangle Community Foundation
The Winston-Salem Foundation

North Dakota
Community Foundation of Grand Forks, East Grand
    Forks, & Region
Fargo-Moorhead Area Foundation
North Dakota Community Foundation

Ohio
Akron Community Foundation
Archbold Area Foundation

Ashland County Community Foundation
The Athens Foundation
Belpre Area Community Foundation
Bowling Green Community Foundation
Bratenahl Community Foundation
Bryan Area Foundation
Bucyrus Area Community Foundation
The Carroll County Foundation
The Cleveland Foundation
Clinton County Foundation
Columbiana Community Foundation
The Columbus Foundation
Community Foundation of Delaware County
The Community Foundation of Greater
    Lorain County
The Community Foundation of Jefferson
    County, Inc.
The Community Foundation of Sidney &
    Shelby County
Community Foundation of Union County, Inc.
Coshocton Foundation
The Dayton Foundation
Edgerton Area Foundation
Fairfield County Foundation
Fayette County Charitable Foundation
Findlay-Hancock County Community Foundation
The Foundation for Appalachian Ohio
Granville Foundation
The Greater Cincinnati Foundation
The Greater Wayne County Foundation, Inc.
Hamilton Community Foundation
Hardin County Community Foundation
Henry County Community Foundation
The Licking County Foundation
Lisbon Community Foundation
London Community Foundation
Marietta Community Foundation

Marion Community Foundation
Mercer County Civic Foundation
Middletown Community Foundation
Monroe Area Community Foundation
Montpelier Area Foundation
Mount Vernon/Knox County Community Trust
The Muskingum County Community Foundation
New Albany Community Foundation
Oxford Community Foundation
The Portage Foundation
Richland County Foundation
Salem Community Foundation
The Sandusky/Erie County Community Foundation
Scioto County Area Foundation
Sebring-West Branch Community Foundation
Sharon Community Trusts
The Springfield Foundation
Stark Community Foundation
St. Clair Foundation
St. Mary's Community Foundation
The Tiffin Charitable Foundation, Inc.
The Toledo Community Foundation
The Troy Foundation
Urbana Foundation
Wapakoneta Area Community Foundation
Warren County Foundation
Yellow Springs Community Foundation
Youngstown Foundation

Oklahoma
Broken Arrow Community Foundation, Inc.
The Norman Community Foundation
Oklahoma City Community Foundation
Tulsa Community Foundation

Oregon
Benton County Foundation
Milton-Freewater Area Foundation
Newberg Community Foundation
The Oregon Community Foundation
Philomath Community Foundation
Salem Foundation
Western Lane Community Foundation

Pennsylvania
Adams County Foundation
The Beaver County Foundation
Berks County Community Foundation
Blair County Community Endowment
Bucks County Foundation
Centre County Community Foundation, Inc.
Chester County Community Foundation
Clinton County Community Foundation
Community Foundation of Westmoreland County
Community Foundation Serving Bedford, Cambria & Somerset Counties
Elk County Community Foundation
The Emporium Foundation, Inc.
The Erie Community Foundation
The Greater Harrisburg Foundation
Greensburg Foundation Fund
Grove City Foundation
Lancaster County Foundation
Lehigh Valley Community Foundation
The Luzerne Foundation
Montgomery County Foundation
The Philadelphia Foundation
The Pittsburgh Foundation
Schuylkill Community Foundation
Scranton Area Foundation, Inc.
Shenango Valley Foundation

Three Rivers Community Fund
Venango Area Community Foundation
The Warren Foundation
Washington County Community Foundation
Wayne County Community Foundation
Williamsport-Lycoming Foundation
York Foundation

Rhode Island
The Rhode Island Foundation

South Carolina
Central Carolina Community Foundation
Community Foundation of Greater Greenville
The Community Foundation Serving Coastal South
    Carolina
Edgefield County Foundation
Hilton Head Island Foundation, Inc.
The Spartanburg County Foundation
Waccamaw Community Foundation

South Dakota
Milbank Community Foundation
Sioux Falls Area Community Foundation
South Dakota Community Foundation
Watertown Community Foundation

Tennessee
Community Foundation of Greater
    Chattanooga, Inc.
Community Foundation of Greater Memphis
The Community Foundation of Middle Tennessee
Community Foundation of Obion County
East Tennessee Foundation

Texas
Amarillo Area Foundation, Inc.
Archer Community Foundation
Austin Community Foundation for the Capital Area,
    Inc.
Brownsville Community Foundation, Inc.
Coastal Bend Community Foundation
Communities Foundation of Texas
Community Foundation of Abilene
Community Foundation of Brazoria County
Community Foundation of North Texas
Community Foundation of the Texas
    Hill Country
The Dallas Foundation
East Texas Communities Foundation
El Paso Community Foundation
Foundation for Southeast Texas
Greater Houston Community Foundation
Heart of Texas Community Foundation
Hill Country Community Foundation
Lubbock Area Foundation, Inc.
Matagorda County Community
    Foundation
Montgomery County Community
    Foundation
Navarro Community Foundation
Permian Basin Area Foundation
San Antonio Area Foundation
The Waco Foundation
Wichita Falls Area Community
    Foundation

Utah
The Salt Lake Foundation

Vermont

The Vermont Community Foundation

Virginia

Arlington Community Foundation
Bedford Community Health Foundation
Charlottesville-Albermarle Community Foundation
Community Foundation of Rappahannock River
    Region
Community Foundation of the New River Valley
The Community Foundation Serving Richmond &
    Central Virginia
DPC Community Foundation
The Foundation For Roanoke Valley, Inc.
The Greater Lynchburg Community Trust
The Norfolk Foundation
Northern Virginia Community Foundation
Portsmouth Community Foundation & Trust
Staunton Augusta Waynesboro Community
    Foundation
The Virginia Beach Foundation

Washington

Blue Mountain Area Foundation
Columbia Basin Foundation
The Community Foundation
Community Foundation for Southwest Washington
Foundation Northwest
Grays Harbor Community Foundation
The Greater Tacoma Community Foundation
Greater Wenatchee Community Foundation
Kitsap Community Foundation
Orcas Island Community Foundation
Pride Foundation
The Seattle Foundation

Whatcom Community Foundation

West Virginia

Barbour County Community Foundation, Inc.
Beckley Area Foundation, Inc.
Bluefield Area Foundation, Inc.
The Community Foundation for the Ohio
    Valley, Inc.
Eastern West Virginia Community Foundation
The Greater Kanawha Valley Foundation
The Parkersburg Area Community Foundation
Tucker Community Endowment Foundation

Wisconsin

Black River Falls Area Foundation
Community Foundation for the Fox Valley Region,
    Inc.
Community Foundation of Portage County
Community Foundation of Southern Wisconsin, Inc.
Community Foundation of South Wood County
Eau Claire Area Foundation
Fond du Lac Area Foundation
The Greater Beloit Community Foundation
Greater Green Bay Community Foundation, Inc.
Greater Kenosha Area Foundation
Greater Menomonie Area Community Foundation
La Crosse Community Foundation
Madison Community Foundation
Marshfield Area Community Foundation
Milwaukee Community Foundation
The New Richmond Community Foundation, Inc.
Oshkosh Community Foundation
Racine Community Foundation, Inc.
St. Croix Valley Community Foundation
Watertown Area Community Foundation
Wausau Area Community Foundation, Inc.

Wyoming

The Community Foundation of Jackson Hole
Wyoming Community Foundation

Information about Federal Government Grants

Literally thousands of federal government grant opportunities are just waiting for nonprofit managers. If you visit the Web site *www.non-profit.gov/resource/support.html* you will find valuable information posted by the federal government regarding funding opportunities. For example, take a look at what one grant program—**the 2001 Challenge America: Positive Alternatives for Youth**—funded by the National Endowment for the Arts helped accomplish. This federal agency awarded 196 grants totaling $1,735,000. The following state-by-state listing of the grant winners gives an overview of each program funded. Keep in mind that this listing of grants is from only one program in one government agency. Plenty of others are out there, too!

Alabama

Jefferson County Committee for Economic Opportunity
Birmingham, AL
FIELD/DISCIPLINE: Musical Theater
$10,000

To support a partnership with SEPIA, Inc. and the Alabama Jazz Hall for the YES Ambassadors Theatrical Troupe Project, a musical theater training and performance program for youth ages twelve to seventeen. Some participants suffer from hearing and visual impairments and learning disabilities, and others have been exposed to substance abuse and domestic violence. After training in writing, dramatic presentation, dance, music, and set design, the group will perform for inner-city and rural youth at local venues, including the historical Carver Theater.

Montgomery Museum of Fine Arts Association
Montgomery, AL
FIELD/DISCIPLINE: Visual Arts
$10,000

To support a partnership with Bellingrath Junior High School and Cloverdale Junior High School for the program "In My View" that offers students hour-long classes in photography, verbal description of visual images, Web design, and museum field trips. Both schools are struggling to improve poor student academic performance. The museum's Assistant Curator of Education will coordinate the interaction of local professional resident artists, school teachers, and key staff, and the youth participants.

Total Grants Awarded: 2
Total Dollars Awarded: $20,000

Alaska

Cultural Heritage and Education Institute (CHEI)
Fairbanks, AK
FIELD/DISCIPLINE: Visual Arts
$10,000

To support a partnership with the Alaska Rural Systemic Initiative, North Star Borough School District and Minto School for students in a small, rural Alaskan native village. Through the project, village Elders will share oral histories with students, then visiting artists will teach the students to draw and paint traditional sites in the Minto area, which will be scanned and posted on the Cultural Atlas Web site and shared with other students in the area.

Total Grants Awarded: 1
Total Dollars Awarded: $10,000

Arizona
Free Arts for Abused Children of Arizona
Phoenix, AZ
FIELD/DISCIPLINE: Multidisciplinary
$5,000

To support a partnership with Youth Etc., the Salvation Army's Family Shelter, Brownstone Care, Family Support Resources, and the Sunshine Group for the Multicultural Arts Camp. The summer camp provides training in art, music, drama, and dance of cultures around the world to children ages twelve to seventeen who have been abused and neglected, are homeless, or live in residential treatment centers, group homes, and shelters throughout the Phoenix area. The project concludes with performances and exhibits to celebrate the children's accomplishments.

LFC, Inc. (Bank One Tucson International Mariachi Conference)
Tucson, AZ
FIELD/DISCIPLINE: Folk & Traditional Arts
$10,000

To support a partnership with the Tucson Unified School District, the Metro Tucson Convention and Visitors Bureau, the Tucson/Pima Arts Council, the Tucson Convention Center, and Bank One to provide beginning, intermediate, and advanced training in mariachi music and Mexican dance for predominantly Mexican American children in grades six to twelve, many of whom come from low-income and single-parent families.

The Navajo Arts and Humanities Council
Lukachukai, AZ
FIELD/DISCIPLINE: Multidisciplinary
$10,000

To support a partnership with the Tsaile Public School and the Dine College Music Club to bring professional Navajo authors and singer-songwriters together with youth from the rural Tsaile area on the Navajo Nation. Due to its isolation from any metropolitan area, children from Tsaile have little access to the performing arts and experience high levels of poverty.

Total Grants Awarded: 3
Total Dollars Awarded: $25,000

Arkansas
Batesville Area Arts Council
Batesville, AR
FIELD/DISCIPLINE: Multidisciplinary
$10,000

To support a partnership with the Batesville School and the Batesville Non-Profit Roundtable to provide training in theater, choir, music ensemble, and visual arts activities through after-school arts programs for fifth and sixth grade children who are at-risk due to poor academic performance, lack of supervision at home, or who have behavior problems at school. Artists will work in an educational setting and create a vibrant learning environment in cooperation with classroom teachers.

Total Grants Awarded: 1
Total Dollars Awarded: $10,000

California

Armenian American Faith Charity
Fresno, CA
FIELD/DISCIPLINE: Folk & Traditional Arts
$5,000

To support a project of artist-led activities in partnership with Padrinos Folklorico of the Roosevelt School of the Arts for an after-school program for ethnically and racially diverse students enrolled at Fresno's Roosevelt High School. Students will study the origins of the music, dances, costumes, and instruments specific to the many geographic regions of Mexico. The program culminates in school and community performances.

California Institute of the Arts (CalArts)
Valencia, CA
FIELD/DISCIPLINE: Multidisciplinary
$10,000

To support the Community Arts Partnership with the Watts Tower Arts Center. The program provides multicultural after-school and weekend, artist-led programs for students ages twelve to eighteen living in the mostly Latino and African American community of Watts in Los Angeles. Special challenges in Watts include chronic unemployment, teen pregnancy, and illegal gang activity.

East Bay Center for the Performing Arts
Richmond, CA
FIELD/DISCIPLINE: Multidisciplinary
$10,000

To support a partnership project with the Summit Center and the Chris Adams Girls Center (both juvenile residential treatment centers) for The Living Mission. This program provides boys and girls ages twelve to eighteen who have been through the court system with workshops in drumming, West African dance, and video production to better realize their creative spirit and discourage recidivism. At the end of each session, the participants present workshop performances to an audience of friends, family, and peers.

Fallbrook Union High School District
Fallbrook, CA
FIELD/DISCIPLINE: Multidisciplinary
$5,000

To support a partnership project with the California Center for the Arts in Escondido and California State University at San Marcos for SUAVE (Socios Unidos Para Artes Educacion/United Communities for Arts in Education). This program features an arts-integrated approach to teaching and learning in multicultural and multilingual settings for students at Fallbrook, Ivy, and Oasis High Schools. SUAVE brings community artists to the classroom and provides professional development for teachers in rural northern San Diego County.

Floricanto Dance Theatre
Whittier, CA
FIELD/DISCIPLINE: Folk & Traditional Arts
$10,000

To support a partnership project with Bravo Medical High School in East Los Angeles to provide after-school folklorico dance. Francisco Bravo Medical Magnet High School is an ethnically diverse, inner-city, science-focused magnet school whose goals are to increase both student literacy in the biomedical sciences and the rate of students entering the health professions.

Fresno Arts Council
Fresno, CA
FIELD/DISCIPLINE: Multidisciplinary
$10,000

To support a partnership project with the Fresno Unified School District and the Southeast Intersession School to provide students in grades three through six with curriculum-based arts activities led by professional artists. These students have been or are at risk for retention. The Fresno Unified School District is the sixth most impoverished district in the state with a population of many ethnic groups that have limited proficiency in English.

Hmong Cultural Arts, Crafts, Teaching and Museum Project
Elverta, CA
FIELD/DISCIPLINE: Folk & Traditional Arts
$10,000

To support a partnership project with the Del Paso Heights and Robla school districts to provide classes in traditional Hmong pa dao (embroidery), qeej (reed instrument) and folk dance to students ages six to eighteen from low-income neighborhoods with high exposure to gangs. It is estimated that 70 percent of Hmong adults who came to the United States as refugees in the 1980s have limited English proficiency. The folk art activities give the children a greater appreciation for Hmong heritage as well as improve their self-esteem and ability to succeed.

Imagination Workshop, Inc.
Los Angles, CA
FIELD/DISCIPLINE: Theater
$10,000

To support a partnership project with Walgrove and Grandview schools, the Accelerated School, the Olympic School, the MacLaren School, and the UCLA Trauma Psychiatry Program. The project will provide age-appropriate training in playwriting and theater arts for students, grades K to 6, from South Central Los Angeles and Santa Monica. The project will be led by professional theater artists and culminate in public performances. Youth targeted by this program are ethnically diverse, have learning disabilities and emotional problems, and are exposed to drugs and gang-related activities.

Inner-City Arts
Los Angeles, CA
FIELD/DISCIPLINE: Multidisciplinary
$10,000

To support a partnership project with schools in the Los Angeles Unified School District and Para Los Niños (an inner-city child care organization) that provides elementary school students from diverse ethnic and racial backgrounds with classes in dance, music, choir, and visual arts. Recent tests suggest that students participating in this program perform better in subjects such as English and math, despite being exposed to poverty, homelessness, gang violence, and crime.

Inside Out Community Arts
Los Angeles, CA
FIELD/DISCIPLINE: Theater
$10,000

To support a partnership project with the Boys & Girls Club of Venice for the Neighborhood Arts Project, a theater-based, after-school program serving middle-school students from the Oakwood District of Los Angeles. Through this program, the students—who are exposed daily to high levels of poverty and drug and gang-related violence—write plays inspired by important issues in their lives and then perform their work.

Kern County Youth Mariachi Foundation
Bakersfield, CA
FIELD/DISCIPLINE: Folk & Traditional Arts
$10,000

To support a partnership project with Hall Ambulance, Kern County Superintendent of Schools, Kern County Department of Human Services, Family Motors Foundation, Oasis Air Conditioning, and Kern County Hispanic Chamber of Commerce. The project will provide after-school training in traditional mariachi music (along with tutoring and higher education guidance) for mostly Mexican American youth ages seven to nineteen living in the inner city and rural areas of Bakersfield and the surrounding areas of East Bakersfield, Richgrove, Lamont, Delano, McFarland, and Santa Maria.

L.A. Theatre Works
Los Angeles, CA
FIELD/DISCIPLINE: Visual Arts
$10,000

To support a partnership with the Los Angeles County Probation Department and the Los Angeles County Office of Education, to engage youth ages fourteen to eighteen in mounting a colored tile mural on the outside wall of the Hope Center in Compton. These young people are first-time offenders or are returning from incarceration.

Museum of Children's Art
Oakland, CA
FIELD/DISCIPLINE: Multidisciplinary
$10,000

To support a partnership with Cole Elementary School and the Oakland Housing Authority for Project YIELD (Youth in Education and Leadership Development), an after-school program that integrates computer graphics, multimedia, and Web page design for fourth through eighth graders from an area marked by low-income and poor academic performance.

Playwrights Project
San Diego, CA
FIELD/DISCPLINE: Theater
$10,000

To support a partnership with Castle Rock Middle School in Chula Vista, that provides teacher training through the Professional Development for Classroom Teachers component of SEEDS (Stimulating Educational Excellence through Drama Standards) including workshops; access to teaching artists; and use of Stage Write, Playwrights Project's recently published playwriting curriculum. Chula Vista is an area of San Diego County marked by high levels of drug-related deaths, teen suicides, and incarcerated youth.

San Diego Dance Institute
San Diego, CA
FIELD/DISCPLINE: Dance
$5,000

To support a partnership project with Edison, Baker Montessori, Harley Knox, Rosa Parks, and Paradise Hills elementary schools; the Nubia Leadership Academy; Wilson Middle Schools; and the University of California at San Diego for City Moves! This project provides an after-school dance program for fifth through eighth grade students from predominately single-family homes in neighborhoods of immigrants from Mexico, Vietnam, Laos, and Somalia. These neighborhoods are marked by drugs and violence, and residents are encumbered by limited English proficiency. At the end of the program, the children perform their original work at school assemblies and evening performances.

San Jose Repertory Theatre
San Jose, CA
FIELD/DISCIPLINE: Theater
$10,000

To support a partnership with the Foundry School, an alternative high school for youth who have been through the court system, and the Red Ladder Theater Company. The program provides students with interactive theater workshops designed to help them build life skills and self-esteem through improvisational exercises, theater games, and dramatic scenarios. Students at The Foundry School encounter violence, abuse, homelessness, and gang pressures.

Shasta County Arts Council
Redding, CA
FIELD/DISCIPLINE: Multidisciplinary
$10,000

To support a partnership project with Northern Valley Catholic Social Services for Kids Arts Recreation and Education (KARE), a program that provides children living in transitional housing with after-school and summer dance classes and visual arts activities to foster skills in socialization and positive interaction.

Theatre and Arts Foundation of San Diego County
La Jolla, CA
FIELD/DISCIPLINE: Theater
$10,000

To support a partnership project with La Jolla Playhouse; the California Youth Authority's Gang Violence Reduction Project in liaison with the San Diego Police Department; and PIPER Partners in Prevention for Project Turnaround. The project provides professional play development instruction for middle school students identified as "high risk" for gang involvement. The teens participating in the project are from an area of central San Diego marked by low income, violent crime, and Latino and African American gangs.

Trinity County Arts Council
Weaverville, CA
FIELD/DISCIPLINE: Folk & Traditional Art
$10,000

To support a partnership project with Trinity Occupational Training that provides summer employment and training in mural arts for youth ages fifteen through eighteen living in the isolated and mountainous area of Trinity County. The project will result in a large mural on the wall around the public swimming pool at Lowden Park in Weaverville. The program targets youth who are confronted by poverty, poor academic achievement, homelessness, and other serious problems.

Total Grants Awarded: 19
Total Dollars Awarded: $175,000

Colorado
Aspen Ballet Company and School
Aspen, CO
FIELD/DISCIPLINE: Dance
$5,000

To support a partnership project with Carbondale and Besalt Middle Schools for Celebrate the Beat, a highly effective in-school dance program developed by the National Dance Institute and celebrated educator and dancer Jacques d'Amboise. This project is targeted to elementary and middle-school students who live in the down-valley communities near Aspen, where many families are new residents of Latino descent who struggle with low-income status and legal and language barriers.

Colorado Dance Festival
Boulder, CO
FIELD/DISCIPLINE: Dance
$10,000

To support a partnership project with the Dairy Center for the Arts, the Collage Children's Museum, the City of Boulder Youth Opportunities Advisory Board, and the Institute of African American Leadership for The Youth Dance Project. This project supports a community-based collaboration of educational, arts, and social science organizations to provide youth ages eleven to eighteen with classes in Latino, African, and African American dance.

Kim Robards Dance
Denver, CO
FIELD/DISCIPLINE: Dance
$10,000

To support a partnership project with the Teen Quest program of the Denver Area Youth Service, a juvenile detention facility, and Kinetic Connection. This project provides incarcerated girls, ages thirteen to eighteen, with a series of classes in ballet, jazz, modern, and tap as well as peer mentoring by specially selected and trained teenage girls from the Kim Robards Dance Company. The classes are designed to cultivate physical, mental, and social skills for girls who lack self-esteem as victims of physical and emotional abuse, in order to assist them in succeeding when they are released from the center.

The Piñon Project
Cortez, CO
FIELD/DISCIPLINE: Visual Arts
$5,000

To support a partnership project with the Art Juice Studio, the Sunrise Youth Shelter, the Mancos Family Center, and the Dolores Club House for The Family Drawing Together project. This project provides Native American youth ages six to twelve in rural southwestern Colorado with trips to remote areas of the Ute Mountain Tribal Land and the rural countryside outside Mancos. Participating youth will write and visually record their experience through painting. Family members, mentors, and Native American dignitaries also participate in this program.

Total Grants Awarded: 4
Total Dollars Awarded: $30,000

Connecticut
Curbstone Press
Willimantic, CT
FIELD/DISCIPLINE: Literature
$10,000

To support a partnership project with Windham High School and the Windham Heights Housing Project that provides after-school workshops in writing and public reading for teen residents. The workshops will be led by bilingual guest authors such as Jack Agueros, Naomi Ayala, and Danielle Georges. An isolated area of Connecticut, Windham has large numbers of Latino residents, many with limited English proficiency who are coping with poverty and unemployment.

Farmington Valley Arts Center
Avon, CT
FIELD/DISCIPLINE: Visual Arts
$10,000

To support a partnership project with Our Piece of the Pie (Southend Community Services) for the Creative Youth Business Partnership (CYBP). This year-round program enables urban middle school students to create and market art products, receive internships and part-time employment in schools and galleries, as well as discuss careers options with professional artists in nearby Hartford. The children are recruited through local social agencies such as foster care, juvenile programs, and the Girl Scouts of America, are mostly African American and Latino, and typically reside in low-income and single-parent families making them often at risk for poor academic achievement and high dropout rates.

International Festival of Arts and Ideas
New Haven, CT
FIELD/DISCIPLINE: Dance
$10,000

To support a partnership project with the Arts Council of Greater New Haven to bring nationally renowned artists, Urban Bush Women, to lead workshops for youth that celebrate the history, culture, and spiritual traditions of the African American community. The workshops take place at schools, community centers, and churches in the Dixwell neighborhood of New Haven. Dixwell is a culturally historic African American community that has begun to experience some poverty, unemployment, and high crime.

New Britain Museum of American Art
New Britain, CT
FIELD/DISCIPLINE: Visual Arts
$10,000

To support a partnership project with Greater New Britain YWCA's Pathways/Senderos (a teenage pregnancy prevention program) and STRIVE (an anti-substance abuse program) for The Youth Studio Project. This project provides after-school visual arts classes to children, in grades six to twelve, in the low-income Arch Street neighborhood.

Total Grants Awarded: 4
Total Dollars Awarded: $40,000

Delaware
Delaware Theatre Company
Wilmington, DE
FIELD/DISCIPLINE: Multidisciplinary
$10,000

To support a partnership project with the Ferris School, a maximum security facility, for improvisational playwriting residencies that incorporate writing skills, acting, directing, and stage design for incarcerated boys between the ages of fourteen and eighteen. This program offers the incarcerated youth the opportunity for self-expression as well as enhancing self-esteem and self-analysis, which the school considers essential to rehabilitation.

Wilmington Music School
Wilmington, DE
FIELD/DISCIPLINE: Multidisciplinary
$5,000

To support a partnership project with the Cole Ensemble, an ensemble for cello, piano, and percussion, and actors Akin Babatunde and Georgina Corbo to perform two musical theatre works. These are Of Ebony Embers-Vignettes of the Harlem Renaissance, which explores the cultural legacy of the Harlem Renaissance period, and Tres Vidas, a celebration of Latin American women. A number of locations within Wilmington's low-income, west center city area, including the Christina Cultural Arts Center, the Cab Calloway School of the Arts, and the Latin American Community Center, will host the residency activities.

Total Grants Awarded: 2
Total Dollars Awarded: $15,000

District of Columbia
Beacon House Community Ministry, Inc.
Washington, D.C.
FIELD/DISCIPLINE: Multidisciplinary
$10,000

To support a partnership project with the Levine School of Music and Dance Place, for after-school and summer camp programs in music and dance for children ages five to eighteen living in the Edgewood Terrace community. The project culminates in public performances. Ward 5, where Edgewood Terrace is located, is a community with a high incidence of poverty, malnutrition, drugs, violence, gangs, and low performance on standardized tests in math and reading.

Washington Drama Society, Inc.
Washington, D.C.
FIELD/DISCIPLINE: Theater
$10,000

To support a partnership project with the Maya Angelou Public Charter School, an alternative school for children who have been through the court system or are identified as at risk of becoming criminally involved. The project brings artists from the Living Stage Theatre Company to perform and conduct workshops for students ages fourteen to eighteen. Many of the youth, who are predominately African American and Latino and have been involved with substance abuse, are encouraged to explore issues faced in their everyday lives.

Total Grants Awarded: 2
Total Dollars Awarded: $20,000

Florida
Asian Cultural Association of Central Florida
Longwood, FL

FIELD/DISCIPLINE: Folk & Traditional Arts
$10,000

To support a partnership project with Midway Elementary School, Rollins College, Stetson University, and Seminole County Public Schools for the acclaimed santoor musician, teacher, and tri-county area resident, Nandkishore Muley. Muley will conduct lectures and demonstrations of the music of India for students in Seminole, Orange, and Brevard counties. Students participating in this program are typically from lower-income families. This music program is designed to help youth expand their communication skills and improve their self-esteem.

Cultural Council of Greater Jacksonville, Inc.
Jacksonville, FL
FIELD/DISCIPLINE: Multidisciplinary
$10,000

To support a partnership project with the State Attorney's Office and Inside Outside, Inc. that provides weekly arts classes for youth ages fourteen to twenty-five who have been recently released from incarceration, been through the court system as adults, or are currently incarcerated in the Duval County Jail. Through Inside Outside, youth participate in programs conducted by professional artists and justice staff, concluding with events open to prison staff, friends, mentors, and volunteers. In addition to after-school programs, the youth make field trips and attend performances and museum exhibits.

Laura (Riding) Jackson Home Preservation Foundation, Inc.
Vero Beach, FL
FIELD/DISCIPLINE: Literature
$10,000

To support a partnership project with College Application Consultants, the School District of Indian River County, and the School Board of St. Lucie County for Teen Writers Workshops, a program led by professional authors and independent publishers for students in grades nine to twelve in Indian River County, a rural retirement community.

Metropolitan Dade County (Miami-Dade Art in Public Places)

Miami, FL
FIELD/DISCIPLINE: Visual Arts
$10,000

To support a partnership project with the Miami-Dade Department of Cultural Affairs and Bay Point Schools, a residential school for moderate-risk juvenile offenders for ArtCare: Tile Mural Project. Led by local artists Carlos Alves and J. C. Carroll, the project engages youth in the mounting of a mosaic tile mural in a common living/dining area of the school.

Plant City Children's Theatre Guild, Inc.

Plant City, FL
FIELD/DISCIPLINE: Multidisciplinary
$5,000

To support a partnership project with the Arts Council of Plant City for the Peacemaker Performing Arts Team, a rigorous after-school program providing training in the performing arts, including ballet, jazz, gymnastics, folk dancing, and creating production costumes and scenery. The project involves children in grades six through twelve residing in the rural area of eastern Hillsborough County. The area is home to many low-income and migrant families that do not have access to the performing arts. The training and activities culminate in two public performances presented by the Plant City Children's Theatre.

United Arts Council of Collier County

Naples, FL
FIELD/DISCIPLINE: Visual Arts
$10,000

To support a partnership project with Collier County Parks and Recreation and PACE Center for Girls, and New Beginnings for The Pottery Adventure Program. This series of classes and workshops for teens is led by professional studio artists in ceramics arts and the business of marketing crafts in the largely Mexican American, southwestern Florida migrant farm community of Immokalee.

Total Grants Awarded: 6
Total Dollars Awarded: $55,000

Georgia
Atlanta Contemporary Arts Center

Atlanta, GA
FIELD/DISCIPLINE: Visual Arts
$10,000

To support a partnership project with Georgia State University, Department of Education; the Boys & Girls Club of Metro Atlanta; and the Atlanta Housing Authority for As Seen Through Teens, a series of workshops led by professional photographers and writers for teens. The project results in a professionally mounted exhibition of the students' photographs and their own literary descriptions installed at the Atlanta Contemporary Art Center. The exhibition will travel to a number of local business centers, during which opening receptions will honor the students and their families.

Total Grants Awarded: 1
Total Dollars Awarded: $10,000

Hawaii
Honolulu Theatre for Youth
Honolulu, HI
FIELD/DISCIPLINE: Theater
$10,000

To support a partnership project with Molokai High and Intermediate School for the Pacific Young Playwrights–Theaterfest, a series of classroom play-writing workshops and after-school public readings for youth ages thirteen to twenty living in the sparsely populated and generally poor island of Moloka'i.

Maui Community Arts and Cultural Center
Kahului, HI
FIELD/DISCIPLINE: Dance
$10,000

To support a partnership project with The Maui Dance Council; the Department of Education, Maui District; and the Hana School for Chance to Dance, a series of residencies by Maui Dance Council artists and other visiting artists for children in grades six to twelve. The children live in the remote, rural, and ethnically diverse communities of Maui County, Moloka'i, and Lana'i.

Total Grants Awarded: 2
Total Dollars Awarded: $20,000

Idaho
Community Youth Connection, Inc.
Boise, ID
FIELD/DISCIPLINE: Multidisciplinary
$10,000

To support a partnership with The Boise City Arts Commission, the Idaho Youth Ranch, and the Community Gang Prevention Team for Youth Speaks Out Arts Initiative, a multidisciplinary arts program

for young people, ages twelve to eighteen. Youth participants are referred by the Idaho Youth Ranch, a facility for troubled, delinquent and abused youth, as well as the Ada County Sheriff's Office Patrol Division Diversion Program. The participating young people develop technical and creative skills with African djembe and Australian didjeridoo instruments, songwriting and recording workshops, and mural art activities.

Festival Dance and Performing Arts Association, Inc.
Moscow, ID
FIELD/DISCIPLINE: Dance
$5,000

To support a partnership project with Troy and Potlatch elementary schools for the Discover Dance Project, a series of in-school classes in jazz, modern, and African dance taught by professional dance instructors for third, fourth, and fifth graders in remote rural communities throughout the region.

Lava Revitalization Team
Lava Hot Springs, ID
FIELD/DISCIPLINE: Multidisciplinary
$5,000

To support a partnership project with The South Bannock County Historical Society, Lava Elementary School, the State Foundation, and the Bannock County Sheriff's Department for Our Youth, Our River, Our Resources. This program of in-school and after-school workshops in storytelling and visual arts involves grades K through twelve students in the rural and isolated area of Lava, Idaho. The children in this region have no other school art programs.

Log Cabin Literary Center, Inc.
Boise, ID

FIELD/DISCIPLINE: Literature
$5,000

To support a partnership project with Idaho Health and Human Services Road to Recovery, the Boise Art Museum, Zoo Boise, the Idaho Historical Museum, the Morrison-Knudsen Nature Center, the Boise Public Library, and the Boise Department of Parks and Recreation for a series of field trips and workshops for students ages nine to fourteen to learn to write about their experiences. The children participating in this project are mostly Mexican Americans who reside in rural, agriculture communities where there is a high dropout rate.

Total Grants Awarded 4
Total Dollars Awarded $25,000

Illinois
Boulevard Art Center
Chicago, IL
FIELD/DISCIPLINE: Visual Arts
$10,000

To support a partnership project with Yale School, Gallery 37, the Chicago Public Schools, the Mayor's Office of Workforce Development, and the Chicago Department of Human Services to engage forty youth ages six through seventeen. The young people will be led by local artists in the production of a mural in the inner-city, low-income, African American Englewood neighborhood. The mural is part of a city plan to transform a vacant lot, currently a refuge for gangs, into a campus park.

Lifeline Productions, Inc.
Chicago, IL
FIELD/DISCIPLINE: Theater
$10,000

To support a partnership project with Joyce Kilmer Elementary School to expand an ongoing artist residency program for seventh and eighth graders to include grades five and six. The residency will teach dramatic storytelling to build literacy, encourage creativity, strengthen self-confidence, and foster an appreciation for other points of view by having students write and present their personal stories. Most of the students at Kilmer School come from low-income families and over half have underdeveloped English proficiency and language skills.

Performing Arts Chicago
Chicago, IL
FIELD/DISCIPLINE: Theater
$10,000

To support a partnership project with Albany Park Theater Project for a performing arts education serving youth in the racially diverse and economically disadvantaged community of Albany Park in northwest Chicago. Participants will learn theater techniques, and improve communication and problem-solving skills by working with professional artists to create and present dramatic works.

Rockford Area Arts Council
Rockford, IL
FIELD/DISCIPLINE: Multidisciplinary
$10,000

To support a partnership project with New American Theater and Rockford Public Schools for teens in Rockford and the surrounding low-income rural areas. Students will serve as apprentices to professional artists as well as create original visual art and small theater works.

Sun Foundation for the Advancement in the Environmental Sciences and the Arts
Washburn, IL
FIELD/DISCIPLINE: Multidisciplinary
$5,000

To support a partnership project with the Illinois Arts Council, Hallmark Metamora Woodworking, Metamora Telephone Company, Caterpillar Foundation, Peoria Community Foundation, and Dick Blick Company to provide 325 students in grades six through twelve with art classes led by artists. Students are from eight underserved communities in the Central Illinois River Valley. The project will culminate in public exhibitions and performances of the youths' work.

Young Chicago Authors
Glencoe, IL
FIELD/DISCIPLINE: Literature
$10,000

To support a partnership with The East Village Youth Program schools in the Chicago Public School District and several west-side community organizations. The project will provide classes in writing, photography, and publication design, field trips, and participation in public readings for 250 teenagers from underserved communities in Chicago's south and west sides.

Total Grants Awarded: 6
Total Dollars Awarded: $55,000

Indiana
Fischoff Chamber Music Association, Inc.
South Bend, IN
FIELD/DISCIPLINE: Music
$10,000

To support a partnership project with South Bend Community School Corporation, Elkhart Community Schools, Penn-Harris-Madison School Corporation, St. Joseph School Corporation, and the 21st Century Community Learning Center at Harrison Elementary for chamber music classes for high school students. Participants will form chamber ensembles that perform for third through sixth graders in underserved South Bend elementary schools.

Muncie Center for the Arts, Inc.
South Bend, IN
FIELD/DISCIPLINE: Music
$10,000

To support a partnership project with Muncie Indiana Transit System, Motivate Our Minds, South Madison Community Center, Ross Community Center, Buley Community Center, Ball State University Student Volunteer Services, and Muncie Community Schools for the Macdonald's Conley Kids After-School Arts Adventure Program. The program supports a series of after-school classes in the visual arts, dance, and music for children ages five to thirteen who come from ethnically diverse, low-income neighborhoods.

Total Grants Awarded: 2
Total Dollars Awarded: $20,000

Iowa
Red Cedar Chamber Music, Inc.
Marion, IA
FIELD/DISCIPLINE: Music
$10,000

To support a partnership with Four Oaks, a community service organization for children, for music activities for children and their senior citizen mentors that will include an introduction to the music heritage of various ethnic groups in Iowa. Participants will make unique instruments from found objects and compose a musical work. Youth targeted for this program are racially diverse, many coming from low-income and single-parent families.

The Sioux City Symphony Orchestra Association
Sioux City, IA
FIELD/DISCIPLINE: Music
$5,000

To support a partnership project with the Sioux City Community School District for Music Explorers, an after-school program for at-risk students grades seven through eleven in the ethnically diverse, rural community. Under the guidance of teachers and musicians, targeted youth will investigate Latin American, Native American, Laotian, Caribbean, and Vietnamese musical traditions, receive instruction on traditional instruments, and form ensembles that will perform for the school community, fostering greater cultural awareness and understanding.

Total Grants Awarded: 2
Total Dollars Awarded: $15,000

Kansas
Filipino Association of Greater Kansas City
Overland Park, KS
FIELD/DISCIPLINE: Folk & Traditional Arts
$10,000

To support a partnership project with Racela Educational & Charitable Foundation and Medical Missions Foundation, Inc. to develop a program in Filipino dance and a rondalla (traditional string ensemble) for Filipino American and other interested youth in grades six to twelve from the Greater Kansas City area. Participants will meet at the Filipino Cultural

Center for eighteen fall and spring sessions. Classes will culminate in performances that will highlight traditional and contemporary Filipino dance and music.

Kaw Valley Arts & Humanities, Inc.
Kansas City, KS
FIELD/DISCIPLINE: Multidisciplinary
$10,000

To support a partnership project with YWCA of Kansas City and the Chameleon Theatre Company for Destination Creation, an arts-based, skill-building day camp for sixty youth ages eleven to sixteen who live in public housing adjacent to the YWCA. The summer program will provide instruction in the arts as a means to develop such skills as creativity, planning, problem-solving, teamwork, and workplace protocol.

Total Grants Awarded: 2
Total Dollars Awarded: $20,000

Kentucky
Americana Community Center, Inc.
Louisville, KY
FIELD/DISCIPLINE: Visual Arts
$10,000

To support a partnership project with Kentucky Theater Project, Iroquois Amphitheater Association, and the City of Louisville Office of International and Cultural Affairs for workshops in photography, oral history, and Web publishing for middle and high school youth. The young people live in a Louisville transitional housing complex for recent immigrant and political refugee families. Through digital photography, storytelling, and Web design activities, participants will explore their relationships with their peers leading to improved understanding and communication, a greater appreciation of diversity, and more effective teamwork.

Kentucky Center for the Arts
Louisville, KY
FIELD/DISCIPLINE: Visual Arts
$10,000

To support a partnership project with City of Louisville Metro Parks Department, Iroquois High Community School, and Meyzeek Community School for after-school art instruction to middle- and high-school students in Louisville's south and central sections of the city. The project will introduce techniques such as collage, assemblage, fiber, and etching with a different project/medium offered each quarter, and culminate in a student exhibition.

Total Grants Awarded: 2
Total Dollars Awarded: $20,000

Louisiana
Contemporary Arts Center
New Orleans, LA
FIELD/DISCIPLINE: Music
$10,000

To support a partnership project with the Street Academy Charter School (an alternative school for youth at risk for academic failure) for ongoing weekend training for Circle of Ten, an ensemble of inner-city students ages thirteen to eighteen. Classes will be taught by jazz musician and composer Hannibal Lukumbe. Objectives will be to help students develop a positive self-image, gain appreciation and skill in music and visual arts, and learn about the relevance of music as a vehicle of individual and community expression.

Louisiana Philharmonic Orchestra
New Orleans, LA
FIELD/DISCIPLINE: Music
$10,000

To support a partnership project with the Good Shepherd School to develop a comprehensive music education program. Good Shepherd School, a new, relatively small school targeting at-risk youth from local inner-city neighborhoods who are living below the poverty line, opens its kindergarten and first grade classes in the fall of 2001.

New Orleans Video Access Center, Inc.
New Orleans, LA
FIELD/DISCIPLINE: Media Arts
$10,000

To support a partnership project with Louisiana Office of Public Health for Listen Up, a nationally recognized series of workshops in video production led by award-winning media artists. The project engages youth ages thirteen to eighteen in various production workshops that lead to the creation of public service announcements directed to teenagers.

Saint Joseph Arts, Inc.
Saint Joseph, LA
FIELD/DISCIPLINE: Music
$5,000

To support a partnership project with Northeast Louisiana Arts Council, Work Force Development (Tensas Parish Office), Tensas Parish Public Schools, Macon Ridge Economic Development Group, and Loving Cup Counseling for music workshops for children in grades K through twelve in Tensas Parish. Participants who generally cannot afford music instruction or instrument rentals will receive scholarships for private and group music lessons. Selected participants will have the chance to play in the Saint Joseph Orchestra, a unique training opportunity for students from a region where music education is seldom available in public schools.

Total Grants Awarded: 4
Total Dollars Awarded: $35,000

Maine
Hancock County Auditorium Associates
Ellsworth, ME
FIELD/DISCIPLINE: Music
$10,000

To support a partnership project with Ellsworth High School, Bull Hill Consolidated School, and the Maine Alliance for Arts Education for an artist residency of the Los Angeles Brass Quintet. The quintet will serve seven rural school districts of Hancock County. This program will enhance students' understanding and appreciation of music through workshops, coaching, and private lessons.

Maine Alliance for Arts Education
Augusta, ME
FIELD/DISCIPLINE: Theater
$10,000

To support a partnership project with nineteen high schools of Penobscot and Piscataquis counties, Acadia Hospital, University of Maine School of Education, and National Center for Student Aspirations for an in-school residency program in theater arts for high school students in the rural districts in the Penquis region. Led by professional theater and movement artists from throughout the state, students will create original work.

Total Grants Awarded: 2
Total Dollars Awarded: $20,000

Maryland
Mayor's Advisory Committee on Art and Culture
Baltimore, MD
FIELD/DISCIPLINE: Visual Arts
$10,000

To support a partnership project with School 33 Arts Center, Thomas Johnson Elementary School, Federal Hill Elementary School, and Francis Scott Key Elementary and Middle Schools for an after-school art program for youth ages eight to fifteen in inner-city south Baltimore neighborhoods. Students receive instruction by professional artists in photography, ceramics, painting, and drawing.

Somerset County Local Management Board
Princess Anne, MD
FIELD/DISCIPLINE: Multidisciplinary
$10,000

To support a partnership project with Somerset County Arts Council, Somerset County Board of Education, and Somerset County Health Department for visits by The FUN-mobile, a mobile after-school enrichment program to school-age children in the rural and economically depressed county. Local artists who are members of the Somerset County Arts Council will lead the students in a wide variety of arts activities.

Total Grants Awarded: 2
Total Dollars Awarded: $20,000

Massachusetts
Artspace Community Arts Center
Greenfield, MA
FIELD/DISCIPLINE: Multidisciplinary
$10,000

To support a partnership project with the Greenfield Housing Authority for ABCs of the Arts, for children and their families residing at Oak Courts, a low-income housing project in rural western Massachusetts. This program consists of a preliminary arts festival designed to inform and recruit participants to attend a two sixteen-week series of age-appropriate art, music, and theater classes, and monthly arts-based activities taught by qualified artists and teachers selected by Artspace.

Barrington Stage Company, Inc.
Great Barrington, MA
FIELD/DISCIPLINE: Theater
$10,000

To support a partnership project with Railroad Street Youth Project and Southern Berkshire Regional School District for the Playwright Mentoring Project, a theater program for students in grades ten to twelve. The program will be led by award-winning director Julianne Boyd and other theater professionals in rural, largely low-income southern Berkshire County in western Massachusetts. The project will culminate in a full-length revue, written and presented by students, that is intended for county-wide touring.

Community Music School of Springfield, Inc.
Springfield, MA
FIELD/DISCIPLINE: Music
$10,000

To support a partnership with the Springfield Housing Authority for Jump Start, a series of after-school and weekend workshops in hip-hop music and music video production led by professional musicians and videographers. This project will serve Springfield youth living in low-income housing developments.

DeCordova Museum and Sculpture Park
Lincoln, MA

FIELD/DISCIPLINE: Visual Arts
$10,000

To support a partnership project with the Alston Branch Public Library for local resident and quilter Clara Wainwright to work with eighth graders from two local schools in the racially and ethnically diverse Boston neighborhood. Ms. Wainwright will help youth create a quilt that will reflect in both theme and design an aspect of the community. The quilt will be permanently displayed at the library.

Music & Art Development
Jamaica Plain, MA
FIELD/DISCIPLINE: Multidisciplinary
$10,000

To support a partnership project with the Bird Street Community Center, Jamaica Plain Community Center, Boston Housing Authority, and Agassiz Community Center for The PeaceDrum Project, an after-school arts and leadership training program for twenty inner-city teenagers. The project includes oral history interviews, drum making, drumming, and a culminating exhibition of drums decorated with visual images resulting from the oral histories gathered from community elders.

Spinner Publications
New Bedford, MA
FIELD/DISCIPLINE: Multidisciplinary
$10,000

To support a partnership project with ArtWorks!, New Directions, the New Bedford Whaling National Park, and the Massachusetts Department of Mental Retardation for the New Bedford Teen Arts Coalition. The project supports a series of summer and after-school art classes including visual arts, graphic design, pottery, journalism, and creative writing for culturally and ethnically diverse, low-income high school students. Participants include youth from Portuguese, Cape Verdean, Latino, African American, and European communities.

Total Grants Awarded: 6
Total Dollars Awarded: $60,000

Michigan
All the World's a Stage
Clinton Township, MI
FIELD/DISCIPLINE: Theater
$10,000

To support a partnership project with Michigan State University Macomb County Extension, and Creating a Healthier Macomb for workshops in theater arts leading to performances of original theater works. The plays will explore relevant social issues of interest to the students who are in grades six to twelve residing in this rural, generally poor county.

Flint Community Schools (on behalf of Flint Youth Theatre)
Flint, MI
FIELD/DISCIPLINE: Theater
$10,000

To support a partnership with Pierce Cultural Center School and Longway Planetarium for classes in playwriting and theater arts for fifth and sixth graders leading to production of a performance by twenty of the students. The teachers are theater professionals associated with Flint Youth Theater. Students at Pierce Cultural Center School are from urban, ethnically diverse communities.

Genessee Intermediate School District
Flint, MI

FIELD/DISCIPLINE: Multidisciplinary
$10,000

To support a partnership project with Very Special Arts of Michigan—Genesee County for an artist-in-residence program serving the Genessee Intermediate School District's special education programs. Hands-on workshops in music, visual and literary arts, creative movement, and drama will give students with a wide range of disabilities new tools for learning and alternative avenues for communication and personal growth.

Liberty Children's Art Project
Negaunee, MI
FIELD/DISCIPLINE: Visual Arts
$10,000

To support a partnership project with the Sault Saint Marie Tribe of Chippewa Indians for an artist-in-residence position to lead a photography program for middle school students. Granger was formerly the Native American Education Coordinator at Marquette Senior High School. Most of the students are Native Americans residents of Michigan's rural and isolated Upper Peninsula.

Mosaic Youth Theatre of Detroit
Detroit, MI
FIELD/DISCIPLINE: Theater
$10,000

To support a partnership project with University of Michigan Arts of Citizenship Program and Performance Network of Ann Arbor for Youth Ensemble, a program providing free training for 105 multiethnic middle- and high-school students in Greater Detroit. The ensemble is directed by Mosaic's theater professionals who conduct intensive workshops and prepare students for culminating performances at schools and local theaters.

Total Grants Awarded: 5
Total Dollars Awarded: $50,000

Minnesota
The Center for Arts Criticism
St. Paul, MN
FIELD/DISCIPLINE: Media
$10,000

To support a partnership project with Na Esh Equay, an Ojibwe women's art cooperative, and Cass Lake Bena High School for Sisters in Leadership, a program in digital photography, videography, and computer editing designed for young Native American women from Leech Lake Nation and the township of Cass Lake in north central Minnesota. Approximately fifteen young women will learn to create artwork using new technologies, write about the issues and themes addressed in their work, and present their media work to the community.

Stages Theatre Company, Inc.
Hopkins, MN
FIELD/DISCIPLINE: Theater
$5,000

To support a partnership project with South Elementary School and East Junior High School in rural central Minnesota for a collaboration between resident professional artists and teachers. This project will incorporate theater into the schools' curriculum, develop students' dramatic skills and appreciation of theater, and produce a play based on folktales of several cultures.

White Earth Land Recovery Project
Ponsford, MN
FIELD/DISCIPLINE: Multidisciplinary
$10,000

To support a partnership project with Minnesota Alliance for Arts Education, Headwaters School of Music and the Arts, Episcopal Church, Naytahwaush Sports Complex, and Detroit Lakes Title 9 Indian Education Programs for after-school and summer arts programs in the rural Naytahwaush and Rice Lake areas. The project involving Native American youth ages twelve to eighteen, will support the learning of traditional Ojibwe storytelling, drumming, art, music, and dance as well as nontraditional art forms.

Total Grants Awarded: 3
Total Dollars Awarded: $25,000

Mississippi
Foundation for the Revitalization of Artesia, MS, Inc.
Artesia, MS
FIELD/DISCIPLINE: Music
$5,000

To support a partnership with Columbus Arts Council and the Town of Artesia for a ten-week after-school and weekend residency for blues musician Johnnie Billington to teach youth in grades six to twelve in the low-income, rural community of east central Mississippi. Billington has been named a Master Folk Artist by the Mississippi Arts Commission and has received a W.C. Handy Blues Award for his dedication to teaching blues music to young people since the 1970s.

Mississippi Cultural Crossroads
Port Gibson, MS
FIELD/DISCIPLINE: Multidisciplinary
$10,000

To support a partnership project with Cornerstone Theater, University of Mississippi Center for Oral History & Cultural Heritage, Mississippi

Library Commission, City of Port Gibson, Claiborne County Supervisors, and Hattiesburg Arts Council for Peanut Butter & Jelly Theater, a literacy and theater project led by Cornerstone Theater of Los Angeles, CA. In addition, local youth in this largely African American community will participate in Taking Their Place: Young Person's Documentary Project, which offers workshops in oral interviews, photo documentation, essay writing for publication in local newspapers, desktop publishing, and Web page design.

Walk of Faith Ministry
Mound Bayou, MS
FIELD/DISCIPLINE: Music
$10,000

To support a partnership project with the Delta Blues Education Fund, public schools in Mound Bayou, North Bolivar and West Bolivar, Youth Focus Initiative, and Mound Bayou Police Department for after-school music instruction and summer programs for youth ages eight to eighteen. Youth from this rural Mississippi Delta community will be instructed in a wide range of music classes including production of audio recordings, African drumming, and blues music.

Total Grants Awarded: 3
Total Dollars Awarded: $25,000

Missouri
Adair County Family YMCA
Kirksville, MO
FIELD/DISCIPLINE: Multidisciplinary
$10,000

To support a partnership project with Kirksville Arts Association for Kreative Kids, an after-school and summer day camp arts program open to children in grades three through eight from the rural community

of Adair County. With the Kirksville Arts Association providing the selection process, regional artists and arts educators will provide instruction. All activities will take place at the YMCA facility.

Kansas City Ballet Association
Kansas City, MO
FIELD/DISCIPLINE: Dance
$10,000

To support a partnership project with Primitivo Garcia World Language School for Reach Out and Dance, a unique in-school arts education program for low-income, inner-city youth in grades four and five using the dance method devised by nationally recognized dancer and educator Jacques D'Amboise. Through exposure to dance movement, youth participants will develop a sense of team dynamics, trust, and discipline.

Kansas City Friends of Alvin Ailey
Kansas City, MO
FIELD/DISCIPLINE: Dance
$10,000

To support a partnership project with Kaw Valley Arts and Humanities, Inc., and Unified School District 500 for a six-week, dance-based summer arts camp for youth ages eleven to fourteen from Wyandotte County, which has the highest percentage of families living below the poverty line in the state. Led by professional artists and educators, the Ailey Camp is based on the premise that dance not only exposes children to creativity but also improves their self-discipline, listening, critical thinking, and communication skills.

Lyric Opera of Kansas City, Inc.
Kansas City, MO
FIELD/DISCIPLINE: Opera
$10,000

To support a partnership project with Kansas City School District in Kansas City, KS and Park University in Parkville, MO for one-week artist residencies in eight middle schools in Kansas City, KS on the opera production The Orphan Train. The subject matter offers participants lessons about slavery, the Civil War, pioneer life, and westward migration. Students will learn basic conventions of opera, work with professional singers to learn excerpts and act out parts of the opera, and attend public performances of the Lyric's opera production at Park University.

The Salvation Army
Independence, MO
FIELD/DISCIPLINE: Multidisciplinary
$10,000
To support a partnership project with Independence School District, Music/Arts Institute and the Children's Art Institute for music lessons and visual arts instruction for low-income children ages six to eight. The Salvation Army offers free instruction as well as art materials, music, and loaner instruments at no cost to participants. Through this partnership and among several music resources, students will receive both weekly after-school classes and private lessons during the summer months.

St. Louis African Chorus
St. Louis, MO
FIELD/DISCIPLINE: Music
$5,000
To support a partnership project with Loyola Academy of Saint Louis for an after-school choral program for nearly forty middle school students at the Loyola Boys Academy of St. Louis that targets African American boys from low-income families. Project activities include training clinics with choral director,

Boniface Mgaga of Kenya. The chorus will meet three afternoons a week after school, presenting monthly mini-concerts for faculty and parents and two school-wide performances in December and April.

Total Grants Awarded: 6
Total Dollars Awarded: $55,000

Montana
Alberta Bair Theater for the Performing Arts
Billings, MT
FIELD/DISCIPLINE: Multidisciplinary
$10,000
To support a partnership project with The Writer's Voice of the Billings Family YMCA, Billings Public Schools, Yellowstone Art Museum, The Billings Symphony, and The Moss Mansion to expand the ongoing Stories Project currently offered to students at two middle schools to include an alternative school. The program participants have been identified by school personnel as needing special assistance and new avenues for creative expression. The project offers in-school classes in music, creative writing, and the visual arts with field trips to collaborating arts and cultural organizations.

Hill County School District
Harve, MT
FIELD/DISCIPLINE: Visual Arts
$10,000
To support a partnership project with Stone Child College, Rocky Boy Indian Reservation, and the H. Earl Clack Museum to implement a photography project for high-school students. The project is designed to teach photography skills, increase communication, and establish better cultural understanding between youth living in Havre and tribal youth living on the Rocky Boy

Indian Reservation, where unemployment is nearly 80 percent. The project will culminate with a traveling exhibition and accompanying catalogue. Graduating art students from Stone Child College near the Rocky Boy Reservation will teach photography as well as cultural aspects of the Chippewa-Cree traditions to youth from both nontribal and tribal communities.

Missoula Writing Collaborative
Missoula, MT
FIELD/DISCIPLINE: Literature
$5,000

To support a partnership project with the Two Eagle River School (an alternative high school on the Flathead Indian Reservation) and the Lone Rock School District for workshops in poetry, fiction, and personal essays. Led by professional writers, the project will publish an anthology of works by youth participants who represent this low-income, rural, and predominately Native American population.

Wakina Sky Learning Circle
Helena, MT
FIELD/DISCIPLINE: Folk & Traditional Arts
$10,000

To support a partnership project with Helena Indian Alliance and the Holter Museum of Art for after-school activities targeting Native American youth living in rural and low-income Lewis and Clark, Jefferson, and Broadwater counties. A team of distinguished traditional artists, including drummer/drum maker Al Chandlers and traditional dancers Nyleta Belgarde and Ken Walton, will lead the project. The program seeks to address and inspire a broader awareness of the disparate cultural histories and shared artistic traditions represented in and among the tribal populations in Montana.

Youth, Inc.
White Sulphur Springs, MT
FIELD/DISCIPLINE: Multidisciplinary
$10,000

To support a partnership project with Meagher County Arts Council, Meagher County Public Television, and Vid-Kid Productions for The Arts are Central Project to expand Youth, Inc.'s existing programs of after-school and summer arts activities to include youth in grades seven to twelve. The project will involve these youth in creating a video documentary about Montana arts resources designed to interest other youth in this age range to participate in the arts. All video will be shot digitally and mastered under the direction of Vid-Kid, a youth-operated video production group, and the executive director of the local public television station. The county is located in a geographically remote area and has a landmass comparable to the size of the state of Delaware.

Total Grants Awarded: 5
Total Dollars Awarded: $45,000

Nebraska
Opera Omaha, Inc.
Omaha, NE
FIELD/DISCIPLINE: Opera
$10,000

To support a partnership project with Omaha South High School and Durham Western Heritage Museum for a composer-in-residence program with composer Deb Tyson. Ms. Tyson will work with teachers, history professionals, and high-school students in preparation for a residency. During Ms. Tyson's visits, she will teach a workshop at the high school on writing lyrics as well as conduct preliminary work on the score with instrumental and vocal students.

Total Grants Awarded: 1
Total Dollars Awarded: $10,000

Nevada
Clark County Nevada
Las Vegas, NV
FIELD/DISCIPLINE: Multidisciplinary
$10,000

To support a partnership project with the City of Las Vegas Cultural & Community Affairs Division and the Reed Whipple Cultural Center for intensive workshops in theater, creative writing, and the visual arts for youth ages thirteen to seventeen. This will take place at the Spring Mountain Youth Camp, a residency for both juvenile offenders and for youth who have been through the court system who are living in halfway homes. Resident artists have been selected from the Nevada Arts Council's roster of qualified artists and have experience in working with youth.

Total Grants Awarded: 1
Total Dollars Awarded: $10,000

New Hamphsire
Manchester New Hampshire School District
Manchester, NH
FIELD/DISCIPLINE: Multidisciplinary
$5,000

To support a partnership project with the New Hampshire Institute of Arts and the Manchester Community Music School for the After School Art and Music Club, a music and arts program targeted for fifth graders from low-income neighborhoods. Up to fifty students, primarily from the underserved Glosser Park community, will participate in the project.

Moving Company Dance Center
Keene, NH
FIELD/DISCIPLINE: Multidisciplinary
$10,000

To support a partnership project with Keene Institute of Music and Related Arts, ACTING OUT (a drama center of the Monadnock Family Services), Savings Bank of Walpole, Monadnock Developmental Services, and the City of Keene Youth Services Division for Creative Arts at Keene, a summer arts program of intensive multidisciplinary workshops for youth ages nine to fifteen living in rural southwestern New Hampshire. During a five-week summer program, a team of professional artists will provide classes in creative writing, music, dance, drama, and visual arts.

Total Grants Awarded: 2
Total Dollars Awarded: $15,000

New Jersey
Appel Farm Arts & Music Center
Elmer, NJ
FIELD/DISCIPLINE: Visual Arts
$10,000

To support a partnership with Arthur B. Schalick High School to hire Ava Blitz, a Philadelphia artist working in sculpture and landscape architecture. Ms. Blitz will serve an eighteen-month residency at the Center, located on 176 acres in rural, southwestern New Jersey. Under the guidance of the artist, students will be involved in fabricating and installing Beauty and the Beast, a large-scale outdoor sculpture. Students of other area high schools and adults from the community also will assist in phases of the project.

Arts Horizons, Inc.
Englewood, NJ

FIELD/DISCIPLINE: Multidisciplinary
$10,000

To support a partnership with the City of Orange Township Board of Education. Arts Horizons will conduct an after-school "safe haven" project, serving low-income, primarily African American students ages eleven to thirteen. Artists and classroom teachers will work with the children through music, dance, theater, and visual arts activities to foster creativity, constructive self-expression, and skills in problem-solving and cooperation.

Total Grants Awarded: 2
Total Dollars Awarded: $20,000

New Mexico
Branigan Cultural Center Foundation
Las Cruces, NM
FIELD/DISCIPLINE: Multidisciplinary
$10,000

To support a partnership with the Las Cruces school system, two cultural museums, and New Mexico State University's theater company. The Foundation will administer Another Planet, a collaborative arts project for 750 middle school students at three schools in this predominately Mexican American town located fifty miles from the Mexican border. During classroom residencies, writers, dancers, musicians, and visual and theater artists from southwestern New Mexico will guide pupils in making artwork, honing their academic skills, and exploring their heritage.

Farmington Municipal School District/Advisory of Arts & Culture
Farmington, NM
FIELD/DISCIPLINE: Multidisciplinary
$10,000

To support a partnership with Farmington Gateway Museum, San Juan College, and Anthony Emerson (artist & gallery) for Navajo Artlinks. This program will enroll approximately 160 students from four middle schools in an after-school, arts discipline-based curriculum. The program, which targets students with academic and behavior problems, will feature professional instruction in Navajo arts and culture, demonstrations of student learning, and public art projects for placement in each community.

La Jicarita Enterprise Community
Peñasco, NM
FIELD/DISCIPLINE: Folk & Traditional Arts
$10,000

To support a partnership with the Peñasco school, the district, and an artists' cooperative to sponsor the Intergenerational Arts Mentorship program for the low-income, largely Mexican American community. The project will connect practitioners of regional craft traditions (woodcrafts, pottery, visual arts, and metal sculpture) with local students. The program has two components: a summer rural arts institute for about sixty middle- and high-school students involving classes taught by six local artists; and a fall semester initiative to enhance the curriculum, pairing area artisans with art teachers in the classroom.

Outside In Productions
Santa Fe, NM
FIELD/DISCIPLINE: Multidisciplinary
$10,000

To support a partnership with El Museo Cultural for the Creative Arts for Youth With Promise project to offer classes to young juvenile offenders and other troubled youngsters, most of whom are from low-income Hispanic and Native American families.

Participants will receive free weekly guitar lessons through the local Boys & Girls Club using instruments donated by the Bonnie Raitt/Fender Guitar Program. Also, workshops will be provided in hip-hop dance and mural painting.

Reach 2000/Unity Center
Roswell, NM
FIELD/DISCIPLINE: Multidisciplinary
$10,000

To support a partnership between two New Mexico community organizations, Unity Center in Roswell and Rocky Mountain Youth Corps in Taos, to sponsor woodworking apprenticeship programs that guide participating youths in production of hand-crafted products while teaching them self-reliance and entrepreneurship. The apprentices, staff, and visiting artists of both programs will join in a series of six two-day workshops to exchange craft construction, marketing, and capacity-building expertise.

Total Grants Awarded: 5
Total Dollars Awarded : $50,000

New York
Amas Musical Theatre, Inc.
New York, NY
FIELD/DISCIPLINE: Musical Theater
$5,000

To support a partnership with Beacon Program: Pathways for Youth project, an after-school performance program serving elementary-school students from throughout the Bronx. Under the direction of seasoned professionals, including Christopher Scott, participants will study singing techniques, learn choral and solo numbers, and perform popular Broadway show tunes in public musical revues.

Arts Center of the Capital Region
Troy, NY
FIELD/DISCIPLINE: Multidisciplinary
$10,000

To support a partnership with the Troy Rehabilitation and Improvement Program to offer creative art experiences to seventy-five economically disadvantaged youth living in the underserved north central section of the Troy. During summer, midwinter, and spring breaks, youngsters will attend week-long day camps led by a range of professional artist-teachers and counselors. Participants will be immersed in a multidisciplinary arts environment.

Asian American Writers' Workshop/CreateNow Youth Writing Program
New York, NY
FIELD/DISCIPLINE: Literature
$10,000

To support a partnership with Harlem Overheard, the Workshop will host a ten-week Saturday writing session for up to twenty-five New York City public high school students. Teen participants, who are selected based on writing samples, will benefit from exposure to professional writers such as American Book Award winner, Kimiko Hahn. The CreateNow program seeks to establish a community of young authors who seek opportunities to write, perform, and publish works under the supervision of professional writers and independent publishers.

Ballet Artists of WNY
Buffalo, NY
FIELD/DISCIPLINE: Dance
$5,000

To support a partnership with the bilingual Herman Badillo Community School located in the inner city, twenty third- to fifth-grade students will receive ballet lessons from Spanish-speaking dancers through the CityDance project. CityDance's objectives are to encourage the children's interest in ballet, classic Spanish dance, and associated music while promoting self-discipline through choreographed movement and purposeful listening.

Brooklyn Information & Culture/ The Rotunda Gallery
Brooklyn, NY
FIELD/DISCIPLINE: Visual Arts
$10,000

To support a partnership with the Rotunda Gallery and William Gaynor Intermediate School that will enable artist-educators to work with the school's pupils to create a series of changing exhibitions for display in the school's Mini-Museum, a specially designed gallery constructed by the partners. Through researching thematic information, creating works in various media, selecting and organizing pieces for display, preparing informational materials, and conducting tours, students develop creative, analytical, and social skills. The school is located in the low-income Bushwick section of Brooklyn, which is a largely Latino and African American community.

Center for the Arts at Ithaca
Ithaca, NY
FIELD/DISCIPLINE: Theater
$10,000

To support a partnership between the Hangar Theatre and the Austin MacCormick Secure Center, which is a long-term (usually four or more years) juvenile detention facility. The project will include artist-led activities by staff of the Hangar Theatre for a six-month artistic residency workshop. Through exposure to writing and theater arts, residents will have the opportunity to perform an original work demonstrating their creative expression and mutual collaboration.

DanceWorks, Inc./Pentacle
New York, NY
FIELD/DISCIPLINE: Dance
$5,000

To support a partnership with Satellite Academy High School-Forsyth Campus through which Pentacle's three teaching artists will serve in a dance residency during nonschool hours. This project serves students who have been transferred due to unsuccessful performance at previous schools. Volunteers must be willing to commit to the scheduled ten-hour course of instruction. At the semester's end, the pupils will perform in a lecture/demonstration of their work.

Dancing in the Streets, Inc.
New York, NY
FIELD/DISCIPLINE: Dance
$10,000

To support a partnership with Good Shepherd Services, School for Leadership in the Environment, South Brooklyn Community High School, and Red Hook Community Center Beacon (at P.S.15) for educational workshops in dance through Dancing in the Schools. This project links art with community and a place to nurture a sense of achievement, cultural exploration, and civic pride in the young dancers who live in the low-income, relatively isolated Red Hook area of Brooklyn.

DreamYard Drama Project, Inc.
New York, NY
FIELD/DISCIPLINE: Multidisciplinary
$10,000

To support a partnership with Ping Chong and Company, who will produce his community response production, Undesirable Elements, featuring local youth. Ping Chong has a track record of successfully producing this dance-music-theater work reflecting the life stories and cultural history of the host community in which it is staged. Supervised by teachers and a team of artists, fifteen teenagers from Harlem, East Harlem, and the Bronx will work on all aspects of the production, which culminates in performances at several city venues including schools.

Elders Share the Arts
Brooklyn, NY
FIELD/DISCIPLINE: Visual Arts
$10,000

To support a partnership to expand Legacy Works, a living history arts project, to a new site, the Casita Maria Settlement House. Twelve teenagers living in Carver Houses, an East Harlem public housing project, will be selected to partner with up to twenty of Carver's homebound elderly residents served by Casita Maria. During the six-month program, the youngsters will learn to produce written stories and visual collages on a designated theme, work with elders to express their biographies in visual form, collaboratively evaluate the results of this process, and mount an exhibition at Carver.

Global Action Project
New York, NY
FIELD/DISCIPLINE: Media Arts
$10,000

To support a partnership with the International Rescue Committee and the International Trauma Studies Department of New York University, Global Action Project (GAP) will lead teen immigrants and refugees in an exploration of displacement, exile, shifting identities, and intergroup relations through the creation of short videos, stories, poetry, and photography. A multinational core group of twelve to sixteen youths, two media artists, and youth audiences will participate in this ongoing project.

Long Island Traditions
Port Washington, NY
FIELD/DISCIPLINE: Visual Arts
$5,000

To support a partnership with the Shinnecock Indian Nation, Long Island Traditions will develop a six-week arts and culture component of the Shinnecock reservation's after-school program for about twenty tribal students in grades six to ten. Three master artists will guide the young people's creation of a quilt and a mural documenting their perceptions of the traditional Shinnecock powwow, for display in the new Family Preservation Center.

Manhattan Theatre Club
New York, NY
FIELD/DISCIPLINE: Theater
$10,000

To support a partnership project with two Rikers Island juvenile facilities, Island Academy and Riker's Island Educational Facility. The Theatre will conduct a playwriting residency, Write on the Edge II, for incarcerated youth ages fourteen to eighteen. A team of theater professionals and classroom English teachers will supervise the students in preliminary study and in writing and revising their scripts, which then will be performed by professional actors.

Mill Street Loft, Inc.
Poughkeepsie, NY

FIELD/DISCIPLINE: Visual Arts
$10,000

To support a partnership with the New Day Repertory Company and the Poughkeepsie City School District, thirty students participating in Mill Street Loft's Project ABLE, an arts-based job skills training program, will design and produce a mural for permanent installation in the Board of Education meeting room of the Poughkeepsie City School District offices. Visual artist Nestor Madalengoitia and Project ABLE's program director, a professional wood craftsman, will supervise the design and construction of the wood mural. In addition, Joan Henry, a Native American storyteller, and the Repertory Company's artistic director will engage youth in other related programming.

Police Athletic League, Inc.
New York, NY
FIELD/DISCIPLINE: Music
$10,000

To support a partnership with the Brooklyn Philharmonic and Coalition for the Homeless. The project will support free, sequential instrumental music instruction for thirty homeless youngsters in four Brooklyn shelters. The Coalition's composer-in-residence Kevin James initiated the project. Professional musicians will teach weekly Saturday lessons at the Police Athletic League's Schwartz Center and after-school workshops in the shelters located in the Bushwick neighborhood. Also, the Philharmonic will contribute monthly off-site performance events.

Puerto Rican Traveling Theatre
New York, NY
FIELD/DISCIPLINE: Theater
$10,000

To support a partnership with Campos Community Center, the Theatre's training unit will continue to conduct a bilingual after-school program of acting, singing, dancing, and visual arts classes for youths from low-income Latino and African American families. The program, which emphasizes reading and other academic learning skills, also promotes responsibility, leadership, and character building.

Teachers & Writers Collaborative
New York, NY
FIELD/DISCIPLINE: Literature
$10,000

To support a partnership with Youth Speaks and the Educational Alliance's Pride Site One (PS1) to offer literary arts programs for PS1's residents, who are sixteen- to twenty-year-old males with drug and alcohol dependency problems. Within the controlled environment of PS1, which is a yearlong residency program, participants will be encouraged to produce literary projects as an outlet for creative expression through poetry, fiction, and the spoken word as potential transforming instruments of their rehabilitation process.

Working Playground, Inc.
Hastings, NY
FIELD/DISCIPLINE: Multidisciplinary
$10,000

To support a partnership with New York City's East Side Community High School, Working Playground will direct a program of arts studio classes. The youth participants are 78 percent Latino and 19 percent African American. Artists and arts educators will teach eight disciplines (acting, playwriting, computer art, dance, design, poetry, video production, and visual arts) to groups averaging seventeen members each, to address a curriculum structured to help seventh- through twelfth-grade pupils excel in English and language arts, mathematics, and science.

Writers & Books, Inc.
Rochester, NY
FIELD/DISCIPLINE: Literature
$5,000

To support a partnership with Hillside Children's Center, a facility that offers community-based treatment and emergency services to children with behavioral and mental health problems. The project will be led by Writer-in-Residence Todd Beer, who has more than fifteen years experience in both traditional and alternative settings. He will be accompanied by a teacher and teacher's aide. Beer will conduct two six-week writing sessions, each for students ages thirteen to eighteen, resulting in a published anthology of their work. The project seeks to provide students with exposure to the creative writing process and instill confidence in this form of self-expression.

YMCA of Greater Syracuse, Inc.
Syracuse, NY
FIELD/DISCIPLINE: Multidisciplinary
$10,000

To support a partnership with the After School Arts Program at Elmwood Elementary School to provide instruction to over 100 children ages eight to fourteen in choir, dance, storytelling, and visual art, consistent with New York State Standards for Arts Learning. Led by the Y's director, Phillip Memmer, who is a published poet, writer, and literary editor, the program, which operates two ten-week terms, reinforces skills the students need to tackle other academic subjects successfully. Elmwood Elementary

School's enrollment is drawn from a low-income, crime-ridden section of downtown Syracuse.

Total Grants Awarded: 20
Total Dollars Awarded: $175,000

North Carolina
Asheville Art Museum Association, Inc.
Asheville, NC
FIELD/DISCIPLINE: Visual Arts
$10,000

To support a partnership with the City Parks and Recreation Department for Art Where I Live, a thirty-six-week course of visual arts activities for teenagers affiliated with an after-school program for low-income residents. Linked to objectives in North Carolina's Standard Course of Study, activities will include four projects at the museum's galleries and new art resource center (making paper and books, masks, puppets, and silkscreen designs), as well as the creation of murals in four community centers. The museum will display participants' works in a culminating exhibition.

Mint Museum of Art
Charlotte, NC
FIELD/DISCIPLINE: Visual Arts
$5,000

To support a partnership with the Charlotte-Mecklenburg Schools in which the Mint Museum of Craft + Design, a new Mint facility, will develop a curriculum-based program, Science of Ceramics. Art, science, and math teachers will work with ceramists on a cross-disciplinary approach to teaching chemistry, physics, and mathematics concepts to students. Pilot implementation will begin with artist residencies in Independence and West Mecklenburg High Schools.

Total Grants Awarded: 2
Total Dollars Awarded: $15,000

North Dakota
FutureBuilders/Trollwood Performing Arts School
Fargo, ND
FIELD/DISCIPLINE: Multidisciplinary
$10,000

To support a partnership between North Dakota East Central District Juvenile Court; Dakota Boys Ranch; Fargo Housing & Redevelopment Authority; Clay County (Minnesota) WrapAround Process; and Trollwood Performing Arts School, a summer program of Fargo Public Schools and the Fargo Parks District. This project will support the STAR (STudents At Risk) project for sixth to twelfth graders with learning disabilities, behavior difficulties, and challenges aggravated by poverty or recent immigration. Aided by a one-to-three mentor-to-student ratio, STAR participants will learn through instruction in dramatic writing, technical theater, and video production.

Nelson County Arts Council
Pekin, ND
FIELD/DISCIPLINE: Multidisciplinary
$5,000

To support a partnership with Nelson County Stump Lake Park Management and Dakota Prairie School District for a summer arts camp for youth from Nelson County and surrounding areas. Pekin is a small town (population 101), yet the County Arts Council has sponsored a regional art exhibit that has attracted more than fifty artists from North Dakota as well as three neighboring states. In 1999, the council initiated the Arts Camp for which some parents drive eighty miles roundtrip daily, and registration has been at overflow capacity for each of its two years of opera-

tion. Under the direction of experienced arts instructors, students study visual and performing arts, and present a culminating public event.

North Dakota Museum of Art
Grand Forks, ND
FIELD/DISCIPLINE: Visual Arts
$10,000

To support a partnership with two middle schools and two elementary schools whose students will attend After School at the Museum, a program bringing together professional artists and youngsters ages eight to fourteen for sessions to acquaint them with the visual arts. Fifteen students from each of the four partner public schools will be selected to participate in a six-week session, during which they will examine contemporary works and learn about the range of techniques used by visual artists, writers, musicians, and actors. The activities are intended to stimulate critical thinking, creative expression, and communication and offer a cultural context for participants, some who have minimal exposure to professional arts resources.

Total Grants Awarded: 3
Total Dollars Awarded: $25,000

Ohio
Jefferson Academy of Music
Columbus, OH
FIELD/DISCIPLINE: Music
$10,000

To support a partnership with the Ohio State University School of Music to expand to weekends the Academy's Jefferson at OSU, a ten-week string music instruction program for area students. By adding Saturday instruction for three ten-week terms, 100 additional inner-city and rural youth, selected from schools in seven central Ohio counties, will have access to private study, master classes with OSU faculty, and performance opportunities. Only 25 percent of Ohio school districts offer string instruction. Tuition assistance and instruments will be provided for potential students targeted with the assistance of Columbus's school personnel and will be available to other potential students.

Mad River Theater Works
West Liberty, OH
FIELD/DISCIPLINE: Theater
$10,000

To support a partnership with Adriel School and Ben-El Child Development Center, the theater will direct YouthWorks, a collaborative project involving youth with special needs. Four residencies for theater artists will take place at the Adriel School complex, based in rural Logan County. The school is a residential care facility for young people who are struggling with disabling psychological and behavioral challenges. Each student group will learn elements of theater and, based on local history, students will develop an original play to be performed as a culminating event for their families, fellow outpatients/residents, and service agency staff.

Portsmouth Public Library
Portsmouth, OH
FIELD/DISCIPLINE: Theater
$10,000

To support a partnership with Community Action Organization and Shawnee State University, the library will host TheatreWorks!, a summer theater education and jobs program for underserved Appalachian youth ages fourteen to twenty. Components of the project

include workshops in commedia dell'arte, mask making, voice, movement, improvisation, and costume design. The second component, apprenticeships, will provide in-depth commedia training, paid employment, career counseling, and rehearsals and performances.

Toledo Museum of Art
Toledo, OH
FIELD/DISCIPLINE: Visual Arts
$10,000

To support a partnership with Toledo Public Schools, the museum and its business sector partners will offer two semesters of job training in design and visual art fields to selected vocational education students. During the first semester, the youths will serve as studio assistants in the School of Art and Design and may take art courses there on scholarship. After preparation in a carefully chosen medium, they will be placed as apprentices in private local firms (architecture, glass manufacturing, advertising) to begin to apply their new crafts.

Total Grants Awarded: 4
Total Dollars Awarded: $40,000

Oklahoma
Cheyenne Cultural Center
Clinton, OK
FIELD/DISCIPLINE: Visual Arts
$10,000

To support a partnership between the Black Kettle Museum, Plains Indian and Pioneer Museum, the Village Within, the Washita National Battlefield and the Fort Supply Historic Sites, Roman Nose State Park, and Fort Reno Visitors Center. The Center and project partners, located in central west Oklahoma, will sponsor Project VALUE, a mentorship project in which sixteen Cheyenne and Arapaho artists will guide local Indian public-school students in creating sixteen commissioned paintings depicting tribal historical events. The youths will gain knowledge about tribal cultural heritage and be involved in the creative process. Initiated and unveiled with traditional ceremonies, the paintings will be housed as part of a permanent exhibit.

Kaw Nation of Oklahoma
Kaw City, OK
FIELD/DISCIPLINE: Multidisciplinary
$5,000

To support a partnership with the Kanza Museum, Ponca City Cultural Center, Ponca City Association, Ponca Arts & Humanities Council, Kaw Dependent School District, and Standing Bear Foundation. The Kaw Nation will host an artist residency as part of its summer Youth Activity and Nutrition program, which primarily serves youth living in public housing.

Arthur Short Bull, a Lakota Sioux visual artist, storyteller, poet, and educator, will engage the Kaw youth grades K through twelve in classes in traditional songs, dance, and Kaw language. Prior to the residency, students will take field trips to visit the various partner arts organizations.

Total Grants Awarded: 2
Total Dollars Awarded: $15,000

Oregon
Artists Repertory Theatre
Portland, OR
FIELD/DISCIPLINE: Theater
$5,000

To support a partnership with the Youth Opportunity Center to enable underserved teenagers to create, produce, and perform original musical theater pieces. Classes of sixteen students from two Portland high schools located in low-income neighborhoods will participate in a twelve-week series of theater workshops. As a basis for career exploration, there will be instruction by drama and music specialists with additional presentations by designers of sets, lighting, sound, and costumes, and by arts administrators.

Crossroads Creative and Performing Arts Center, Inc.
Baker City, OR
FIELD/DISCIPLINE: Multidisciplinary
$10,000

To support a partnership between Baker School District 5J, the Commission on Children and Families, Mountain Valley Mental Health, New Directions Northwest, and the American Association of University Women, during which the Center's Artspeak project will expand its after-school and summer programming. Classes are conducted for pre-kindergarten to twelfth graders who live in this isolated, rural locale in northeastern Oregon. From what began as a dance class for juvenile offenders, the program now offers instruction in visual arts, dance, poetry, and theater.

The International Refugee Center of Oregon (IRCO)
Portland, OR
FIELD/DISCIPLINE: Folk & Traditional Arts
$10,000

To support a partnership between IRCO's Arts for New Immigrants Program and the Oregon Historical Society Folklife Project Program to sponsor a series of traditional arts classes for youth. Master folk artists-in-residence representing various cultures will teach primarily sixth through twelfth graders from the same cultural community during nonschool hours. The programs will culminate in a public arts event showcasing the students' work. IRCO serves immigrant populations from Southeast Asia, Eastern Europe, Africa, and the Middle East.

Lane Arts Council
Eugene, OR
FIELD/DISCIPLINE: Multidisciplinary
$10,000

To support a partnership with Looking Glass Youth Services and the City of Eugene's Amazon Community Center, the council will sponsor arts programming for homeless, runaway, and troubled youth ages eleven to twenty. Artist residencies will be extended into longer residencies at each of the three participating sites: Station 7 Crisis Shelter, New Roads Access Center, and Amazon Community Center. Through work with a team of mentoring artists, young people acquire creative self-expression and the ability to involve themselves more constructively within the community.

Total Grants Awarded: 4
Total Dollars Awarded: $35,000

Pennslyvania
Abington Art Center
Jenkintown, PA
FIELD/DISCIPLINE: Visual Arts
$5,000

To support a partnership with the Montgomery County Youth Center and County Juvenile Probation Division and the Abington Police Department that will sponsor a delinquency prevention initiative. Abington Art Center (AAC) will establish a visual arts internship program for twelve to fifteen students from Abington junior and senior high schools in suburban Philadelphia. Under the guidance of

AAC staff, artists and local business professionals working in related fields (e.g., journalism, graphic design, printing), the teenagers will produce a visual art magazine.

Associated Artists of Pittsburgh
Pittsburgh, PA
FIELD/DISCIPLINE: Visual Arts
$5,000

To support a partnership with the Visual Arts Career Orientation Partnership (VACOP), operated by Associated Artists of Pittsburgh with four area high schools. VACOP introduces students to the variety of career paths in the visual arts. Successful local artists will offer realistic perspectives on rewards and challenges associated with their respective disciplines, while overseeing the pupils' individual and collaborative art projects. Twenty youths with artistic ability and interest, who may need intervention to keep them on track, will be chosen from each school to ensure a diverse representation of racial, ethnic, and socioeconomic backgrounds.

Berks Art Council
Reading, PA
FIELD/DISCIPLINE: Multidisciplinary
$5,000

To support a partnership with the Institute of the Arts, Berks Community Television, and Lauer's Park Elementary School to administer Arts Camp on the Air for elementary children. Poet Craig Czury, sculptor Angelo DiMaria, and Full Circle Music Society will lead televised courses in their respective disciplines. The project supports a three-week series offering literature, sculpture, and music classes conducted in the studio for broadcast by Berks Community Television. The Wyomissing Institute of Fine Arts will help supply teachers for the inner-city students of Lauers Park Elementary School, twenty of whom will serve as the interactive audience.

COSACOSA art at large, Inc.
Philadelphia, PA
FIELD/DISCIPLINE: Multidisciplinary
$5,000

To support a partnership with Temple Children's Medical Center to sponsor artist Pedro Ospina for a three-month residency at the Medical Center working with young patients to create Safe Harbor, an installation work. Youths ages ten to eighteen from adjacent African American, Latino, and racially mixed neighborhoods, including patients, will fashion milagros (miracles), figural metal amulets symbolic of their lives that, when attached to a large sculptural piece, will symbolize the connection of art and healing.

Philadelphia School District/High School for Creative and Performing Arts
Philadelphia, PA
FIELD/DISCIPLINE: Folk & Traditional Arts
$10,000

To support a partnership with the Philadelphia Folklore Project to sponsor four fifteen-week artist residencies at CAPA. Masters of traditional African continental and African diaspora dance will conduct classes for dance students as well as mount a public performance. A magnet school, CAPA's enrollment includes many students of all races from low-income families. This project highlights cultural artistry that has not been previously available in the dance curriculum.

Total Grants Awarded: 5
Total Dollars Awarded: $30,000

Rhode Island
Island Art Center, Inc.
Newport, RI
FIELD/DISCIPLINE: Multidisciplinary
$10,000

To support a partnership with the Martin Luther King, Jr. Center, a Newport-based social service agency, to offer professional-level photography instruction to low-income African American and Latino teenagers who are students at Rogers High School. Twice a week in after-school and summer sessions, the youths will learn fundamental camera techniques and film processing from a team of professional photographers and arts educators, producing work for a community exhibition. After-school counselors of the MLK Center, art department staff at Rogers High School, staff of the Stopover Services, and experienced staff of the Art Center will assist in identifying student participants.

Total Grants Awarded: 1
Total Dollars Awarded: $10,000

South Carolina
Columbia City Jazz Company
Columbia, SC
FIELD/DISCIPLINE: Dance
$10,000

To support a partnership with John Ford Elementary School to benefit sixth to eighth graders in rural Calhoun County to participate in weekly after-school dance lessons during the academic year. Participants also may include students from nearby Sandy Run Elementary School. Students will learn original choreography. Businesses will defray the cost of shoes, tights, and leotards for the young dancers, who come mainly from poor, African American households in a jurisdiction where organized recreational and cultural activities for youth are generally unavailable.

Creative Spark, Inc.
Mt. Pleasant, SC
FIELD/DISCIPLINE: Multidisciplinary
$5,000

To support a partnership with three elementary schools, the Ron McNair School, Jennie Moore School, and Cainhoy School, to provide residencies for artists affiliated with the South Carolina Arts Commission's roster program. The program seeks to inform children about forms of cultural expression, enliven the study of history and geography, and enrich the standard curriculum. Each participating school represents an underserved population: rural African Americans, inner-city tenants of public housing, and residents of a rural area undergoing both modernization as well as the arrival of new immigrants.

Darlington County Cities in Schools/Puck's Theatre
Hartsville, SC
FIELD/DISCIPLINE: Multidisciplinary
$10,000

To support a partnership with Puck's Theater and Communities in the School to provide after-school art sessions during the academic year for selected fifth through ninth grade students in six Darlington County public schools. Participants will be chosen according to their need for help, such as poor grades or low attendance, difficult home environment, or encounters with the police. Students will participate in an integrated program of dance, music, and theater, offering an artist to student ratio of one to ten. As a culminating activity, students will be able to participate in a presentation for families and the general public.

Greenville Symphony Association
Greenville, SC
FIELD/DISCIPLINE: Music
$10,000

To support a partnership with the School District of Greenville County and the Greenville County YMCA to expand the Symphony's LARK program, which provides music education for middle-school students who live in public and low-income housing. LARK enables youngsters to participate in school bands, orchestras, and strings groups by furnishing instruments, supplies, uniforms, and fees.

Total Grants Awarded: 4
Total Dollars Awarded: $35,000

South Dakota
South Dakota Symphony Orchestra
Sioux Falls, SD
FIELD/DISCIPLINE: Music
$10,000

To support a partnership with South Dakotans for the Arts and the Short Grass Arts Council to allow the Orchestra's touring groups, a string quartet, and a wind quintet, to conduct after-school residencies in two Pierre public schools. At the Pierre Indian Learning Center, attended by 250 pupils in kindergarten through eighth grade, the musicians will introduce European classical music and instruments. While at Riggs High School, musicians will work one-on-one with the 170 members of the school band.

Total Grants Awarded: 1
Total Dollars Awarded: $10,000

Tennessee
Jefferson County School System

Dandridge, TN
FIELD/DISCIPLINE: Visual Arts
$10,000

To support a partnership with the Tennessee Arts Commission, BankFirst, and the St. Mary's Foundation to sponsor the LINK program, designed to benefit newly arriving high-school freshmen. This program utilizes the visual arts to build and strengthen academic and social skills students require to help make a successful transition into high school. Families living in this Appalachian region cope with a traditional lack of access to economic and cultural resources.

Jubilee Project, Inc.
Sneedville, TN
FIELD/DISCIPLINE: Theater
$5,000

To support a partnership with Sneedville/Hancock Community Partners, Hancock High School, the Women's Clubs of Sneedville and Hancock, and the Rose Center in Morristown, to initiate JET-Arts (Jubilee Empowerment through Theater Arts), a course of theater workshops for troubled youths ages eleven to eighteen in Hancock County, a poor, rural Appalachian area. Instruction will begin in the summer and continue until December. The program is designed to permit participating youngsters to learn about the creative process, as well as provide them with the experience of setting and attaining goals.

Total Grants Awarded: 2
Total Dollars Awarded: $15,000

Texas
Arts for Everyone, Inc.
Encinal, TX
FIELD/DISCIPLINE: Visual Arts
$10,000

To support a partnership with the Encinal Community Team and the City of Encinal to conduct more than twenty artist-led workshops providing sixth through eighth-grade students with the opportunity to learn from experienced visual and media artists, create artwork, and showcase their work in a community exhibit. The project provides a unique and creative experience for children living in a rural, isolated community.

San Antonio Youth Opportunity Program
San Antonio, TX
FIELD/DISCIPLINE: Dance
$5,000

To support a partnership with the San Antonio Housing Authority and the Carver Development Board to bring renowned Capoeira master, Jaire Mansur, to teach six weeks of Capoeira classes for students living in public housing. It provides an opportunity for the largely Hispanic and African American students to participate in a study of a relevant cultural form, promoting pride and deeper understanding of heritage.

SAY SÍ
San Antonio, TX
FIELD/DISCIPLINE: Multidisciplinary
$10,000

To support a partnership with the San Antonio Independent School District to support a weekly Working Artists and Mentors (WAM) visual and media arts program aimed at artistically talented middle-school students. Under the tutelage of professional artists, WAM gives students an opportunity to develop artistic and social skills, while providing the senior students an opportunity to share their developing skills and act as mentors.

Several Dancers
Houston, TX
FIELD/DISCIPLINE: Dance
$10,000

To support a partnership with the Battered Women's Shelter of the Houston Area Women's Center and the Children's Assessment Center to continue the Rising Stars Creative Arts Program that serves children at both centers. The program provides children ages five to fifteen with the opportunity for creativity, learning, and fun through movement and dance. The program offers positive interactions with adults who care about them, helping abused children begin to heal and improve self-esteem.

Southwestern Alternative Media Projects, Inc.
Houston, TX
FIELD/DISCIPLINE: Media Arts
$10,000

To support a partnership with Talento Bilingüe de Houston to sponsor the Storytelling on the Internet Project serving young people in a low-income, inner-city, primarily Latino community where residents have limited access to computers. The project provides children with an opportunity to work with media artists and to use technology as a vehicle for creative expression and communication.

Teatro Humanidad Cansada
Austin, TX
FIELD/DISCIPLINE: Theatre
$10,000

To support a partnership with the Austin/Travis Co. Summer Youth Employment Program, the University of Texas, the Texas Commission on the Arts, and the Milagro Foundation to provide low-income, minority, middle- and high-school students with employment in the arts as apprentice actors, designers, and technicians in Teatro's acclaimed Youth Theatre Program. The participants have an opportunity to earn money while learning theatre arts through workshops and drama activities in an after-school setting at the University of Texas campus.

Writer's Garret, Inc.
Dallas, TX
FIELD/DISCIPLINE: Literature
$10,000

To support a partnership with a variety of organizations including Southern Methodist University, Dallas Independent School District, and Artspartners to expand the successful Make A Write Turn after-school program for youth grades two through twelve. The program serves mainly inner-city, low-income Latino and African American children, providing them the opportunity to learn from writers in a workshop setting, develop a student journal, and participate in a writing contest resulting in potential scholarships.

Total Grants Awarded: 7
Total Dollars Awarded: $65,000

Utah
Moab Arts Festival
Moab, UT
FIELD/DISCIPLINE: Multidisciplinary
$10,000

To support a partnership with the Grand County School District, KZMU Community Radio, and the Dan O'Laurie Museum to support Voices of Youth, an interactive, community-based photography and radio project designed to deepen teenagers' understanding of culture and community. The project aims to reinstill in both the participating youth and the community an appreciation of Moab's unique cultural heritage.

Moab Music Festival
Moab, UT
FIELD/DISCIPLINE: Music
$10,000

To support a partnership with the Grand County School District to provide an Educational Outreach Program to bring Chinese Composers-in-Residence, Chen Yi and Zhou Long, to Moab schools for teacher workshops, presentations, and school assemblies. The Moab Music Festival's Outreach Program provides an opportunity for students in a rural, isolated, and low-income area to participate in comprehensive music programs.

Utah Opera Company
Salt Lake City, UT
FIELD/DISCIPLINE: Opera
$5,000

To support a partnership with the Rock Springs Community Arts Center and the Sevier County Arts Alliance to provide five-day residencies in schools in remote communities of Utah, Idaho, Nevada, and Wyoming, reaching children with little or no access to the arts. Residencies are conducted by members of Utah Opera's Ensemble Program, a prestigious training program serving young professional vocalists from throughout from North America.

Art Access/VSA Arts of Utah
Salt Lake City, UT
FIELD/DISCIPLINE: Multidisciplinary
$10,000

To support a partnership project with the Utah Arts Council and Horizonte Instruction and Training Center, an alternative school, for a folklorist-led project in the use of masks in traditional culture followed by a workshop in the construction of fused glass masks led by artists from Powell Brothers and Sons. Project activities are targeted for the ethnically diverse students of Horizonte Center. Students with limited English proficiency comprise 62 percent of the population.

Total Grants Awarded: 4
Total Dollars Awarded: $35,000

Vermont
Flynn Theatre for the Performing Arts
Burlington, VT
FIELD/DISCIPLINE: Music
$10,000

To support a partnership with two inner-city youth organizations, the King Street Youth Center and the Sarah Holbrook Community Center, to support a five-week intensive residency with percussionist/composer/educator Donald Knaack. The residency will serve teenage youth from Burlington's urban, poor, multiethnic neighborhoods and culminate with a student performance at Burlington's Discover Jazz festival.

Onion River Arts Council
Montpelier, VT
FIELD/DISCIPLINE: Multidisciplinary
$10,000

To support a partnership with the Washington County Youth Service Bureau/Boys & Girls Club and the Cityscape Consortium to continue support for artist residencies in a community-based after-school program serving approximately 200 fifth to eighth graders. The Cityscape Program provides an opportunity for students in a rural and low-income area to work with artists selected by the Onion River Arts Council.

Total Grants Awarded: 2
Total Dollars Awarded: $20,000

Virgina
Northern Virginia Youth Symphony Association
Annandale, VA
FIELD/DISCIPLINE: Music
$10,000

To support a partnership with the Fairfax County Public Schools to expand the Music Buddies Mentorship program that provides one-on-one, peer-to-peer weekly music instruction from advanced teenage musicians to middle-school students. The students being mentored are identified as having financial, social, or academic challenges and attend one of three middle schools with large ethnic populations. Music Buddies provides these students with an opportunity to develop musical skills and build stronger relationships with their peers.

The Barter Foundation, Inc.
Abingdon, VA
FIELD/DISCIPLINE: Theatre
$5,000

To support a partnership with the Olney Theatre and several public schools to create a Young Playwright's Workshop and Festival for students in rural Appalachia, offering artistic opportunities that were previously unavailable to these students. The program will guide high-school students in development of critical writing skills and give them the experience of seeing works presented on stage at the Youth Playwright's Festival.

Southampton County Assembly, Inc.
Newsoms, VA
FIELD/DISCIPLINE: Multidisciplinary
$10,000

To support a partnership with the Suwabi African Ballet and the City of Franklin Department of Parks and Recreation to develop a Rites of Passage Project to provide year-round, after-school and weekend classes in traditional African dance and drums at the local community center for youth from the sixth through twelfth grades, in rural Southampton and Isle of Wright Counties and the city of Franklin. The project will use traditional African folk arts and cultural heritage to assist youth from largely low-income, African Americans communities in their transition from childhood to adulthood.

Total Grants Awarded: 3
Total Dollars Awarded: $25,000

Virgin Islands
School of Visual Arts and Careers
St. Thomas, U.S. Virgin Islands
FIELD/DISCIPLINE: Visual Arts
$5,000

To support a partnership with the Fort Christian Museum and the St. Thomas-St. John Arts Council to support an after-school and summer art program. The project will provide intensive training in the visual arts and related careers for students in seventh through twelfth grades. Most of the students live in public housing and do not have access to the opportunities the program provides, such as creative self-expression, self-exploration though the arts, vocational training, and some paid internships.

Total Grants Awarded: 1
Total Dollars Awarded: $5,000

Washington
Arts Council of Snohomish County
Everett, WA
FIELD/DISCIPLINE: Visual Arts
$5,000

To support a partnership with the Denney Juvenile Justice Center, the Cocoon School, and the Everett School District to provide incarcerated and homeless teens with weekly art classes, led by a professional art instructor. The art classes are designed to improve both the academic and art skills of the participants as well as provide youth with positive interactions with caring adults.

Blue Mountain Art Alliance
Walla Walla, WA
FIELD/DISCIPLINE: Multidisciplinary
$5,000

To support a partnership with the Walla Walla Community, the City of Walla Walla, the Walla Walla Community Center for Youth, and the Walla Walla Community Network to support arts education programming at the Community Center for Youth, providing after-school and weekend activities for students in this rural community in southeast Washington. Participants, largely from low-income families and several of whom have already been through the court system, will have an opportunity to improve their art skills, with artists selected by Blue Mountain Arts Alliance, while having positive interactions with their peers.

Kitsap County Consolidated Housing
Silverdale, WA
FIELD/DISCIPLINE: Multidisciplinary
$10,000

To support a partnership with the West Sound Academy to create Forms of Identity, a pilot project designed to engage students, ages eleven to eighteen, by intensively exploring different art forms. The students, who are residents of low-income communities, will participate in artist-led workshops, create an outdoor sculpture, design a Web page for a Homework Club, and serve as mentors to younger students. The program will not only enhance their artistic skills but also develop leadership skills through mentoring the younger children.

Tears of Joy Theatre
Vancouver, WA
FIELD/DISCIPLINE: Multidisciplinary
$10,000

To support a partnership with Joy Theatre, the Northwest Afrikan American Ballet, the Ockley Green Community School, and the Youth Services Consortium to continue an after-school arts-based student success program housed at an inner-city, low-income, largely ethnic middle school. Participants in this program engage in challenging experiences with professional artists geared to enhance creativity and self-expression, practice discipline, manage responsibility, and develop communication skills.

Unidentified Moving Objects, Inc.
Vashon, WA
FIELD/DISCIPLINE: Theatre
$5,000

To support a partnership with the Ruth Dykeman Children's Home to provide an art-in education initiative for young people who are victims of violence, neglect, trauma, abandonment, and abuse. Participants will learn writing techniques from a poet and creative writing teacher, eventually writing original poetry, songs, and stories that will be published in a booklet. In addition, the youth will make masks and learn improvisation and performance techniques. By learning alternative modes of expression through performance and writing techniques, the young participants will be less afraid to confront issues of self-awareness and improve their self-esteem.

Total Grants Awarded: 5
Total Dollars Awarded: $35,000

West Virgina
High Rocks Educational Corporation
Hillsboro, WV
FIELD/DISCIPLINE: Multidisciplinary
$10,000

To support a partnership with Carnegie Hall to integrate an arts-in-education component into High Rocks' Use Your Noodle Club, a community service program developed by high school girls in rural, poor counties in West Virginia. Carnegie Hall will provide visual and dramatic arts instructors to teach teenagers, some of who will then serve as apprentices with the artists in classes for elementary-age children.

Huntington Museum of Art
Huntington, WV
FIELD/DISCIPLINE: Visual Arts
$10,000

To support a partnership with the Huntington Housing Authority to support ArtWorks, a project to provide visual arts instruction to teens ages fourteen to eighteen living in the Huntington Housing Authority. The students will work on a public mural in the summer and a tile project in the winter. ArtWorks provides participating teens with an opportunity to create work as well as practice successful coping strategies and enhance communication skills.

Morgan Arts Council
Berkeley Springs, WV
FIELD/DISCIPLINE: Theatre
$10,000

To support a partnership with the Boys & Girls Club of Morgan County and the Ice House School of the World to establish a youth summer theatre camp and after-school theatre arts classes. The programs will teach playwriting, teen drama, stage craft, and movement, providing an opportunity for youth living in a low-income, rural area of West Virginia to receive theatre arts training as well as provide them with high-quality, enriching after-school and summer activities.

Upshur County Youth Council, Inc.
Buckhannon, WV
FIELD/DISCIPLINE: Folk & Traditional Arts
$5,000

To support a partnership with the Buckhannon Community Theatre, Upshur County Arts Alliance, Augusta Youth Ballet Company, and the Upshur County Family Resource Network to provide a four-week series of summer performance and visual arts education programs, focused on regional Appalachian arts and culture, to youth in sixth through eighth grades. These programs provide area youth, living in an isolated, rural, low-income area of Appalachia with limited exposure to the arts, with an opportunity to increase awareness and appreciation of art and their own culture, develop new skills, and explore future opportunities in the visual and performing arts.

Total Grants Awarded: 4
Total Dollars Awarded: $35,000

Wisconsin
Center for the Deaf and Hard of Hearing, Inc.
Brookfield, WI
FIELD/DISCIPLINE: Multidisciplinary

$10,000

To support a partnership with the Milwaukee Public Theater, Danceworks, Inc., and the Milwaukee Sign Language School to support a one-week, full-day, multicultural arts camp for deaf and hard-of-hearing youth. The camp will incorporate three components of creative expression that are accessible to deaf and hard-of-hearing children: rhythm and dance, music (drumming), and visual arts, while focusing on Asian, African and deaf cultures. This project will be an opportunity for children to overcome communication barriers and gain exposure to the arts.

Fresh Tracks Discovery Center
Danbury, WI
FIELD/DISCIPLINE: Musical Theatre
$5,000

To support a partnership with the Siren and Webster School Districts and Communities United in Education to support an artist-in-residency project bringing performing artists from the Big Top Chautauqua into the Siren and Webster High Schools to work with band and choir students, culminating in their performance with the Big Top. The project's students reside in a low-income, rural, and isolated area of Wisconsin, with very limited access to art and music resources.

John C. Cudahy YMCA
Milwaukee, WI
FIELD/DISCIPLINE: Multidisciplinary
$10,000

To support a partnership with the Milwaukee Public Theatre, Milwaukee Repertory Theater, Wisconsin Conservatory of Music, and Kairo Communications to support ArtsAlive, an after-school arts program for middle- and high-school students in the North Meadows low-income housing community. A diverse roster of pro-

fessional artists and organizations from the greater Milwaukee area will participate in the program, helping to expand the students' awareness of and engagement in the visual and performing arts. The project will be launched in collaboration with the local Gear Up Program aimed at helping low-income students prepare for college.

Latino Arts, Inc.
Milwaukee, WI
FIELD/DISCIPLINE: Multidisciplinary
$10,000

To support a partnership with the Milwaukee Public Theatre to support after-school cultural arts workshops for low-income, primarily Latino youth. The workshops will include sessions in visual arts, theater, and flamenco dance and will center around three Latino cultural events. The program seeks to be a source of cultural appreciation and enrichment for the young participants and for the community as a whole.

Milwaukee Institute of Art and Design
Milwaukee, WI
FIELD/DISCIPLINE: Multidisciplinary
$10,000

To support a partnership with the Neighborhood House of Milwaukee to support an after-school arts program serving an inner-city, low-income Milwaukee neighborhood. The program provides a safe, supervised, and educational after-school venue while its interdisciplinary approach helps students use art and design to explore literacy, technology, and arts careers.

Northern Lakes Center for the Arts
Amery, WI
FIELD/DISCIPLINE: Multidisciplinary
$5,000

To support a partnership with the Amery Public School District, Northern Lakes Writers' Guild, Northern Lakes Theater Guild, ICN Radio, and the Amery Area United Way to support an artists' residency program to bring actors and writers into language arts and literature classes in public schools located in a rural, isolated area in northwestern Wisconsin. The program will help students in grades four, six, eight, and ten write, produce, and perform a series of radio plays.

Oneida Nation Arts Program
Oneida, WI
FIELD/DISCIPLINE: Multidisciplinary
$10,000
To support a partnership with Youth Educational Services, Cultural Heritage Department, Oneida Community Health, and Workforce and Job Placement to support Nurturing Roots and Spreading Wings, a ten-week arts job training program for tribal youth. Tribal youth will be hired as apprentices to work with three resident artists in sculpture and video animation. The project addresses the community's need to provide meaningful youth employment, teach job skills, and expose tribal youth to new and positive experiences.

Total Grants Awarded: 7
Total Dollars Awarded: $60,000

Wyoming
Community Visual Arts Association
Jackson, WY
FIELD/DISCIPLINE: Design
$10,000
To support a partnership with Western Wyoming High School to develop an after-school art and design studio for young people, providing advanced arts training and being equipped to produce marketable works of art. The project will offer talented young people in this rural, isolated community professional opportunities in the visual arts and experience in implementing and managing an art design studio.

Region V BOCES
Wilson, WY
FIELD/DISCIPLINE: Multidisciplinary
$5,000
To support a partnership with Community Visual Arts Association, the Martin Harris Gallery, and the Dancer's Workshop to support a program offering multidisciplinary art opportunities for youth at C-V Ranch, a residential special education school. The program will be led by community artists and arts-related professionals and will afford the participants an opportunity to enhance creative skills as well as improve self-esteem.

Young Musicians
Evanston, WY
FIELD/DISCIPLINE: Music
$10,000
To support a partnership with the Davis Middle School Music Department to support a Summer Music Program bringing visiting professional musicians from as far away as New York and California to educate and perform for rural southwest Wyoming and areas of rural Utah and Idaho. This week-long program offers unique educational and performance opportunities to youth in grades six to twelve that are currently unavailable through any other regional source.

Total Grants Awarded: 3
Total Dollars Awarded: $25,000

In addition, the following regional arts organizations may be able to help you with grants:

State and Jurisdictional Arts Agencies
Alabama State Council on the Arts
One Dexter Avenue
Montgomery, AL 36130
334-242-4076
TT-Relay: 1-800-548-2546

Alaska State Council on the Arts
411 West 4th Avenue, Suite 1E
Anchorage, AK 99501-2343
907-269-6610
asca@alaska.net

**American Samoa Council on
Arts, Culture & Humanities**
P.O. Box 1540
Pago Pago, American Samoa 96799
011-684-633-4347

Arizona Commission on the Arts
417 West Roosevelt
Phoenix, AZ 85003
602-255-5882
general@ArizonaArts.org

Arkansas Arts Council
1500 Tower Building
323 Center Street
Little Rock, AR 72201
501-324-9766
info@dah.state.ar.us

California Arts Council
1300 I Street, #930
Sacramento, CA 95814
916-322-6555
TT: 916-322-6569
cac@cwo.com

Colorado Council on the Arts
750 Pennsylvania Street
Denver, CO 80203-3699
303-894-2617
TT: 303-894-2664
coloarts@artswire.org

Western States Arts Federation
1543 Champa Street, Suite 220
Denver, CO 80202
303-629-1166
staff@westaf.org

Connecticut Commission on the Arts
Gold Building 755 Main Street
Hartford, CT 06103
860-566-4770

Delaware Division of the Arts
State Office Building
820 North French Street
Wilmington, DE 19801
302-577-8278 (from New Castle County)
302-739-5304 (from Kent or Sussex Counties)
TT-Relay: 1-800-232-5460
delarts@artswire.org

District of Columbia Commission on the Arts & Humanities
410 8th Street, NW
Washington, DC 20004
202-724-5613
TT: 202-727-3148
carrien@tmn.com

Division of Cultural Affairs
Florida Department of State
The Capitol
Tallahassee, FL 32399-0250
850-487-2980
TT: 904-488-5779

Georgia Council for the Arts
260 14th Street, Suite 401
Atlanta, GA 30318
404-685-2787
gca@gwins.campus.mci.net

Southern Arts Federation
1401 Peachtree Street, Suite 460
Atlanta, GA 30309
404-874-7244
TT: 404-876-6240
saf@southarts.org

Guam Council on the Arts & Humanities
Office of the Governor
P.O. Box 2950
Agana, GU 96910
011-671-647-2242
arts@ns.gov.nu

Consortium for Pacific Arts & Cultures
2141C Atherton Road
Honolulu, HI 96822
808-946-7381

State Foundation on Culture & the Arts
250 South Hotel Street, 2nd Floor
Honolulu, HI 96813
808-586-0300
TTD: 808-586-0740
sfca@sfca.state.hi.us

Idaho Commission on the Arts
P.O. Box 83720
Boise, ID 83720-0008
208-334-2119
idarts@artswire.org

Illinois Arts Council
State of Illinois Center
100 West Randolph, Suite 10-500
Chicago, IL 60601
312-814-6750
TT: 312-814-4831
ilarts@artswire.org

Indiana Arts Commission
402 West Washington Street, Room 072
Indianapolis, IN 46204-2741
317-232-1268
TT: 317-233-3001
inarts@aol.com

Iowa Arts Council
600 East Locust
State Capitol Complex
Des Moines, IA 50319
515-281-4451
jbailey@max.state.ia.us

Kansas Arts Commission
Jayhawk Tower
700 Jackson, Suite 1004
Topeka, KS 66603
785-296-3335
TT-Relay: 1-800-766-3777
KAC@arts.state.ks.us

Kentucky Arts Council
31 Fountain Place
Frankfort, KY 40601
502-564-3757

Division of the Arts
Louisiana Department of Culture, Recreation, &
Tourism
1051 North 3rd Street
P.O. Box 44247
Baton Rouge, LA 70804
225-342-8180
*arts@crt.state.la.us***Maine Arts Commission**
55 Capitol Street
State House Station 25
Augusta, ME 04333
207-287-2724
TT: 207-287-5613

Maryland State Arts Council
175 West Ostend, Suite E
Baltimore, MD 21230
410-767-6555
TDD: 410-333-4519
moliver@mdbusiness.state.md.us

Mid Atlantic Arts Foundation
22 Light Street, #330
Baltimore, MD 21202
410-539-6656
TT: 410-539-4241
maaf@midatlanticarts.org

Massachusetts Cultural Council
10 Street James Avenue, 3rd Floor
Boston, MA 02116-3803
617-727-3668
TT: 617-338-9153

New England Foundation for the Arts
266 Summer Street, 2nd Floor
Boston, MA 02210
617-951-0010
info@nefa.org

Michigan Council for Arts and Cultural Affairs
525 West Ottawa Street
P.O. Box 30705
Lansing, MI 48909-8205
517-241-4011

Arts Midwest
2908 Hennepin Avenue, Suite 200
Minneapolis, MN 55408-1954
612-341-0755
TT/Voice: 612-341-0901
general@artsmidwest.org

Minnesota State Arts Board
Park Square Court
400 Sibley Street, Suite 200
St. Paul, MN 55101-1949
651-215-1600
800-8MN-ARTS
TT-Relay: 612-297-5353
msab@tc.umn.edu

Mississippi Arts Commission
239 North Lamar Street, Second Floor
Jackson, MS 39201
601-359-6030

Missouri Arts Council
Wainwright Office Complex
111 North Seventh Street, Suite 105
St. Louis, MO 63101
314-340-6845
moarts@mail.state.mo.us

Mid-America Arts Alliance
912 Baltimore Avenue, Suite 700
Kansas City, MO 64105
816-421-1388

Commonwealth Council for Arts & Culture
P.O. Box 553, CHRB
CNMI Convention Center
Commonwealth of the Northern Mariana Islands
Saipan, MP 96950
9-011-670-322-9982

Montana Arts Council
316 North Park Avenue
Room 252
Helena, MT 59620
406-444-6430
TT-Relay: 800-833-8503
mac@state.mt.us

Nebraska Arts Council
The Joslyn Castle Carriage House
3838 Davenport Street
Omaha, NE 68131-2329
402-595-2122
TT-Voice: 402-595-2122
nacart@synergy.net

Nevada Arts Council
716 North Curry Street Suite A
Carson City, NV 89703
775-687-6680

New Hampshire State Council on the Arts
Phenix Hall
40 North Main Street
Concord, NH 03301
603-271-2789
TT-Relay: 800-735-2964

New Jersey State Council on the Arts
225 West State Street
P.O. Box 306
Trenton, NJ 08625-0306
609-292-6130
TT: 609-633-1186

New Mexico Arts Division
228 East Palace Avenue
Santa Fe, NM 87501
505-827-6490
TT: 505-827-6925
artadmin@oca.state.nm.us

New York State Council on the Arts
915 Broadway
New York, NY 10010
212-387-7000
TT: 212-387-7049
nysca@artswire.org

North Carolina Arts Council
Mail Service Center 4632
Raleigh, NC 27699-4632
919-733-2111

North Dakota Council on the Arts
418 East Broadway Avenue, Suite 70
Bismarck, ND 58501-4086
701-328-3954
comserv@state.nd.us

Ohio Arts Council
727 East Main Street
Columbus, OH 43205
614-466-2613
TT: 614-466-4541
bfisher@mail.oac.ohio.gov
wlawson@mail.oac.ohio.gov

Oklahoma Arts Council
P.O. Box 52001-2001
Oklahoma City, OK 73152-2001
405-521-2931
okarts@tmn.com

Oregon Arts Commission
775 Summer Street, NE
Salem, OR 97310
503-986-0082
TT: 503-378-3772
oregon.artscomm@State.OR.US

Commonwealth of Pennsylvania Council on the Arts
Finance Building, Room 216A
Harrisburg, PA 17120
717-787-6883
TT-Relay: 800-654-5984

Institute of Puerto Rican Culture
Apartado Postal 4184
San Juan, PR 00902-4184
809-723-2115

Rhode Island State Council on the Arts
83 Park Street, 6th Floor
Providence, RI 02903-1037
401-222-3880
TT: 401-277-3880
info@risca.state.ri.us

South Carolina Arts Commission
1800 Gervais Street
Columbia, SC 29201
803-734-8696
kenmay@scsn.net

South Dakota Arts Council
Office of Arts
800 Governors Drive
Pierre, SD 57501-2294
605-773-3131
TT-Relay: 800-622-1770
sdac@stlib.state.sd.us

Tennessee Arts Commission
Citizens Plaza
401 Charlotte Avenue
Nashville, TN 37243-0780
615-741-1701
btarleton@mail.state.tn.us

Texas Commission on the Arts
P.O. Box 13406
Austin, TX 78711-3406
512-463-5535
TTY: 512-475-3327
front.desk@arts.state.tx.us

Utah Arts Council
617 East South Temple Street
Salt Lake City, UT 84102
801-236-7555

Vermont Arts Council
136 State Street
Montpelier, VT 05633-6001
802-828-3291
TT-Relay: 800-253-0191
info@arts.vca.state.vt.us

Virginia Commission for the Arts
223 Governor Street
Richmond, VA 23219
804-225-3132
TT: 804-225-3132
vacomm@artswire.org

Virgin Islands Council on the Arts
41-42 Norre Gade, 2nd Floor
P.O. Box 103
St. Thomas, VI 00802
340-774-5984

Washington State Arts Commission
234 East 8th Avenue
P.O. Box 42675
Olympia, WA 98504-2675
360-753-3860
TT-Relay: 206-554-7400 or 800-833-6388
wsac@artswire.org

Arts & Humanities Section
West Virginia Division of Culture & History
1900 Kanawha Blvd. East
Capitol Complex
Charleston, WV 25305-0300
304-558-0220
TT: 304-348-0220

Wisconsin Arts Board
101 East Wilson Street, 1st Floor
Madison, WI 53702
608-266-0190
TT: 608-267-9629

Wyoming Arts Council
2320 Capitol Avenue
Cheyenne, WY 82002
307-777-7742
TT: 307-777-5964
wyoarts@artswire.org

For more information on this topic, visit our Web site at www.businesstown.com

Index

John Riddle

John Riddle is a freelance writer and author. His byline has appeared in the *Washington Post*, the *New York Times*, and dozens of other publications. Mr. Riddle has over ten years of experience in the non-profit arena, both as a fundraising manager and a nonprofit management consultant.

Tere Drenth

Tere Drenth, an award-winning author and editor, serves as an adjunct English faculty member at Franklin College (Franklin, Indiana) and has edited more than fifty general-reference books. Ms. Drenth is author of the upcoming *The Everything® Budgeting Book*.

Also available from Adams Media

STREETWISE® BOOKS

24 Hour MBA
$17.95
ISBN 1-58062-256-9

Achieving Wealth Through Franchising
$19.95
ISBN 1-58062-503-7

Business Forms w/CD-ROM
$24.95
ISBN 1-58062-132-5

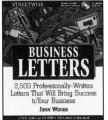

Business Letters w/CD-ROM
$24.95
ISBN 1-58062-133-3

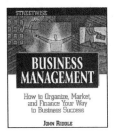

Business Management
$19.95
ISBN 1-58062-540-1

Complete Business Plan
$19.95
ISBN 1-55850-845-7

Customer-Focused Selling
$19.95
ISBN 1-55850-725-6

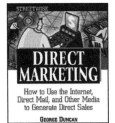

Direct Marketing
$19.95
ISBN 1-58062-439-1

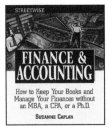

Do-It-Yourself Advertising
$17.95
ISBN 1-55850-727-2

Finance & Accounting
$17.95
ISBN 1-58062-196-1

Get Your Business Online
$19.95
ISBN 1-58062-368-9

Hiring Top Performers
$17.95
ISBN 1-58062-684-5

Available wherever books are sold.

For more information, or to order, call 800-872-5627 or visit adamsmedia.com

Adams Media Corporation, 57 Littlefield Street, Avon, MA 02322

Adams Streetwise® books for growing your business

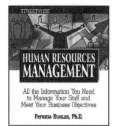

**Human Resources
Management**
$19.95
ISBN 1-58062-699-8

Independent Consulting
$17.95
ISBN 1-55850-728-0

Internet Business Plan
$19.95
ISBN 1-58062-502-9

**Low-Cost Web Site
Promotion**
$19.95
ISBN 1-58062-501-0

Managing People
$17.95
ISBN 1-55850-726-4

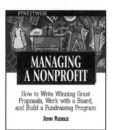

Managing a Nonprofit
$19.95
ISBN 1-58062-698-X

Marketing Plan
$17.95
ISBN 1-58062-268-2

**Maximize Web
Site Traffic**
$19.95
ISBN 1-55850-369-7

**Motivating & Rewarding
Employees**
$17.95
ISBN 1-58062-130-9

**Relationship Marketing
on the Internet**
$17.95
ISBN 1-58062-255-0

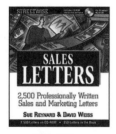

**Sales Letters
w/CD-ROM**
$24.95
ISBN 1-58062-440-5

Selling Your Business
$19.95
ISBN 1-58062-602-5

Small Business Start-Up
$17.95
ISBN 1-55850-581-4

**Small Business
Success Kit**
$19.95
ISBN 1-58062-367-0

**Small Business
Turnaround**
$17.95
ISBN 1-58062-195-3

**Start Your Own
Business Workbook**
$9.95
ISBN 1-58062-506-1

**Take Your Business
Online Workbook**
$9.95
ISBN 1-58062-507-X

Time Management
$17.95
ISBN 1-58062-131-7

FIND MORE ON THIS TOPIC BY VISITING
BusinessTown.com
The Web's big site for growing businesses!

- ☑ **Separate channels on all aspects of starting and running a business**
- ☑ **Lots of info on how to do business online**
- ☑ **1,000+ pages of savvy business advice**
- ☑ **Complete Web guide to thousands of useful business sites**
- ☑ **Free e-mail newsletter**
- ☑ **Question and answer forums, and more!**

businesstown.com